THE GIFTED AMATEUR (Part 1 of 2)
Life and the Military
(A memoir of a Welsh bloke and Sexagenarian)

Nigel M Sainsbury

Copyright © 2020 Nigel M Sainsbury

All rights reserved. No part of this book may be reproduced or transmitted in any form or by any means, electronic or mechanical, including photocopying, recording or by any information storage and retrieval system without permission in writing from the publisher.

Publisher: Nigel Sainsbury Consulting LLC - Fairfax, VA
ISBN: 978-1-7349665-0-3
Library of Congress Control Number: 2020907949
Title: The Gifted Amateur
Author: Nigel M Sainsbury
Website: *www.mybikerauthor.com*
Digital distribution | 2020
Paperback | 2020
Printed in the USA

The stories in this autobiography reflect the author's recollection of events. Some names, locations, and identifying characteristics have been changed to protect the privacy of those depicted.

Front cover:
'Jake' caricature of Nigel Sainsbury 2004

Dedication

Inspired by my dear friend Squadron Leader Peter Michael Kingwill, RAF, who whilst terminally ill, wrote about his own life for his unborn grandson. Peter peacefully departed us on April 11th, 2011 aged just 64, shortly after the birth of his grandson, Alfie Mark Newton Kingwill.

Rosie & Peter Kingwill and Me, UK, 2010

For my children; Dan, Josh and Sian, their children, and their children's children.

To all my family, friends, and the wonderful people I have been privileged to meet over my 60 years - you know who you are. And finally, to all my new friends, who will hopefully connect with me through reading this book.

Acknowledgements

To my work colleagues for their blunt and honest feedback, and my dear friend Bob Morgan for his foreword, continued support to my writing exploits, and correcting my Welshisms.

Newbookauthors.com for keeping me on the straight and narrow, and Google and Wikipedia for being my fact checker.

Finally, to my wife Carol, for continuing to believe in me, and giving me the encouragement needed to get the job done.

Table of Contents

Dedication iii
Acknowledgements v
Preface ix
Forword xi
Chapter 1 *Humble Beginnings* 1
Chapter 2 *Experiential Learning* 28
Chapter 3 *Tough Love* 52
Chapter 4 *The Military Effect* 62
Chapter 5 *Career Pause* 81
Chapter 6 *Pushing the Boundries* 113
Chapter 7 *Dreams, Duty and Decisions* 125
Chapter 8 *Switching Lanes* 152
Chapter 9 *Drinking from a Fire Hose* 173
Chapter 10 *Balancing Act* 201
Chapter 11 *Samsonite Wariors* 234

Preface

From early childhood we deal with life's trials and tribulations often armed with little to no knowledge of what we are really facing, yet we do our best and hope for a good outcome. Decisions and choices are made on a combination of experience, advice from others and our best judgement under the circumstances at the time. The path we pursue from those decisions, shape our lives going forward and help make us who we are today. As a teenager in the military, the learning of basic life skills is reinforced through a combination of leadership training and enforced discipline that is rarely experienced in other walks of life. This promotes an outward mindset and builds a self-confidence enabling individuals to pursue their dreams and fulfil their career aspirations whilst facing personal and professional challenges head on. Unfortunately, success is never guaranteed, but nothing is ever a total failure. Military people simply view setbacks as the new start point for moving forward. Making sound decisions by adapting successes and applying lessons learnt from past failures, simply makes them *'Gifted Amateurs'*.

Nigel M Sainsbury

| 1960 | 1964 | 1977 | 2016 |

'Success is the ability to move from one failure to another with no loss of enthusiasm' - Winston Churchill

Foreword

Nigel's story begins with his childhood upbringing in the coal mining valleys of South Wales during the 60s and 70s, at a time where the rise and popularity of oil was surpassing the need for coal. Nigel's plan was to move away from village life and join the military. However, his career almost ended soon after it had started when he suffered a terrible road traffic accident. Nigel digs deep to get his life and career back on track. With support from family and friends, and his infectious positive attitude, he begins to realise his true potential. Recognising that no two military careers are ever the same, Nigel tells his own unique story of life in uniform over a career that spans several decades and through some significant global events. From an extremely young age, all his experiences both positive and negative have been valuable life learning opportunities, each having influence on his decision making going forward. Nigel describes all this with a wicked sense of humour and a natural Welsh self-depriving tone that becomes a common thread throughout the book. Always wanting to do the right thing, he admits that he doesn't always get things right, but does his best whilst having fun along the way. The stories encourage the reader to reflect hard on their own life learning, through their own successes and failures, against this bloke from the Welsh valleys. As Nigel suggests, perhaps we are all just 'Gifted Amateurs'.

Bob Morgan (Nigel's Friend)

In the beginning ……

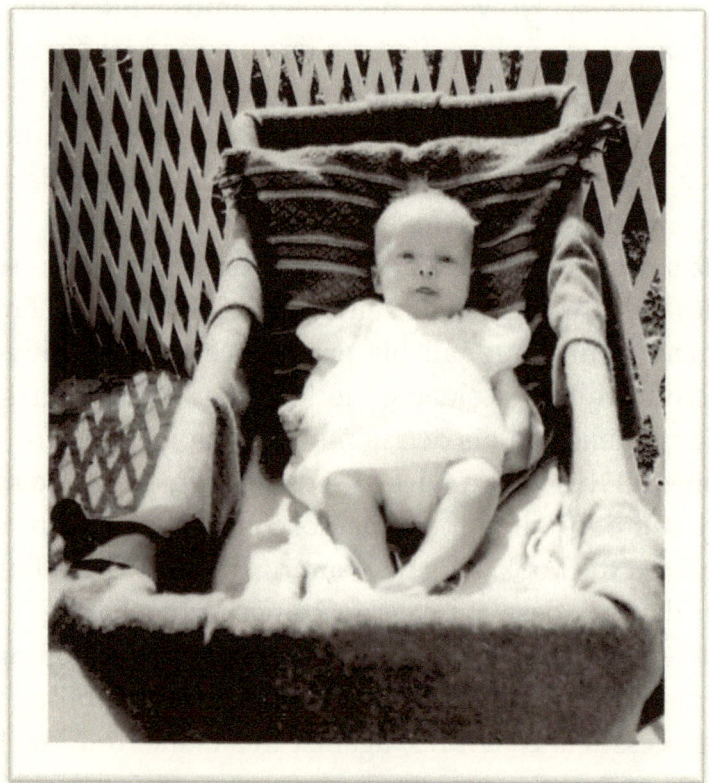

Nigel M Sainsbury, Cwmfelinfach, Wales, June 1960

Chapter 1
Humble Beginnings

Farting in a tin bath shared with my older brother Paul, is something few people have ever experienced. After all, not many people even know who my brother is. Growing up in the 1960s and early 70s in a small Welsh mining village was a completely different experience compared to my children who grew up in the luxury (comparatively speaking) of the 90s and the millennium. Milk was delivered daily to your front door by a milkman. Newspapers and magazines were also delivered direct to your home by the paperboy through the oblong hole in the front door called a *'letter box'*. You paid the milkman cash on a Friday night or you wouldn't get your milk the following week. You paid the village newsagent weekly or whenever you had money; everyone in the village had a tab open with the newsagent.

The milkman drove an electric milk float, not the kind of lightweight streamlined high-tech electric vehicles of today, but a gigantic set of lead acid batteries loosely bolted onto truck axles. It looked more like a mobile electrical sub-station from a Mary Shelly novel than a milk float. The milkman only delivered pre-ordered one-pint glass milk bottles but carried tubs of cream and containers of orange juice for those who could afford it. Each milk bottle was sealed by a very thin and shiny aluminium cap that you just pressed your finger through to get to the milk. There were gold and blue tops too, but we always had the silver top, that was the normal full fat milk - and the cheapest. The flimsy aluminium tops were no match for a bird's beak. The local crows and magpies would follow the milkman like seagulls following a fishing boat bringing home its catch. Once the milkman had placed the bottle on your doorstep and moved away, the birds would simply strut up to the milk, shove their beaks through the aluminium top and syphon off the cream that sat at the top. When they had finished, they would simply shit on your doorstep as a

Me & Paul, Cwmfelinfach, Wales, 1962

'thank you/fuck you' gesture before moving on. The milk man would normally do his rounds between 5am and 7am, so if you got up early enough and discovered that the crows had beaten you to the milk, it was local protocol to nip next door and swap your neighbours bottle for the one violated by the birds. All children had family chores growing up, and one of mine was to wash and put the empty milk bottles out for the milkman to collect in the morning. This was recycling, but we never called it that, it was simply what you did. If we wanted to cancel the milk for the next day or we needed extra, you carefully placed a rolled-up note in the top of the empty bottle and the milkman would oblige. Whoever got up first in the morning usually got the *'Milk In'* and did the bottle swap with next door as required.

The letterbox was an interesting device, a multi-function oblong shaped contraption located roughly halfway down and in the centre of the front door. The letterbox had a spring-loaded flap that served as a primitive reverse air conditioner letting out the little heat you had in winter and replacing it with cold damp outside air. The letter box also acted as a loudspeaker. It was perfect for pushing open with your two thumbs, crouching down and shouting directly into the house. It was the quickest and easiest way to get your mates attention to come out and play. Finally, of course, it could be used to deliver letters from the postman and your daily newspaper which would usually become tomorrow's toilet paper. Everyone knew the postman and he knew everyone's business, that is how it worked in the village. If you wanted to know anything, ask the postman. If you wanted financial information, ask the newsagent.

Grocery stores, not supermarkets, existed in the small Welsh villages and the *'co-op'* (Co-operative) store or *'Spar'* Store was the place where you bought the food you needed daily. Most families never had fridges to store perishables. In reality, the terraced houses were so cold you didn't need a fridge, the whole house was one big fridge. Biscuits (cookies) were sold individually and out of exceptionally large biscuit tins. Broken biscuits were heavily discounted. I was in my teenage years before I realised biscuits were made in symmetrical shapes with individual flavours. Other than the local chapel and church, nothing else was open on a Sunday and few people drove cars.

Our approach to personal hygiene was interesting. Once a week, normally on a Saturday, mum would unhook the tin bath that would be hanging on the lime painted outside wall of the house and put it into the middle of the living room and half fill it with water warmed on the fire place. Whether we needed a bath or not - we bathed. This weekly ritual was to make us look nice for Sunday School at the local Presbyterian chapel, and of course to prepare us for normal school the following week. If we did get dirty on Monday, then that dirt would be on us until we washed it off the following Saturday.

The toilet (singular) was outside and located at the end of the garden path, some 60 feet away (about 18 meters) - the metric system did not replace the imperial units of measurement until 1971. Having a toilet so far away was not that bad in the summer, but you really hung onto your number ones and twos in the wintertime and only went down there when you really needed to. We didn't know it then, but this was good training for bladder and bowel control that would be needed later in life.

Black and white television, when we eventually got it, was a real luxury for just a few hours a day. National broadcasts were timed to last just a bit shorter than the time it took for the television to overheat and break down. The thick glass protruding grey screen looked like a refined giant milk bottle bottom, but that was just a fraction of the size of the contraption it was mounted in. It would make all sorts of noises when you first switched it on, and you had to switch it on a good five minutes before you wanted to watch something to give it a chance to warm up. The large glass vacuum tubes along with the thick glass screen would quickly suck the electricity dimming the living room light momentarily. Not sure if this was a power surge or dodgy house electrics. We had an additional box on the side of ours that swallowed our money every hour to pay for its rental, as buying such a luxury was well outside mum and dad's budget. There was so much static coming off the screen that your hair would stand on end if you came within a foot of it. However, the warmth emanating from the vacuum tubes in the back were a welcome heat source in winter.

The transistor radio was just as popular as the TV, was less expensive to run and would work almost the moment you switched it on if it was tuned properly. Cassette tapes were a quantum leap forward and allowed you to personalise your listening experience in the 70s. You could even record songs directly from the radio with the new combined radio/cassette recorders, save you buying the vinyl records. This was quite a common and accepted practice in the 70s because nobody ever made a portable record player you could use on the go. The Sony Walkman was a technical revolution for cassette tapes. Recording from the radio was the beginning of the practice of pirate copying of music. We just didn't know it at the time.

Both my mother and father smoked cigarettes until the day they died, or at least until they got so seriously ill it was too late for them to do anything about it. Dad smoked real tar *'cancer generating'* cigarettes called Woodbines, they had no filters of any kind. Mum would smoke the posh, lady like cigarettes called Embassy or Embassy Regal. Our house was like Beijing on a bad day, with smog that would literally burn your eyes and secondary smoke that you could taste and would make you gasp for breath. Smoke would just linger and contaminate the food, your clothes and just about everything in the house. There were no windows, air conditioning or basic ventilation, not even a letter box in the kitchen. The kitchen was located at the back of the house, in the converted *'coal hole'*. The coal hole was a chute and storage area at the back of the ground storey of the house to store coal. The open-hearth fire was the only source of heating in the house (other than the vacuum tubes in the TV) and was completely useless in heating anything that was more than five feet away from the actual fire place, let alone warm up any other room in the house.

All the paintwork, wallpaper and false wood wall boards that covered up the bare stone walls were all a brownish colour with a gooey residue that in places looked and felt like sticky fly strip paper. This byproduct of smoking would blend seamlessly into the deep brown that would cover the artic (rough plaster) covered ceiling. False wall boards and veneered hardboard was trendy in the 60s and 70s and a straightforward way to give a room a makeover, particularly if the room had been previously used to store coal. Oddly, in the summertime, the only relief I got from seasonal allergies or *'hay fever'* was being at home in the smoke-filled living room or kitchen as there was no room for any air borne pollen particles to make me sneeze. It made a pleasant change to have difficulty breathing, but without the sneezing. I must have been around 12 years old and was having tea (the meal you have after lunch but before supper) after school one day around a mate's house in the next village. His mum had prepared us a bowl of bananas and custard and I remember that they tasted so differently to what my mum used to give us, realising that the difference was that his home was smoke free. Not only was I breathing second-hand smoke at home I was eating cigarette smoke soiled bananas and custard too.

In the 60s, it seemed like everyone you met smoked. I was the only member of our family that never smoked. Like most kids, I did try it under duress from other kids at school, but it made me physically sick. Those kids who did smoke thought this was highly entertaining. I was bullied several times to smoke, but the outcome was much the same; choking and coughing followed by retching, watery eyes, and if I had recently eaten, throwing up. It was considered cool to smoke out of school, several of the bullies smoked in school as well. Many believed it was a sign of adulthood to walk around with a tobacco stick hanging out of your mouth or clenched between your fingers. Many cigarette companies of the day were promoting such a culture in their marketing campaigns. To this day, I never understood why you would want to persevere with an activity that made you sick, cost you money, gave you bad breath and made your clothes smell. The smoking habit was perhaps the first time I experienced real peer pressure from others to conform. It was a test of character and a challenge for me.

Avoiding confrontation on the subject and standing my ground worked well, as did my throwing up. Time is your friend in these scenarios, people get bored unbelievably quickly when they realise you are not going to conform. It was perhaps my first realisation that in life you make choices. If you believe in something, then you stand up for it. It helps build your strength of character and allows you to develop your own personal arsenal of defensive mechanisms to deal with negative confrontations.

Anyway, back to the outside toilet. I remember the meticulous preparation dad would go through just to go to the loo. He would gather up his cigarettes, *'England's Glory'* matches, pick up the newspaper and search for some additional *'just in case'* toilet paper. The additional toilet paper was usually the leftovers of yesterday's newspaper that had not been used to light the coal fire. He would then sling the lot under his arm before gracefully walking down the garden path. If you needed to use the toilet when dad was going through this preparation phase, you needed to move quickly because once he was down there, he was there for a while. When he had finished his business, there would be a huge cloud of smoke that would bellow out of the little toilet cubicle when he opened the door. It was dad's way of sending a signal to the rest of the family that he was

Paul, Me & Cousin Carol (outside toilet behind us), Cwmfelinfach, Wales, 1964

done. Much like what the Vatican does today when they appoint a new pope. Dad would smoke several cigarettes whilst he was in there and with no ventilation other than the gap at the top and bottom of the door, and with little light, how he could read a newspaper in those conditions remain a mystery. It would be the early 1970s before we would experience the luxury of an indoor toilet.

Other home advancements like double glazing for the doors and windows we would never see in this house. Single glazed *'Sash'* Windows was the norm at that time. These windows used large iron counterweights on ropes that were placed inside the window frame. On releasing the catch holding the two halves together, you could lift the bottom half of the window which would overlap the top. If the weights had little friction the window would literally fly open leaving a gap that was so large several children could fall out of it at the same time. Health and safety were just a pipe dream and had no influence on the window designers' requirements in those days.

I don't really know why these windows were designed to be opened at all because they were completely useless at stopping even the slightest gust of wind or cold. Our bedroom was always full of damp outside air. During the wintertime, which in the Welsh valleys is about 10 months of the year (the other two months are just miserable), I often thought it would be just as warm to be sleeping outside. The windows would be so ineffective I can remember lying in bed scraping my name and drawing rude body parts with my fingernails on the ice that would form on the inside. This to me was the only advantage of having a bed closest to the window. The single glazed glass was extremely thin and never that securely attached to the frame. Used chewing gum seemed more effective than putty for holding the glass in place. The movement of the window when closed would produce a rattling sound even in the calmest conditions that would send you to sleep on a good night or scare the shit out of you if the wind was gusting.

As an infant, I had my own bedroom and slept in a cot with tall sides. I had developed a habit of rocking my head back and forth before I went to sleep. Not sure why I did this, perhaps it was to keep my body warm because of the ineffective windows, but it did help me sleep. The habit stayed with me well into my late teens and my pillows would look and feel like concrete paving slabs. As a child with a larger than normal head for my age, I could beat the fluffiest of pillows into submission after just a few weeks of head rocking. As an infant, my whole body would rock back and forth and be so violent that I could physically move my cot. One night I had managed to get the cot stuck behind the bedroom door which put mum into a bit of a panic. I think she thought there was something wrong with me and I had been possessed by the baby devil. Dad had the perfect solution, he simply screwed my cot to the floor, a sort of DIY exorcism.

The chamber pot or *'potty'* under the bed was your only means of relief if you woke up during the night. Usually because you thought the windows were just about to shatter and break, or you had started to freeze to death because it was so cold, and your bladder had shrunk to the size of a walnut. A couple of bri-nylon sheets (nylon was the new cotton type fabric of the day) on a plastic covered mattress just don't keep the cold out or the body warmth in. Apart from that, any movement between the sheets caused so much static from your pyjamas it looked like you were trying to sleep amongst the Aurora Borealis. If you touched anything you would earth yourself and get an immediate shock. If the cold and noise failed to wake you, there is nothing like a sharp electric discharge through your extremities to do the job.

Me and my brother were forced to share a bedroom for many years after our sister Jayne arrived. We both had little to no capacity for *'holding on'* until the morning so we made sure we went to the toilet before we headed off to bed. The alternative was to get dressed over your pyjamas, sprint down two flights of stairs and then dash the 60 feet to the outside toilet at the bottom of the garden - in total darkness. I did have a small, aptly named *'Winnie the Pooh'* potty, but quite frankly that was less than useless. Just spitting in it a few times would have filled it up. We figured out that mum's plastic washing bucket was just the job. She never used it every day, so we only needed to empty it when she wanted to use it or when it was getting full. Unfortunately, it never had a lid on it, so our bedroom would often smell like a pub toilet just before closing time.

We lived at No 3 Commercial Road, a small three storey, three-bedroom terraced house in a small village called Cwmfelinfach (comb-fell-in-vac). The *'street'* consisted of two end-of-terraced houses with around 25 houses in between. The posh word for the end of terraced house was semi-detached. This was typical of the time as there was not much flat ground in the valleys, so strips of streets would be built at different elevations within the valley. The streets would all be linked by a road to the front of house and an unsealed dirt track, colloquially known as the *'Back Lane'* connecting the rear. Looking at our house from the back lane you could see all three stories, but from the front, at street level,

Front of Commercial Road (No3 by middle car), Cwmfelinfach. Wales. 2010

they looked like small two storey town houses. There are several memorable moments I recall as a kid, but probably one of the most influential moments I had was in our back lane. It was here that I learnt to ride a bicycle and enjoy the freedom of being on two wheels. It wouldn't be mum or dad who taught me, but Billy Skinner, the middle-aged bachelor man who kept racing pigeons and lived with his mum and uncle about ten houses down the street from us. I had no idea what Billy did for a living; I think he worked in the local Switchgear factory making electrical products. Billy always had time for us kids. He was a lovely man.

The houses in the street were almost identical in design but if there was a kink in the street, as there was in Commercial Road, then the house on the kink would be a little different and often the back of the house at street level would have been a grocery store or warehouse of some kind back in the day. By the sixties though many people had started to modify their houses to incorporate modern technology like running hot water, inside toilets and properly fitted windows and doors. Some even extended out the back to include larger kitchens or small conservatories and others even split the house in two using the third storey as a granny flat. The first storey of all the houses in the street was built into the hill, so it only had external access from the back. It consisted of the coal hole or bunker, a small living room and a kitchen. The coal would be delivered from

Back Lane, Commercial Road, Cwmfelinfach, Wales, 2010

the front of the house on the second level down a chute allowing you to take the coal from the bunker direct to the fireplace in the living room. A steep and very narrow staircase would take you to the second level where there were two rooms; inventively called the front and back middle rooms. The staircase was so tight you could hardly pass wind on it let alone pass anyone coming in the other direction. Mum and dad had connected the two middle rooms to make it one expansive room. They kept with the name *'middle room'* as it was the middle room in the middle of the house. Not a great imaginative name, but things were simple in those days and it worked for us. It was also the biggest room in the house, but we only ever used it at Christmas time. Dad kept his modern Alba radiogram/stereogram here. This was a large wooden contraption that looked like a tabletop cocktail cabinet, but under the lid was a fancy tuneable transistor radio, a record player and a set of 'stereo' speakers. It also held dads' country and western record collection. Mum kept all her *'nick knacks'* in the middle room. Nick knacks were ornaments and objects of little to no use, but they cluttered up the room nicely and complimented dads' stereogram. For me and my siblings, the middle room was just the room you navigated through on your way to and from the bedroom.

Another narrow staircase connected the middle room to the third floor which is where the three bedrooms were. Mum and dad's bedroom looked out the back with a view of the valley and the other two bedrooms looked out the front into a wooded area. The wooded area has since been redeveloped with more affordable housing. All the houses had an attic space as well, but we never utilized ours. Insulation was unheard of when these houses were built and there was nothing but cold air and dust between the slate roof and the ceilings in the bedroom. The walls and ceilings of these terraced houses were made of lath and plaster. Lath was nothing more than thin strips of wood tacked closely together to form a backbone for the plaster to adhere to. It was rarely smooth or straight, but it was a cheap and effective way to make walls and ceilings. It was also easy to damage and terribly messy if anything needed to be repaired or replaced. Wallpaper was common in those days and was remarkably effective in covering up the gaps and poor finish of the lath and plaster whilst adding a little bit of colour and style to any room.

Cwmfelinfach is a small mining village located in the Sirhowy Valley in South East Wales. Cwm (as we called it) was typical of the many South Wales villages of the era, developed as a direct result of the coal mining industry and their exploitation of the vast amounts of coal seams located just below the surface of the Welsh Valleys. In 1947 when the industry was Nationalised, there were some 250 active collieries in Wales. Today (2020) there are none. The last one closed in 2011. The colliery in our village was innovatively named 'Nine Mile Point', so called because it was nine miles from Newport by tram, producing coal from 1902 until its closure in 1964. Dad never worked there, but he did work in other local collieries in his short 48 years.

Road B4251, Running through Cwmfelinfach, Wales, 2010

Cwmfelinfach translated from Welsh means 'valley (Cwm) of the little (Fach) mill (Felin)'. Although, as kids, none of us spoke

Welsh and who cared what it meant anyway. It was just *'Cwm'* to us. The most famous thing about Cwmfelinfach to this day is the burial place of Islwyn, the 19th century Welsh poet who was known as the *'Sweet Singer of Sirhowy'*. He was laid to rest in the grounds of the Babell Chapel in 1869; he was just 46 years old. In fact, his name was William Thomas and he was born in Ynysddu (un-ess-d), the next village up. I guess Cwmfelinfach was a much nicer place to be buried than Ynysddu which in Welsh means "black river meadow".

Few people spoke Welsh in our part of Wales. Indeed, as a kid, I cannot remember anyone ever speaking the language, but I never knew why. Which, on reflection, is a real shame. I am proud to be Welsh and slightly embarrassed by the fact I can't speak a word of my native tongue. We always sang the Welsh National Anthem in Welsh although we had no idea what we were singing about. Other than it was something about the 'Land of our Fathers'. In fact, you can't sing the Welsh anthem in English – it just doesn't work. Evan James wrote the anthem in 1856 in Pontypridd and the music was composed by his son James James. Even naming your kids was kept simple in those days. The anthem is not established in law like many other National Anthems, so I am not sure how it became the definite anthem of Wales. Also, I find it strange that it was written in a part of Wales that does not generally speak Welsh, although 150 years ago they probably did.

My surname *'Sainsbury'* is not an indigenous Welsh name and goes back a little further than the 1960s. In fact, it goes back around 900 years. The name has Anglo-Saxon origin and like many names of the time was derived from an actual place. In this case it was from Saintbury, Broadway in Gloucestershire. Saintbury is listed in the Domesday Book of 1086 as *'Svineberie'* before evolving into *'Seinesbir'* in the 1203 Curia Rolls of Gloucestershire, and finally ending up as *'Seineburia'* in the

1220 Book of Fees. There were few school tests for spelling and grammar in those days, so who knows how many other derivatives there were or could have been. The translation of Sainsbury means fort or fortified manor. I am glad they went with Sainsbury; I prefer Nigel Sainsbury to Nigel Fortmanor. In those days, the lord of the manor and local landowners acquired locational surnames and used them as a means of identification of those who had left their birthplace to settle somewhere else. Other modern surname forms from the same original place of Saintbury are Saintsbury, Sainsberry and Sinisbury. My Sainsbury family found themselves in the Welsh coal mining villages after they had moved up from Wiltshire in the last quarter of the 19th Century. Agricultural work had dried up and the coal fields of the Welsh valleys had started to become productive. In 2019 I did a DNA Ancestry test which confirmed much of my family history. The result showed that I was 84% England, Wales and north-western Europe and 16% Scottish and Irish. Interestingly, my first name, Nigel originated from the Irish Niall which was adopted by the Scandinavians as Njal who introduced the name to Normandy, where the Latin language police made it Nigellus. When William the Conqueror invaded England in 1066 they dropped the unnecessary Latin letters and the name Nigel was born.

Both mum and dad were born at their respective family homes. Home births were common in the 1930s. Their birth places of Wattsville (mum) and Risca (dad), are less than three miles apart and they would live their whole lives within a six-mile radius of where they were both born. What was also common during this time and still is to a certain degree, was that people remained in the same place, moving away only to secure work in a different location. Neither mum nor dad ever ventured overseas during their lifetime although they did go over the Severn Bridge many times into England, but that really doesn't count. Dad always wanted to visit Hawaii one day but sadly the closest he got was to see it on the television.

Dad was born GRAHAM NIGEL SAINSBURY on 19th April 1930 at 5 Taylor Street, Risca, in the county of Monmouthshire. Dad was the first of seven children of Cecil Ivor Sainsbury, a bus driver and Dorothy May Sainsbury (formally Saunders but spelled Sanders). For several centuries, Monmouthshire was referred to as a sort of annex to Wales as it bordered Gloucestershire to the east, Herefordshire to the northeast, Brecknockshire to the north, and Glamorgan to the west. A 50/50 split of English and Welsh.

Me, Dad and Paul, Up the Dingle, Cwmfelinfach, Wales, 1961

This divide may have been the reason why the Welsh language was not widely spoken in this part of the country. Although we know Evan James must have spoken it, as he wrote the National Anthem in Pontypridd and that is only 20 miles away from Risca. Even though it is a short commuting distance by modern day travel, it would have been treated like another country as it sat outside Monmouthshire. The Local Government Act of 1972 confirmed most of the county of Monmouthshire as being part of Wales and with some redistribution of boundaries its name was changed to Gwent.

Number 5 Taylor Street, Risca, is another example of a house built for the coal mining industry. A small two storey terraced house with three small bedrooms. It was home to dad, dad's parents, grandparents, and his Aunt Edna. It was common for young families to be living under the same roof as their parents. However, things were not clear cut in dad's family.

May Sanders, my grandmother (born 1909) was the only girl of six siblings and her parents gave her up to her biological Aunt Benham who was childless at the time. Just two years later, Aunt Benham had a daughter of her own named Edna, so both May and Edna were raised as sisters. It was common for brothers and sisters to *'give up'* or *'adopt'* their own children to their childless siblings. Formal adoption laws in England and Wales did not come into law until 1926 and there was never a formal adoption of May, so her (legal) maiden name remained Sanders. Ivor Sainsbury, my grandfather, had a much simpler family. He was the only boy of four siblings.

Ivor Sainsbury & May Saunders, Wales, 1928

Money was tight, and life was full on at 5 Taylor Street, Risca. Some 18 months after dad was born, he was joined by his first sibling, a brother named Peter. Then in 1934 Eric arrived. The small three-bedroom house was getting a little full now and so May and Ivor eventually moved out and into their own home at 17 Navigation Road, Risca, which was literally a three-minute walk down the hill from 5 Taylor Street. This was just in time, as 18 months after that the fourth sibling, Pamela arrived. Jill, Kay and finally Judith would complete the family. Seven in all.

May had four children in five and half years. As space was tight, dad remained living at 5 Taylor Street with his grandparents and would never move to Navigation Road. Indeed, Pamela and Judith would also live with their grandparents. Although the two homes were close together, my grandfather was never totally happy with his family being split up. I never really got to know my grandfather that well and suspected his relationship with my grandmother was not that great. It was certainly different to the relationship mum and dad had. I have no memory of my grandmother and grandfather talking to each other. As a child, everything that happens seems normal, you have nothing to compare it with. It is only when you grow older that you start questioning this kind of behaviour. Separation and divorce were taboo subjects in those days, and I am not sure if there were any services that helped people who were struggling in marriage, so one can only imagine what used to go on in private. Thankfully, society is much more accepting and open with relationships these days, which is positive progress – life is far too short to tolerate unhappiness.

When he was old enough, dad undertook mandatory military service called *'National Service'* with the Royal Corps of Engineers in the Territorial Army, reaching the rank of Corporal having served for two years, 15 days as a driving instructor and tester. Dad did various jobs over the years including working in the coal mines, operating trains, boilerman in a box making factory and a security guard in a large caravan making factory. He was working in Llanwern Steel works, Newport, when he died prematurely in 1978. Dad often took me to his workplace when I was a young teenager and taught me all sorts of life skills like how to use hand tools, powered wood working tools and how to make things like *'nick-knack'* holders. Dad designed and made these nick-knack holders with the chipboard *'off-cuts'* from the manufacturing of fittings in the caravan factory. It was a simple three-tier shelf that could be screwed to the wall from the top shelf to display ornaments and nick-knacks. The device measured about two feet in length and was about a foot tall. The shelves were around five inches deep and were held equidistant by four pieces of ½ inch dowel. Although the actual measurements varied depending on the available wood and what people wanted; dad would make most of them to order. The whole thing looked classic seventies and after a year or so of usage, these things would begin to sag in winter as they would absorb so much water due to the constant dampness in the house. They would dry out during summer and straighten out a little. They were like wooden barometers. Dad and I must have made 50+ of these things for various people over the time he worked there. Mum loved them and could fill the shelves with all sorts of useless objects and as quick as we could make them.

Dad also taught me how to drive an electric, and the much larger diesel fork truck, during the quiet hours at the box making factory. However, my forklift driving days were short lived when I crashed the small electric fork truck into a cardboard roller and bending machine. Me and my brother were having a bit of a race around the factory when I lost both the race and control of the fork truck. Dad was well pissed with me and quite rightly so. I had a real bollocking for that misdemeanour, but only once he realised that I had not been injured in the accident. I have to say the bollocking was well deserved - I got off lightly. I am still not sure how dad recovered the situation as I had managed to rip the electrical cables out of the main distribution box with the forks of the truck as well as damage the distribution box itself. How I never caused an electrical fire or got an electric shock was pure luck. I also thought that this incident would get dad the sack from his job -

thank goodness, it didn't. In my defence I was 14 years old. I didn't know it at the time, but the fork truck driving lessons and even the crash, were a fantastic grounding for me. Within three years of this event, I would be driving Land Rovers, tractors and towing aircraft as a 17-year-old. All before I would get a licence to drive a car.

Mum and Me, Commercial Road, Cwmfelinfach, Wales, 1960

Mum was born MARION MAUD PHILLIPS on 15th February 1934 at 11 Hafod Tudor Terrace, Wattsville, in the county of Monmouthshire. Second daughter of Catherine and David John Phillips. David was a coal hewer. Cora, her elder sister and only other sibling, was 16 years her senior. Mum's grandmother could not cope with children, so David was brought up by other family members. Not too different to my grandmother on my dad's side. Once again, a sign of the times. I remember Nana Phillips being a tough but very fit and lovely lady to be with. She would constantly talk to you about anything and everything, wore the same pinafore over her clothes, and was always on the move or doing something. My brother and I would usually walk to her house from school on a Tuesday for our tea. It was only two miles from school and about another mile back home from her house. Nan would always have homemade stew, a classic Welsh broth made for our tea. The pot would be sitting on the hotplate at the side of the open-hearth fire. The simmering aroma of cooked meat and fresh garden vegetables would drift through the house and had the effect of making your tummy rumble even if you weren't hungry. Nan would let us rip the soft middle out of a loaf of bread and dip it in the soup. The bread would soak up the juices and if you were lucky, small pieces of tender meat and vegetables would also attach itself to the bread. With your head leaning over the pot to catch the drips, you simply whipped the bread out of the broth and put it straight in your mouth. Nan had a knack of keeping the stew at the right temperature so it wouldn't burn your mouth. It was simply delicious. The stew pot would be sitting in tandem next to a big old kettle of hot water always ready to make a nice cup of tea.

You were constantly drinking tea at nana Phillips house. That along with distinct smell of a burning coal fire and the aromas of the stew was the hallmark of being in nans house and probably many of the houses in that street during the 50s and 60s. These houses were often called *'two up, two down'* terraced houses. Two rooms downstairs and just two bedrooms upstairs. We spent all our time in the small living room/kitchen of nans house. I don't remember ever going upstairs. There was a narrow corridor outside and behind the living room called the scullery. To get there you walked across the extremely small back yard which was about the size of three double beds. The scullery housed the outside toilet, wash basin, rubbing board and mangle for doing the laundry. It always smelt of washing powder and detergent in nans toilet which was much nicer than cigarette smoke and pooh in ours. The clothes drying line used to *'hang out'* your clothes was *'up the back'*, a generic term used to describe an undefined area behind the house you were currently in. To get up the back at nans place, you needed to go up a dozen very steep and narrow stone steps, through a very small and badly fitted wooden gate, cross a thin unsealed back lane and onto a grassy area. This area had a tiny shed fronting up a small allotment that was used for growing your own vegetables. The total distance from the scullery to the clothesline could not have been more than 40 feet. This was another classic coal miner's house.

It was at nans house that I discovered I had an affinity to travel. I would have been about five years old at the time. I used to go out the back of nans house and play with the neighbours big black Labrador dog called *'Blackie'*. He was a lovely placid dog and we were great mates. One day Blackie and I decided we would go on a little adventure beyond the back lane, and we set off with no destination in mind. Clearly, I had no clue where I was going, I was five years old for goodness sake. And Blackie, well, he was a dog and older than me so he should have known better. Anyway, we both went missing. My going walkabout sparked a parental panic for mum, followed by a police alert and search by all the local people. Well, too late, me and Blackie were well on our way heading towards Pontywaun (Pon-tee-wayne), a little village about two miles northeast of Wattsville. We were just enjoying our little adventure when mum's niece's husband, Ron, was driving his lorry from Pontywaun back up towards Wattsville and spotted this little lad walking with a big black dog down the side of the road. What got his attention was the fact this little lad had no adult with him, and as he got closer, he thought to himself, *'this lad looks a lot like our Nigel'*. He stopped his lorry and gave me and Blackie a free ride back to nans house. I didn't know what all the fuss was about. Ron and mum were surprised by how far I had walked, and so quickly. They were lucky I didn't have my passport with me, who knows how far I could have gone. Travel and adventure were in my DNA. This was the genesis of what would be a lifetime of adventures.

Nana Phillips would always repeat herself when she spoke to you, it was quite funny to listen to. She would say, *'our Nigel, go and get my washing in for me please. I say, go and get my washing in"*. I never really understood why she did that until I had my own children and realised how often you repeat yourself to children. It had become habit for nan over the years.

I guess my mother and her sister Cora must have drove nan mad at times for her to get such a habit. It was also quite common to call someone *'our'* before their name. Not sure where that habit originated from, but it is still common in Wales.

Grandad, David John Phillips WW1, Unknown Location, 1915

My grandad, David John Phillips died at 72, I was just four years old. He was a retired colliery traffic manager and coal hewer who had lung cancer. The word hewer (German: Hauer or Häuer) is the name given to a qualified miner who loosens rock and minerals in a mine. Like most men who lived in the village, he was a coal miner. Over the years, I have ended up with responsibility for grandad's military stuff which includes his war medals, pocket watch, horse whip, leather pouch belt and cigarette case. The same whip and leather pouch belt shown in this picture. I was hoping to put a small story together about grandad and gift the lot to a museum, but sadly never did it, I still have all the memorabilia today. I did invest for a one page print out of my grandfather's service in the Army from the UK, National Archives. It was a little vague, but I learnt that David John Phillips – Royal Field Artillery 30385 served in Egypt during the Great War. His service record was stamped in Egypt on 13th July 1915, he would have been just

23 years old. Grandad was awarded three WW1 medals; Pip, Squeak and Wilfred which are the affectionate names given to the three campaign medals. The 1914-15 Star, British War Medal and Victory Medal, respectively. All three medals are worn together and in the same order from left to right when viewed from the front. The medals were issued in the 1920s and they coincided with a popular comic strip published in the Daily Mirror newspaper. Pip was a dog; Squeak was a penguin and Wilfred a young rabbit. Somehow the names of these characters became associated with the three campaign medals.

David John Phillips, WW1 Medals, Dog Tags & Watch, Fairfax, USA, 2016

The 1914-15 Star is made of bronze and was awarded to all who served in any theatre of war against Germany between 5th August 1914 and 31st December 1915. The 1914-15 Star was not awarded alone. The recipient had to have received the British War Medal and the Victory Medal, which of course grandad did. The reverse is plain with grandad's service number, rank, name and unit stamped on it. The British War Medal is made of silver and was awarded to officers and men of the British and Imperial Forces who either entered a theatre of war or entered service overseas between 5th August 1914 and 11th November 1918 inclusive. The head on the medal is of George V. Grandads service number, rank, name and unit are stamped on the rim. After the war, it was decided that each of the allies should issue their own bronze Victory Medal with a similar design, similar equivalent wording and identical ribbon. The front depicts a winged classical figure which represents victory. Eligibility for this medal was more restrictive and not everyone who received the British War Medal received the Victory Medal. Grandads service number, rank, name and unit are stamped on the rim.

There were some 250,000 men that went to war in the British army in 1914. The infantry and cavalry were divided into regiments and specialist troops were grouped into so-called corps such as the Royal Artillery or Royal Engineers. On his records, grandad had several ranks, but I could not identify the dates or places. He was a gunner, and it looks like he was also a sapper, which was the term given to a pioneer or combat engineer who is also a combatant that performs a variety of military engineering duties. My grandad survived that bloody awful war. Thousands did not. Every year on Rememberance Day (November 11th), wherever I am, I always reflect and am grateful for the freedoms we have today because of what my grandfather, and all those who faught in that awful war did. Many paying the ultimate price. Lest we forget.

Apart from bathing in the tin bath, I have few memories of mum and dad from when I was a small child; less than 10 years old. However, two episodes stick in my mind, both of which have influenced my own thinking over the years towards my own children. A not so good memory with my mum and a better one with dad. I had been crying for a while one morning and mum had unsuccessfully tried encouraging me to stop, but she was rapidly approaching her wits end and in a last-ditch attempt to stop me crying, she threatened to take me to the children's home (orphanage) and leave me there. Yep, well done mum, that worked. I had no idea what such a place looked like, you just don't when you are four years old, but if all the bad children were sent there forever like mum had said, then it was not a good place for me to be. Mum always regretted saying that to me, she was full of guilt and remorse as soon as she had said it, but it had been said. Lesson in life, you cannot take back the spoken word to a child. It was akin to looking at a bad picture for me, the image was imprinted on my mind forever and I never blocked it out. We had talked and joked about that moment many times over the years, but it did have a profound effect on both of us. Mum never said anything like that to me again and I swore to myself that if I ever had children, I would never threaten them with anything that would cause them fear.

Mum was quite a strict parent and I would even go so far to say, a hard woman in many ways. Her way or the highway kind of thing. I know my brother had a slightly different relationship with mum, particularly later in life which was not as good as mine. I never forgot the time mum found a condom in the washing machine. She was furious. Both my brother and I swore blind it didn't belong to either of us, it certainly wasn't mine and if it wasn't my brothers then that's one unsolved mystery that will go to the grave. No life lesson here other than the fact that if mum had made light of the situation and had not been so angry, there may have been an admission from one of us, i.e. my brother that it was his.

The episode with dad was much more positive and reflects a dad's love for his children, and in dad's case the not so great relationship he had at times with his own mother. We were celebrating my brothers ninth birthday at nans (dad's mums) house. I would have been five. To my brothers delight I remember him being given a large birthday present from nan. When he opened it, his face lit up with an excited smile as he revealed this magnificent articulated toy lorry. I wanted one too, but there was no present for Nigel. I was absolutely devastated and of course I cried a lot because that's what you did at that age. Dad was furious and then set about giving his mother a scolding about treating all her grandchildren the same. She could have gotten me anything, it would have mattered little, but she had nothing for me at all. I had been forgotten and she never even tried to correct her error. It was not my brother's fault, he was the very first grandchild so by default, was a special child in nans eyes. I was number three of around six grandchildren at that time, but the principle of treating children equally was the lesson here.

The following week, dad came home from work with the corgi book of models (cars, lorries and other vehicles) and asked me which one I liked. I studied it for a while and suggested that the pick-up truck looked good as it had a workable tow hitch and rope which could pull other cars around. It also looked awesome in the small glossy Corgi Book of Vehicles. A week or so after that moment, dad brought me a present home. We sat on the top step of the garden path together whilst I opened it. It was the tow truck. He never said it was for anything, he just wanted me to have it. It was years later I learnt the gift was correcting the wrong his mother had made on my brothers' birthday. Only then did I understand the significance of that moment and how dad must have felt giving that gift to me. I have never forgotten the principle of treating everyone the same and with humility. This is a core value. In my personal and professional life, the tow truck memory is often recalled when I meet people for the first time. I always treat people with respect, in the hope of course that it is reciprocated - sadly, that is not always a given. I now have children of my own, and I understand that there are no favourite children, you love them all the same, and you love them unconditionally. There was a lot of fatherly love in that tow truck, and a life lesson in how to treat others.

Chapter 2
Experiential Learning

Me & Jayne at the Fairground, Wales, 1973

I was born Nigel Mark SAINSBURY on 7 June 1960 at St Woolos Hospital, Newport, Monmouthshire. Sibling to brother Paul David SAINSBURY born 15 July 1956 and later sister Jayne Claire SAINSBURY born 3 July 1968. I share my birthday with Welsh singer Tom Jones who is 20 years older than me and American singer Prince who was two years older than me when he died in April 2016. Clearly, I broke the mould for good singers born on 7th June. Singer Ricky Valance of *'Tell Laura I Love her'* fame was born in the next village of Ynysddu in April 1939 and had his massive hit the same year I was born - so some singing connection there perhaps. Being four years younger than my brother meant that I spent my early years fighting him and being eight years older than my sister meant that I spent my teenage years always fighting her. Being a middle child had both advantages and disadvantages. For example, it was rare for me to get new clothes growing up, I always seem to have hand-me-downs from my brother (luckily, he was a boy). On the positive side, I could (and did) blame things that went wrong, or got broken in the house, on my sister. I was far more streetwise than her, having learnt the lessons from my brother.

Being the one in the middle also gave me a degree of independence from my parents that I don't think my siblings experienced. Paul was the first (spoiled child and first grandchild) and Jayne was the last born (also spoiled of course and was dad's girl). I say this not to discredit my brother or sister, it was not of their doing, it was just the way it was. My perception was my reality. I never felt unloved by my parents but my relationship with them seemed different to my siblings. I loved my parents of course, but I had this burning desire to move away from home and experience life outside our village as soon as I could. I don't remember mum or dad ever encouraging me to stay at home. I always had a bit of a fascination with aeroplanes growing up, this was fuelled by my dad's enthusiasm to take me and my brother every year to the *'At Home Day'* at Royal Air Force (RAF) St Athan. The St Athan at home day was one of many at home days the RAF used to have across the UK. They were a massive recruitment tool for the RAF all through the 50s, 60s, 70s, 80s and 90s. St Athan was the closest, and the date usually fell on the second Saturday in September. With thousands of other aviation enthusiasts, we would spend the morning walking around the static aircraft and ground displays, and as this picture shows, getting the memorable photographs. The significance of this instant polaroid photo of me in the cockpit of a Hunter and its impact was huge. Never underestimate what kind of influence these experiences have

Me in the Cockpit of a Hunter Aircraft, St Athan, Wales, 1968

on children, particularly if they are repeated year on year as was our pilgrimage to St Athan. The cockpit photo of the Hunter aircraft and St Athan would play a much bigger part in my life over the coming decades. Watching the various aircraft displays in the afternoon was inspiring. You either enjoyed the aircraft noise, speed, and aroma of burnt jet fuel or you didn't, there was no in between. I loved it all. Not surprisingly, all this exposure to aircraft had me focused during my latter years in school on joining the RAF. Having completed school in July 1976, I had to wait until January 1977 when I would be 16 1/2 years old. This was predicated on my achieving the relevant qualifications from school and my parents signing the consent for me to join the military.

Unfortunately, my focus on schoolwork did not kick in until early teenage years and by then it was too late to study subjects at the highest level possible since I had failed my 11+ exam. The 11+ was a test for kids (aged 11, oddly enough) to see if they had the academic ability to study subjects in Grammar School at the General Certificate of Education (GCE) *'O Level'* (O = Ordinary) and then progress to *'A Level'*, (A= Advanced) before attending University. Those of us that failed the 11+ would attend the local Secondary Modern School to study at the Certificate of Secondary Education *"CSE Level"*. The CSE was a lower level qualification with little to no opportunity to progress to A Levels and onto University. For me this meant that I had to attend Ynysddu (un-ess-d), Secondary Modern School and not the more prestigious Pontllanfraith (Pont-Lan-Fryth), Grammar School. The major benefit for attending Ynysddu school was that it was much closer to home and I could walk there and back every day (about a mile each way). It would be a daily bus trip to attend Pontllanfraith and a much earlier start and later finish to the day. Furthermore, the subjects were easier at Ynysddu. I was always one to look for the positives.

From my own experience, I see children develop and experiment with all sorts of things at various times as they grow up. I was no different, just a little slower than average perhaps and by the photograph taken in July 1969 for the Prince of Wales Investiture, I was clearly experimenting with my sexuality. I found it fun to dress up in girl's clothes for the fancy-dress party without any sense of embarrassment or concern. Nobody seemed to care in those days, it was fun, and nobody judged you. However, a more significant and memorable event took place when I must have been about 12 years old; I discovered masturbation. In fact, it was something I was taught rather than discovered on my own. There was an older boy who lived in our community called Charlie, an only child, who for some reason, thought it would be a great idea to take me up the dingle (a large wooded area behind our street) and teach me how to masturbate. I was more than a little nervous and not really that interested, but he was persistent. It only happened once, and it really was against my will, but clearly it was more about him than me. I doubt I was his only pupil either. He would never get away with anything like that these days. I never told anyone about the incident, but I knew it was wrong. I never associated this behaviour as bullying, forcing me to smoke a cigarette was bullying. This was different. It felt more

Me in Fancy Dress, Prince Charles Investiture Party, Cwmfelinfach, Wales, 1969

like I was being coerced and harassed rather than bullied, there was no physical harm, and luckily no long-lasting emotional damage - but I never forgot the incident. It was wrong from whatever angle you look at it; today it would be called sexual abuse. He will always be remembered as a wanker in my mind.

My first school was Cwmfelinfach, Junior School. A small village school that combined infants and juniors. It schooled around 250 children and was a mere third of a mile walk from home. During the 1960s there were no such things as pre-schools or nurseries, so at five years old you went to school for the very first time. It was quite an adventure. Part of the adventure I didn't like so much was school milk. The government of the day insisted that every child needed to consume a third of a pint of milk per day to supplement their diet. We would be forced to drink this shit at morning break time. I hated it; most kids did. It was never kept in a fridge so in the summer the milk would warm and begin to curdle by the time we had to drink it, the smell was awful. It was like drinking your own sick. In the winter, icy cream would form on the top and the milk was just lumpy. The ice cream might sound appetising, but it was just bloody gross. After all, who wants to drink ice cold drinks on a freezing cold day. To this day, I almost gag at the thought of drinking neat milk or any flavoured milk drink. Milk in coffee or on cereal is the best I can do.

Going through those early years of primary school I suffered from stuttering, and even when I could speak, I spoke with a slight lisp. Not great social traits but it could have been worse. I would be teased more for my lisp than my stutter, but I don't remember it ever bothering me. The stutter was more irritating than anything else. I also don't remember suffering any real trauma (other than my mother threatening to send me to the children's home) so can only assume that my stutter was inherited from my parents or I had some undiagnosed anxiety disorder. I don't remember having anxiety as a youngster, but then again, I was a youngster and would not have known of the condition anyway. It is hard to stutter if you don't have the natural affliction – try it. It was also quite typical in the day for parents to self-diagnose their own children saying things like *'he will grow out of it'* or *'It's just a phase he's going through'*, referring to just about anything from dribbling whilst chewing your food to stealing cars. Both my stutter and lisp seemed to naturally disappear as I got older. As a young lad in primary school, I had a belief that people only had a finite amount of words they could speak before they ceased talking completely. This belief may have been my coping mechanism for dealing with my stutter and ultimately may have even slowed my development rate in those early years as I was reluctant to speak just for the sake of it. I have since made up for that belief.

It was cool in the 60s and 70s to have a nickname at school. Your nickname was used predominantly in the playground when playing football (soccer) with your mates and it was a name given to you, rather than one you would choose yourself. In my case, I was called *'Fishmonger'*, which was quickly shortened to *'Fisher'* and then to *'Fish'*. That nickname stuck with me all through my school years and is still used when I travel home to Cwmfelinfach and meet up with my old school mates. I don't know the origin of the nickname, but I was given it in the playground by a school mate called Dai. When I joined the RAF, I quickly inherited the nickname *'Tesco'* which came directly from my surname Sainsbury. Both Sainsbury's and Tesco are extremely popular UK supermarkets and it was much easier and less formal for my work mates to call me Tesco than Sainsbury. Calling me Fish just didn't make sense in the adult world. People remember nick names much better than your real name, particularly when it is related to something common. Tesco made me popular during my young adult life, though popularity was not my goal.

While disappointed at my failure to pass the 11+, I thought little about the better education and more about me having an easier life. Because at 11 years old, it is all about you. The CSE grading system was not as widely recognized as an educational foundation stone for further education and was more aligned to students heading into vocational occupations. The positive side of studying in a secondary school was there was no limit on how many CSEs you could study, and it was also easier to get into the rugby team since the school population was smaller.

Students were restricted to the number of O levels they could study in Grammar school (minimum of three, max of six to eight for the brainy kids). The other benefit of CSE was that if you achieved a Grade 1 in a CSE subject, that was (an accepted) equivalent to a C level pass at O Level. The entrant qualification for joining the RAF had both O Level and CSE Grades. Therefore, to ensure that I got the right qualifications to join at the highest level possible, I undertook all 12 CSE's that were available at the time and managed to achieve seven Grade 1: History, Arithmetic, Mathematics, Physics, Scripture Knowledge, Craft and Design (woodwork) and Art and Design; three Grade 2: Chemistry, English and Geography and a Grade 3 in Technical Drawing. I got an Unclassified in French. To this day I can only say *"open a window"*, *"close a door"* and tell someone to *"shut their mouth"* in French. Apart from being able to order a large beer or a glass of wine, what additional French phrases do you really need to know. My French teachers comments on my school reports reflected my attitude towards the subject at that time with remarks like; *'has not exerted himself'* and *'capable of far better, poor attitude to work'*, these words of encouragement were not a good homing for the final exam.

Indeed, his final comments on my last school report summed me up; *"it seems as though Nigel has ceased to make an effort in this subject"*. He was correct. I was not proud of my attitude in the French lessons, but I realized even then, that any additional work and revision effort would be better placed on subjects I enjoyed or had half a chance of success. That decision certainly paid off in the end of year exams. It was a great life learning experience in that sometimes it is better to cut loose those things that demand your time, are of no interest to you and add no value to your goals.

On the other hand, I was particularly good at Art and Design and my teacher, Miss Davies, decided that I was good enough to undertake that subject at O level. As a result, I got a Grade 1 CSE and I passed the O level exam getting a recognized Level C pass. Funny how you remember some teacher's names from school but not others. She was a lovely lady with a large (memorable) chest, because at 14 years old you notice these things in your teachers and these outstanding features can be quite influential when selecting subjects to study. Strangely, I also remembered the French teachers name because he was Italian, our football coach and his initials were MAD. Come to think of it, what the hell was a French speaking Italian doing in a Welsh school. No wonder I struggled with the language. Also, I find it strange that I can remember a teacher's name and initials from the seventies yet struggle to remember what happened three days ago now that I am a sexagenarian.

Notwithstanding this huge (but expected) disappointment in French, I came top of my class and top of the school in 1976 beating the favourite top student who was by far the brightest student throughout my secondary education. It was me who won the 1975-76 Service and Attainment Award. I guess I just came good when it mattered. I don't think I would have performed so well in a Grammar School. Having said that, the adage of being a *'big fish in a small pond'* may have some context here and I may have developed quicker being a 'small fish in a big pond' by going to Grammar School. Who knows. I really enjoyed my secondary education and rarely missed a day. In fact, the only real time I had off school was when I had serious allergies (hay fever) in the spring or when my parents took me out of school to go on the family holiday.

This additional holiday during school term did not happen that often and in the 70s it was not frowned upon to take your children out of school, parents just did it, but for me, it just meant additional work to catch up on when I got back. Taking holidays outside normal school holidays offered cheaper deals in accommodation and car hire, just like they are today. On reflection, it was probably a combination of all things about school and my happy days growing up at home that I did so well in the end. Even suffering setbacks with serious allergies did not deter me. It was always a struggle for me at exam time as that was normally the height of the pollen season and to this day, I hold it as my excuse for failing the 11+ exam in junior school. The lesson here was that there are things in life you have no control over, you just have to live with them. I had no control over my allergies and there were few remedies available in the 60s and 70s, but the allergies were not going to ruin me at final exam time. If that meant locking myself in a cold dark room over the summer, then that's what I would do – and in fact, that's exactly what I did in 1976, it was not difficult to find such a room in our house.

Secondary school was an experiential learning period for me. My focus was not just on school subjects. Music, sport, motorcycles, girls and alcohol all started to influence me at various times. I am still not sure how I determined their priority or when they occurred in my life. Girls and alcohol seem to happen around the same time. I really wanted to learn and play music and was offered the violin at school, but my parents could not afford such an expense. I had a good voice too and was in the school choir for a while, but it was not cool in the 70s at our school for a boy to be in a choir. Peer pressure and my testicles dropping took its toll on my voice, which gave me the perfect excuse to fade out of choir practice to focus on sports and other subjects. I can still sing the first few bars from the old 1940s Rodgers and Hammerstein musical *'Oklahoma'*, albeit in a deeper voice now than back then. The height of my youth singing career saw me knocking out a solo of *'Mary's Boy Child'* in the Christmas service at our local Presbyterian Chapel in 1973. I remember being scared to death at the time, but I did it and it was the only occasion I can remember the congregation clapping; funny the details you remember. I also remember wearing some awful psychedelic large rounded collar shirt during the performance. Perhaps it was my dress shirt they were clapping for and not my singing. I would not feel those kinds of nerves again until a decade later in early 1983 when I joined a rock band as their keyboard player. It is these kinds of moments experienced as a kid that help build your strength of character and confidence to fulfil your dreams. There really are no boundaries to your dreams as a child. However, as we grow older, we seem to suppress those dreams by building invisible obstacles, making crap excuses, or letting ourselves get distracted by other less important things in life.

I have always loved music. Initially, like most people, just listening to songs on the radio, but television quickly trumped radio for the music listening experience. Suddenly you could dress and act like your favourite artist whilst watching them perform your favourite songs on TV. I loved watching Top of the Pops (TOTP) in the 70s and 80s on a Thursday night at 7:30pm on BBC1. It was like a religion to me and I found it quite inspirational. I would often picture myself up on stage performing to my fans - it was a dream that would come true, in a less impressive way in 1983.

TOTP was great entertainment for 30 minutes and the programme would always end with the Number 1 song in the 'Hit Parade" or 'The Charts' as they became known. During the show, you could get to see some shocking performances from several bizarre pop stars' that performed your favourite tunes. The more astute of us knew that they were not actually performing live on stage as the instruments and microphones were never plugged in. And if that wasn't convincing enough, the lip syncing from some of the performers was so shocking you wondered if they were singing the same song as the music you were listening to. TOTP was presented by popular Radio 1 (pop radio channel) DJ's, some of which I remember had faces that were best suited for radio.

I started to really get into music at about age 13. The tune (music rather than the singing) was the attraction to me as I played little attention to the lyrics. Indeed, I used to make my own lyrics up if I couldn't understand what they were singing about, a sort of parody. Often my alternative lyrics would be rude or just stupid and made no sense at all. It didn't really matter because it was my own performance and such random words helped me remember the tune. It would not be until I joined a band that I would get to fully understand and appreciate the meaning behind lyrics and the skill and inspiration that songwriters have for writing and producing a song. To me, music is akin to laughter, it crosses language boundaries and connects people by being a common denominator. Our sense of smell and taste can remind us of an event, a moment, a person or place; music does the same for me. I have always held the belief that if you can play a musical instrument you will always make friends and have a special connection with people. If you can sing as well, that's a bonus.

As a kid growing up, I never felt the need to buy records, I could record songs from the radio onto a cassette recorder, a practise everyone did at the time. Initially using a basic tape recorder with a microphone. Such a device would pick up doors slamming, parents shouting and all sorts of other noises. The introduction of the radio/cassette player combination revolutionised the way you could capture music and increase your music collection. The original *'Boogie Box'* grew from something that was quite personal at the start to something quite monstrous over the years that needed mechanical means to carry it around. Bigger also meant louder and being able to share your music with people that were over a quarter mile away was always a cool thing to do.

I was always attracted to electronic/synthesizer music. In amongst dads' country and western records, was a LP (long Player) record called *"The Amazing Music of The Electronic Arp Synthesizer'*. The tunes were contemporary for the time and included songs like; *'Yellow Submarine'* and *'Raindrops Keep Falling On My Head'*. There was no singing and I found the strange sounds fascinating. The music of people like the Frenchman, *Jean Michel Jarre*, and German bands like *Kraftwerk* became favourites of mine, but I was also inspired by the Punk era and the music of the *Stranglers, Sex Pistols* and the contrasting genre of the New Romantics and bands like *Depeche Mode, Spandau Ballet, Duran Duran* and *Human League*. To this day, some 40 years later, I still have a collection of cassettes tucked away that were either recorded off the radio or more recently (post 1977) from vinyl records. In 2016 I bought a cassette player, so I could listen to the tunes of my youth while converting them into useable digital formats for my phone and car. Not everything is on Spotify.

Rugby was, and still is, a religion in Wales and it seemed that we played it during summer and winter during school terms. Football (soccer) was also popular but more so in the school yard and knocking around at home; I enjoyed playing and was fairly good at both. Rugby sevens which is a sprinting version of normal rugby played with half of the team on a full-size field was also popular. I made the sevens team a few times in my later years in school. Sevens was not quite as rough as Rugby 15 which was why I preferred to play sevens, but you had to be super fit. Unfortunately for me, the racing snakes in our school had all the plum positions on the normal rugby 15 team and that left me wearing the No 2 *'Hooker'* jersey which is not the best position for someone who was quite small. I hated scrums.

Rugby Team (Me Far Left), Ynysddu School, Ynysddu, Wales, 1975

If I could get through the game with just a bloody nose and only having had one or two fights during the scrum, then I was doing well. School boy rugby was a particularly harsh game back in the day and was used to turn Welsh boys into men, albeit broken men in my case. I am not sure it was the *'one thing'* that turned me into a man, but it did teach me the art of survival in a competitive and physical environment. During my last full game in October 1975, just after the photograph above was taken, I broke my right wrist during a ridiculously hard tackle. I didn't even know that I had broken it and continued playing until just before half time when the pain got so bad, I almost passed out. I remember our PE Teacher and referee, Mr Pulsford rolling back my shirt sleeve to expose a very odd-looking wrist before stopping the game completely to take me to the hospital. I only played sevens from then on until I left school. By playing rugby sevens, fitness was not going to be an issue for me in joining the RAF.

Motorcycles have always played a large part in my life. I loved them even before I had even ridden one. An adventure occurs every time I throw my leg over the saddle. I was 13 years old when I owned my first motorcycle. In fact, it was a non-running moped that had been gifted to me by our neighbour. The bike was an NSU Quickly. An odd name for a machine that was anything but quick. With a little bit of supervision/help from dad, I got the thing running. What was significant about owning the NSU was from that day forward there would only be brief periods in my life when I didn't own a motorcycle. As a teenager, I had four-part time jobs that were a good source of pocket money. The Sunday paper round was quite a lucrative job to have as a young lad and the money I got for delivery and tips was excellent. The job was all done and dusted in about four hours. I also had a grocery delivery job on a Friday night. That was easy, just load up the grocery boxes into the store owners Volkswagen Beetle and then go around with her delivering the groceries to the old and infirm people who lived on their own. The third job I had was filling and weighing sugar bags in the same local village 'Spar' shop that I used to do deliveries on a Friday, the fourth one was the delivery of shop leaflets advertising special offers. All this pocket money enabled me to purchase my next motorbike, which was in fact a Scooter, a red Vespa 150 and then soon after that a Honda C50. Earning money and buying motorcycles would be a lifelong habit. These machines were only ridden up and down the back lane. At age 13 when I had the NSU Quickly, I would often 'borrow' my brothers Honda SS 50 moped and travel beyond the back lane without anyone knowing. Mainly in the evening when it was dark so no one would recognise me. I was never caught, and no one ever found out. I was lucky.

Me & My Honda C50, Back Lane, Cwmfelinfach, Wales, 1975

Life was pretty good on Commercial Road. All the adults were called aunty or uncle by the kids, even though most were unrelated; although to be fair, you never really knew for sure. All the households that had kids were just open homes and we regularly spent time in each other's houses when we were not playing outside. Nothing was locked, and we often did things as communities. Life on Commercial Road was just like having an extended family. The concept of time was interesting. We never had watches, so time was determined by the sun and your stomach. If you were going out to play or going somewhere you had to be back by lunch time, teatime or nighttime. It worked; the rules were not complicated.

We used to play all sorts of games in the back lane. Classic games like hide and seek; and there was no shortage of places to hide. *'Kick the Tin'* which was a derivative of hide and seek. You had an empty baked bean tin or plastic bottle that would be placed in an open area of the back lane. The seeker would hide their eyes and count to 100 whilst the others hid. When the seeker found someone, it would be a sprint race to the tin. The seeker had to bang the tin three times stating the name of the person that had just been caught. If you were the person who had been found, you had to come out of hiding and try and get to the tin before the seeker had knocked it three times and shouted your name. As the seeker searched for the others, then the hiding guys could take the opportunity, break cover and run to the tin and kick it down the lane. This released those that had been caught by the seeker, so they could hide again as the seeker recovered the tin and counted to 100 once more with their eyes closed. A great game, we played it for hours and in all weathers.

If we got bored with such innocent games, there were other fun but riskier games we could play. Once such game was called *'Split the Kipper'*, a pretty dangerous game of throwing a sharp dagger between someone's legs, stabbing the ground forcing them to spread eagle until they fall over - if you stabbed their foot, then it was their turn to do it to you. A less dangerous game was called *'Knock up Ginger'*. A simple game which involved daring your friends to go knocking on the front door of someone's house before running away and hiding simply to watch the occupant come out of the house and look for the culprit who knocked their door. Doing it once is no big deal but doing it several times over a 20 to 30-minute period really pisses people off. When you think the occupant is going to hide behind the door to catch you, you simply put some dog pooh or anything you like into a paper bag and set fire to it just before you knock the door for the last time and then run away like a startled banshee. Watching people come out of their houses quickly in bedroom slippers or even bare feet to catch you is the real dare. Once they open the door and see the fire, it instantly takes their mind off chasing you and they immediately set about trying to stamp out the fire. Well, you can imagine the rest if there is dog pooh in the bag and they are wearing nothing but slippers on their feet. It is hilarious to witness. Yes, it was stupid, yes it was irresponsible and no, I am not proud of what we did but when you are growing up in the valleys, this is the kind of stuff that you did for entertainment.

We were also physically fit as kids in the 1960s and 70s. We would have fun just running races against each other in the back lane. We were always climbing trees and making tree swings up the dingle, and in the summer, we would often go on long walks up the local mountains to pick wild berries and pull ground nuts, strangely, out of the ground. Wimberries or bilberries were a great source of nourishment for us, they look like small blueberries, are not very juicy but sweet enough to eat raw. They are not easy to find either, so they were rewarding to eat when you did find them, even though they could have been pissed and shat upon by sheep and wild rabbits. We must have had stomachs of steel as kids, as we quenched our thirst and washed down the digested nuts and berries with water drank directly from the natural stream. God only knows what was in the water. For any berries that made it back home, mum would bake them in a pie. We were also inventive as kids. We would make bows and arrows from tree branches cut with just our pocketknives and for the more technically minded, make boogie carts from old baby prams. A four-wheeled boogie cart was nothing more than three pieces of wood; two smaller pieces to hold the axles of a set of baby pram wheels, and a longer piece to sit on and to connect the two axles together. The front axle would be connected by a single nut and bolt to the long piece allowing it to be steered by your feet and the other axle simply nailed to the long piece of wood into a T shape at the back where you sat. A length of rope was normally attached to the steering axle ends to pull it along when you were walking, but it also doubled up as a means for you to hang on when going around corners whilst giving you some feedback from the steering with your feet. It was like having power assisted steering. Downhill races often led to crashes. Injuries were commonplace as most carts never had brakes. I have realised that the improvisation skills we learnt as kids, were directly transferable into adult life. It's called DIY.

A couple of weeks leading up to Bonfire Night, 5th November, we would spend time after school and weekends going up the dingle to chop down trees and large branches off bigger trees. These would then be dragged to the waste area at the end of Commercial Road before arranging them in a pyramid fashion ready for Bonfire Night. We would take turns staying in the bonfire just in case it got raided (deliberately set on fire) by other local kids. Yes, stupid when I think about it, but we were kids and that is what we did. We would also raid bonfires outside our own area, it was just something you did. I cannot imagine allowing kids these days armed with axes, large wood saws and big knives cutting down pristine wooded areas just so they could burn in memory of some whacko bloke called Guy Fawkes who tried to blow up the Houses of Parliament, London in 1605.

It was common for a week or two before the night to make an effigy of the *'Guy'* and, as kids, we would sit on the corner near the local pub and shops asking, *'penny for the guy'*. The money was usually spent on fireworks which anyone could buy in those days. *'Bangers'* were everyone's favourites, and usually came in boxes of 10 or 20 just like cigarettes. These fireworks were miniature explosives and were much more fun than handheld sparklers or other benign types of fireworks, if there are any benign types. We would light, hold and then throw these bangers at each other just to scare the shit out of ourselves. Not so much fun if you were on the receiving end though. Minor burns were commonplace, that just made it even funnier. Accidents worse than minor burns did happen but taking risks was part of the excitement and fun. It was a common dare to see how long you could hang on to it before you threw it. That kind of fun.

I would never allow my kids to do such stupid things yet, it was ok for me to do it. Dual standards or lessons learnt. Probably a little bit of both. If the bonfire had survived raids and was still standing on 5th November, the Guy would be placed on top of the bonfire. Once it got dark, we would smash the streetlights near the bonfire or shoot them out with a pellet gun before covering the bonfire in paraffin or petrol and setting it alight. The street celebrations would begin soon after; food, fireworks, music and friends just hanging out.

In the 70s, chopping down trees for bonfire night was never frowned upon, it was just something kids did. After all, there were plenty of common wooded areas around. Young trees were good for making bows and arrows and bigger trees on a slope were good for making rope swings, not sit-down ones, but single ropes with knots on the end that you could swing out in an arc from one side to the other. Mum always thought these swings were dangerous and I was told to keep off them. It seemed like everything I enjoyed doing was dangerous to mum. One afternoon, me and my mates were playing on one of these rope swings when I slipped and landed on my abdomen atop an old tree stump. I was badly winded and almost knocked myself out as my head whacked the ground. Worse than that, I had scraped all my stomach and it was bleeding from the grazing. The bruising had started to come out immediately, I felt physically sick and could not get up and walk without pain. How I got home and hid this from mum is still a mystery to me. Coincidentally, I had started to pee red thinking that it was blood. I was worried sick but could not bring myself to tell Mum at first, then I thought I would just tell her about my pee, she didn't need to know about the swing injury. Mum smiled at me and told me that the red pee was probably a result of all the beetroot I had been eating (mum used to pickle her own beetroot and onions) and there was nothing to worry about. I was relieved. Yeah, I thought it must be beetroot not blood; that was a good enough answer for me.

The reason I remember this story is that as a parent, I know from the answers and expressions on my own children's faces that there have been times when things have happened to them that they never told me about or perhaps spun a yarn that was more palatable to me than the real story. Perhaps they were worried about the consequences of my knowing, embarrassed or just thought that I would disapprove of their actions. And I am ok with all that. In life you make decisions, and there can be grave consequences to not telling the whole story or just not telling the truth about something that has happened. Growing up you need to experiment with these choices, and you don't always get it right. Telling the truth can be hurtful and worrying and if there is nothing to be gained by it and the situation is over, then why do it. I am not saying that lying is a good option, merely suggesting that not telling the whole truth can work equally as well in some scenarios. As an adult, I ask myself *'would I have done something different in the swing story?'* Yes, absolutely, I would have told Mum that I had an accident and shown her my injuries, perhaps skipped the part of telling her exactly how it happened, replacing the swing with a fall off my bicycle type of yarn. That is experience shining through, recognising that mum would have been both worried and angry if I had told her the exact truth. In the revised scenario, she only would have been worried about my injuries rather than the activity I was doing that had caused them. Everyone is a winner then. These kinds of events are all good learning opportunities and character building. However, I don't advocate extrapolating this kind of behaviour when dealing with sensitive relationship issues or other matters that really do require the whole truthful story to be told.

Family time seemed to be confined to the weekend, after Sunday School and Sunday lunch. We often spent Sunday afternoon down at nans house (on my dad's side) with our real aunties and uncles visiting. Sunday was a time for catching up with our cousins whilst the grownups would play cards, gossip, smoke cigarettes and drink. Not a great way to spend Sunday as a kid growing up, but we had little choice. Nan's house was full on a Sunday. Dad was the eldest of six children and if they all turned up with kids in tow, it was a crowded living room.

As a kid you are oblivious to grown up talk and adult relationships and it is only when you are all grown up yourself that you begin to understand exactly what was going on in those days. I mentioned earlier that I didn't remember my nan having a good relationship with grandad, but this was normal to me. I learnt later in life that they went for years without speaking to each other - even though they lived in the same house for years. I don't know to this day why it was like that, but in the 60s and early 70s people just seem to stick with it. Divorce was rare. Also, I did notice even at that young age there were several internal family feuds that never seemed to get settled. It was as though they enjoyed fighting and talking behind each other's back. I learnt this just by eavesdropping on mum and dad talking on the way home in the car. Reminds me of the adage, *"You can choose your friends, but you can't choose your family."*

I have never really been excited about cars, even as a kid. However, from an early age my parents suspected that I was going to be an engineer because as a baby I would always take the tyres off my brother's toy cars. This really pissed my brother off as he could never find them afterwards. I only ever took them off, it would be many years later that I would understand the big deal and learn to put them back on.

As a small kid around five years old, I remember running down the back lane to meet dad coming home from work and he would let me sit on his lap and steer the car (a modern-day Austin A35 Van) down the lane into our neighbour's cutaway garden. I loved the experience, but cars would be a secondary means of transport to me growing up. The uncle who lived there was the local butcher and an ex-WWII aircraft rear gunner. He was a lovely friendly man, and both he and his wife always had a smile and the time of day for you. It would be these folks who would put on the Bonfire night party on 5th November. The bonfire was on waste ground right next to their house. BBQ, toffee apples and all sorts of goodies. Good times.

Their son Chris used to have some unusual animals. I have no idea where he got them from, but he always had something of interest. Over the years, he had at least one snake; I had no idea what it was, but it was big. A buzzard and various other birds and reptiles. The one I remember the most was a Tawny Owl that had been 'rescued' and subsequently became domesticated; not that it watched TV, did laundry and cooked meals, just that it lived in the house. Everyone in the street knew it lived there but clearly one of our neighbours was not happy about having an owl living in the neighbourhood and reported Chris to the RSPCA (Royal Society for the Prevention of Cruelty to Animals). The RSPCA came and removed the Owl at least twice, releasing it back into the wild but the bird would find its way back. The owl would sleep in the airing cupboard on top of the hot water cylinder in the living room.

Being a wild animal, the owl would only eat living things. As kids we would chip in some money and go and buy a white mouse from the pet shop in Blackwood, a shopping village just up the valley and then we would go around to see Chris and his owl. Chris would let us release the mouse onto the living room floor and then we would all sit and watch quietly as the owl stalked the mouse. Once the mouse was out in the open and the owl was ready to strike, the owl would gracefully glide from the top of the hot water cylinder, quietly land on the floor of the lounge keeping its wings fully deployed to prevent the mouse running away. Slowly and deliberately the owl would walk to corner the mouse and then when both the mouse and owl were still, the owl seem to hypnotise the mouse for about 20 seconds then, in a blink of an eye, it would lunge forward with its mouth wide open and grab the mouse head first. There was no fuss, no noise, no nothing. The owl would gracefully tilt his head backwards and in two or three gulps would swallow the mouse alive. The last thing you would see is the little pink tail wriggling like a piece of spaghetti draped over the owl's beak before finally disappearing down the owl's throat. The owl would then calmly fold his wings, turn around, strut a few steps into open space and then gracefully flap his wings and take up his position on the hot water cylinder again. The whole event was over in a few minutes. Once the mouse thought it was safe to come out from under the furniture it was game over. It was a surreal experience, just like being in a scene from a Harry Potter movie.

Cars of the 60s and 70s were basic and needed constant attention. They were more functional than anything and not really designed for traveling long distances because people just didn't travel very far in those days. Often underpowered, cold and noisy with vinyl seats that were hard and slippery in the winter and soft and sticky in the summer. You could open the door with a screwdriver and with the same screwdriver in the ignition switch, you could start the engine. You really didn't need keys at all. The headlights were bright enough to illuminate about 10 feet in front of you, and the indicators (on some of dad's older cars) were small arms that flicked out of the side of the door frame. If it rained, the windscreen wipers were about as effective as an ashtray on a motorcycle. The wipers would clear a fraction of the windscreen area and you would be forced to stick your face on the inside of the glass just to see a few feet in front. If it was dark as well, you would be in trouble. Luckily, these cars were incapable of going fast.

I learnt a lot in those days about internal combustion engines, carburation, electrical systems, brakes, exhaust and a range of other things from helping dad service and fix not just his cars, but several troublesome cars my brother seemed to have the knack of buying, and cars of friends and neighbours. It was this education and my enjoyment of motorcycles that would lead me down the path of maintenance engineering. I had decided that I wanted to become a diesel fitter in the RAF, even though I didn't know much about the ground engineering trades - there was no internet to research these things. I simply thought it would be a trade just like working on cars and motorcycles that would keep me close to aeroplanes. However, I was to learn that the RAF recruiting staff had a slightly different idea about the career path I should take. My interest in aeroplanes was a much bigger factor than even I had envisaged.

Chapter 3
Tough Love

Not all kids know what they want to do when they leave school. I was fortunate, I knew exactly what I was going to do. I was hell bent on joining the RAF. Those annual pilgrimages to the St Athan 'At

Me & Lucky, Out the Back, Commercial Road, Cwmfelinfach, Wales, 1975

Home Days' were not wasted on me. Knowing what I needed from an educational standpoint, school would become a major focus for me from around 14 years old until I left at 16. However, I put my whole career at risk even before it had started. Back in 1975 I got mixed up with some unfavourable company. One person was particularly bad news for me and the two of us would go to Newport town centre on a Saturday afternoon and partake in a bit of shoplifting. Real petty things at first, but then as the excitement grew, and the rewards got bigger, so the shoplifting became more serious. It became almost addictive and we also became rather good at it - we thought. We were invincible teenagers. There were no in-store cameras in those days and there was little personal surveillance in the smaller stores. Oddly enough, one of my aunties was a store detective and we would see her on occasions patrolling some of the larger stores. She never recognised me.

I certainly didn't think about the consequences of what we were doing, only the rewards. I never once got caught, but my shoplifting mate got found out, and unbeknown to me at the time, he was also involved in other unfavourable activities. I believe that the father of my shoplifting mate told my dad, but dad never told me his sources. He just knew, and I had no defence. I arrived home on Saturday afternoon after we had been on one of our little business excursions into town, and dad confronted me. He demanded that I bring everything I had stolen to him immediately. He never even asked me if I had been doing anything wrong, he didn't need to. I never thought for one second to argue back, that would have been futile. I knew that he knew, and I went cold. I had been caught and now had to face the consequences.

I remember to this day dad talking to me in a forceful, slightly raised voice but also in a kind of strange and calmly spoken manner. It felt like he was holding back. I am sure he just wanted to strangle me. I had never experienced this tone from dad before and it frightened me. I brought everything I had to him. I had stuff hidden all over the house. Mainly toys and clothes, but other odds and sods, like sew on patches, model making paints, tools and stuff that I would never actually use, sell or even give away. Suddenly, it all seemed so senseless. One by one, he threw everything in the fireplace and burnt the lot. Even stuff that was clearly never going to burn – it didn't matter, he wanted rid of everything. He was making a very clear statement in his actions. Whilst he deliberately chucked things one by one into the fire, he cursed and lectured me on throwing away a career before it had even started, stating that there would be no RAF if I had a police record. He was angry in a way I had never experienced before, and I was left in no doubt that I had let him and mum down big time. I was hoping he would give me a beating and be done with it, but he didn't. Instead he did the opposite, he had nothing to do with me for days (seemed like weeks), he never even spoke or acknowledged me, nothing. I was absolutely devastated. It was terrible punishment.

I was having great difficulty dealing with dad constantly ignoring me, it was as if I didn't exist anymore in his eyes. I begged mum to ask dad to say something to me, his behaviour was breaking my heart, but mum had no influence. It was tough love and I was fairly sure it was killing dad too. I had already apologised for my actions, but I needed to do more. To break the deadlock, I faced up to dad by telling him that not only was I extremely sorry for my actions, I acknowledged that I had let him and mum down big time. I recognised the stupidity of my actions and I would work hard to make things good again. It worked. Dad slowly came around and I swore a promise to him that I would never do anything like that again, ever. To this day, I have stood by that promise to dad. I considered myself lucky to be found out, incredibly lucky indeed.

The shoplifting period was a significant turning point in my young adult life, I learnt a tough lesson that would never, ever be forgotten. I didn't know it then, but I also learnt a lot about risk and the consequences and likelihood of things going wrong. I also learnt about luck. Risk you can mitigate, manage and define. Luck, not so much. You have no control over luck at all, and I have no doubt that my luck would have ran out at some point. Thankfully, dad learnt of my extracurricular activities first. I also learnt that poor decisions and actions can have a profound effect on the people who love you and their relationship with others. Mum and dad were divided on my punishment and I knew it had taken a toll on them both. They were really worried about me and they thought I had started to head down a dark career path. It was a subdued few weeks for everyone. I never thought of the career implications at the time, but boy did I think about them afterwards. Some kids grow up and enter adulthood without any problems or stumbling along the way. Others, like me, needed to learn the boundaries of the acceptable from the unacceptable. Not the best way to learn perhaps, but it is a way in which you never, ever, forget. I also think that as a family, we came out of this better, stronger and perhaps even a little closer.

I left school after the end-of-year exams in July 1976, and after passing all the induction tests for the RAF, my joining was now predicated on my exam results. If I did well, I could join as a fitter. I would join as a mechanic if my results were average. I didn't know the difference at that time and quite honestly it didn't matter to me, I just wanted to join and move away from home. The term fitter described a more academically qualified and advanced trained mechanic. I would not start recruit training until sometime in January 1977, so I had five months to kill.

Around this time dad had started to have a few heart issues, so he and mum decided that they should move to a home that was built on the flat and had two storeys' rather than three. A noble decision, but it would be a decision that would add to dad's stress rather than ease it. They had lived on Commercial Road for over 20 years. They found a new house in Cross Keys in August 1976, a village about four miles away from Cwmfelinfach. We moved in, but the move did not go well. It was a massive upheaval for mum and she never really settled there. I wasn't that bothered, I was moving away with the RAF anyway, but mum's only sibling, her sister Cora, were quite close. Cora and her husband Emlyn lived next door to us at 4 Commercial Road.

Uncle Emlyn used to enjoy his beer and cigarettes, but he also enjoyed spending time with me and, years earlier, with my brother. We would spend hours out the back of the house hanging out over the dividing garden wall just drawing pictures and talking. The time spent on the garden wall was not wasted. Uncle Emlyn was great at drawing anything and it was his teaching me how to draw that piqued my interest in Art and Design classes later in secondary school. Emlyn was also a bit of a comedian and he would teach me how to tell jokes and recite classic daft Welsh phases like; *'you three are a pair if I ever seen one'*. Of course, phrases like that made no sense at all, but if you are Welsh, you get it. Other classic Welsh phrases included *'Who's coat is this jacket.'* and *'we got 300 miles of coastline, and it's all by the sea'*. The one I have probably used more than any other is *'follow me and I'll be right behind you'*. I didn't know it at the time, but these phrases would become good ice breakers for me during adult conversations. My uncle Emlyn was more of an influence on me than he would ever know.

Everyone knew everyone in the street, and it was such a great community and support network. Additionally, all us kids were born and grew up there, so there was a huge emotional attachment to the house and that immediate area. I am convinced that if we had moved to another country, the trauma mum experienced would have been no different than our moving four miles down the road to Cross Keys.

Mum always seemed unhappy in Cross Keys. Dad did his best to make it our new home and he tried hard to make mum happy, but in the end even dad thought that the move had been a mistake. The move took its toll on dad and he would suffer his first heart attack in this house. The irony of the situation. To make matters worse, our next-door neighbour had a daughter that was getting friendly with my brother. She would eventually become a daughter in law, but mum never really warmed to the girl next door and her reservations were to be realised a few years down the line when they got divorced. Although funny, it is perhaps a reflection of my mother's values and strong beliefs, that during my brother's divorce, mum decided to cut off the head of my sister-in-law in all the family photographs including the wedding ones. They really did look odd afterwards as mum never replaced the cut outs, she just left them blank with the jagged edge scissor marks. They were the kind of pictures police investigating a murder would find in a prime suspect's home.

Luckily, nothing happened to my brother's ex-wife after the divorce otherwise mum would have been arrested. After just one year, mum and dad had had enough of Cross Keys and sold up in October 1977 and moved back to Cwmfelinfach. They moved to a two storey three-bedroom terraced house at 23 Arthur Street, about a half mile away from Commercial Road. Things were never the same even though they had moved back to Cwmfelinfach. The move back to the village never really affected me as I was now in the RAF, but I do believe that mum never should have moved away from Commercial Road. There was too much emotional connection to that home for both mum and dad and of course, to us as kids and our pet dog, Lucky.

Lucky was a regrettable name for our family pet. He could be a nasty little bugger at times, but he was the family dog after all, and we loved him. He was a mongrel, a cross between a Terrier and a few other breeds with black and white coloring. He was only about a foot tall, weighing around 20lbs, but boy he was strong, there was likely some Bulldog in his DNA. Not long after dad had died, a local man came to the house one day and told mum that Lucky had been identified as the dog that had bitten his son. Mum refused to accept that it was Lucky and did nothing. The man came back a couple of weeks later and threatened to report mum if she did nothing about Lucky. Now facing a summons from the local authorities, mum had a horrible choice to make. Face the courts and an expensive lawsuit or euthanize Lucky. It was a horrible position for her to be in, she knew Lucky could be unpredictable, and he would have been capable of biting. He had been identified some months previously as one of the village dogs that had been seen chasing sheep. In the 70s, it was normal for family dogs to roam around the streets unsupervised, dog fights were common and there were a lot of dogs looking for fights - including Lucky. A small boy playing outside, as all kids did, would have been easy for him. My brother, Paul, took Lucky to the vet. Several weeks after we had Lucky euthanized, the chap reported to mum that it was probably not Lucky that had bitten his son. Although we were all terribly upset by this, mum and Paul were absolutely devastated.

Mum had also gotten herself engaged into a bitter neighborly feud with the lady next door. The feud seemed to go on all the time she lived there and after dad died had probably gotten worse. On reflection, I wondered if this was just an avenue for mum to focus and express her anger and regret for dads passing after we had moved back to Cwmfelinfach, and everything else that had gone bad since moving away from Commercial Road. Her arguments with her neighbor were always a topic of conversation during a visit back home. It was almost comical, like listening to a Laurel and Hardy skit, but this was real, this was mum's real life not some fictional comedy duo on television. I was glad not to be a part of it.

In Cross Keys, we lived opposite an industrial estate where I landed a job with a heavy engineering firm called 'Wheway Watson'. This company agreed to employ me as casual labour until I joined the RAF. I was a personal apprentice to an engineer who was responsible for replacing a steam turbine in Aberthaw Power Station, Barry. Working on this steam turbine was such a great experience. I learnt the principles of household electricity generation and how industrial turbines work. I would come across these very same principles again during my RAF training as a propulsion engine fitter. The work at Aberthaw was manual and dirty but a lot of fun and I got paid in cash, with bonuses, on a weekly basis. Within a few weeks, I had enough money saved for a deposit for my first legal motorbike; a Yamaha FS1E, which was technically a moped and colloquially called the *'Fizzie'*.

Dad was always supportive of my getting a motorbike. Mum, not so much - in fact, she was dead against it but knew she was fighting a losing battle. I landed a more regular job in October 1976 in a supermarket called ASDA (Associated Dairies) stacking shelves in the sauces and pickles aisles. This job would secure me a regular wage and hence see me earn enough money to make the hire purchase payments on the Yamaha. I was so excited the day dad and I signed the agreement for the Yamaha I could hardly sleep the next few days until I picked it up. It may have only been a moped, but it was a superbike to me. A street legal bike that would give me independence and some kudos with my mates. Dad and I convinced mum that the bike was essential for me to travel back and forth work and of course it would allow me to come home once I had moved away and joined the RAF. Mum was never convinced that a bike was the solution, nor would she ever be, but dad and I tried. Mum never learnt to ride or drive herself and her fears of my riding a motorcycle and having a serious accident would become a self-fulfilling prophecy in a few years' time.

Working in ASDA was the first time that I had worked with other adults as a peer group. The work was easy, all you had to do was to keep the shelves full during your shift and carry out any additional duties that your supervisor wanted you to do. You needed to have a little self-motivation and that was not a problem for me, the time went much quicker when I was busy, but I was really surprised by how many adults acted in the opposite. They seem to go out of their way to avoid work. I found this most unusual and to this day don't understand why folks put more effort into avoiding work when it is much easier just to get on and do it. It's not as if they had anything better to do. There were no smart phones or other handheld gaming devices in those days to distract them.

The other thing I learnt about this environment was that it seemed to be quite normal practice to damage perfectly good stock and then dump it in accordance with company policy and procedures. At the end of the shift, my co-workers would swing by the dumpsters on their way home and recover the damaged goods they had just dumped. Avoiding work and deliberately damaging goods were major lessons in loyalty and trust for me. This was shoplifting by stealth and I knew a thing or two about shoplifting. I asked myself, *'was this the way adult workers really behaved.'* I kept quiet about the things I witnessed as I felt even at that young age, that there would be repercussions for me if I reported what I had seen. Luckily, I was never asked any questions about these activities, so I never told any lies. As a grown up, I would act very differently today. I would most certainly confront my co-workers head on, asking what they were doing and highlighting the consequences of such actions to steer them away from what was clearly theft.

As a grown up 16 ½ year-old I was ready to step up and begin my RAF career. I had clearly made an impression at Asda. The store management were keen to retain me and offered me a pathway into retail management, sponsored 100% by Asda. This would also include a pay increase. It was a great opportunity, I recognised that, but my mind was made up. I was going to join the RAF. I remember the store manager encouraging me to reconsider right up to my last day. He settled in the end for me promising to return to Asda if military service was not for me. I didn't recognise the significance of his offer at the time, but clearly, he had seen something in me that I never saw in myself. All I did was my job, it wasn't hard, but I did recognise in the short time I worked there, that not everyone espoused the same work ethic and core values as I did. I enjoyed my time working in Asda, and I left in the knowledge that returning to retail management would be my career Plan B. I considered myself incredibly lucky to have choices.

Chapter 4
The Military Effect

Joining the military, any service arm of the military, is not for everyone. Those who want to serve do so for many different reasons. Friends and family can be major influencers, as can events like *'At Home Days'*. Some want to physically fight in battle, whilst others like me just wanted to move away from home, train in a trade they enjoyed, and in my case, just be around aeroplanes.

My father had enlisted in the Army under National Service, a mandatory commitment introduced after the war, and my grandfather had been enlisted during the Great War. My brother had enlisted in the Army four years before I joined the Air Force and I am sure other distant relatives of mine would have served in the military too. But these family commitments were not conscious influences in my decision to sign up. Naive as this sounds, fighting in wars and laying down my life for my fellow countrymen was not a real thing to me, but if I had been called upon to do just that, it would not have changed my mind.

The common denominator in all the Services, irrespective of the profession chosen, is that you are part of a special close knit community, a group of likeminded people who share the same core values - the military is a lifestyle not a job. You have the security of a regular wage, subsidised accommodation, health care and a pension (if you serve a full career). As a teenager, these benefits are merely a bonus to moving away from home. The flipside is that your time is not really your own, you serve the government of the day who represent the people. I was a teenager, knew absolutely nothing about politics, so it didn't matter to me what party or colour the government of the day was.

I was enlisted into the Royal Air Force at 9am on Tuesday 18th January 1977 at the Newport, South Wales, Recruitment Office. H8131915, AC Sainsbury, A-Tech-P (Aircraft Technician Propulsion - Under Training), aged just 16 ½ years old reporting for duty – Sir! The next six weeks would be basic recruit training at RAF Swinderby, Lincolnshire which would start the following day. My intake was 36 MP 26. I had no idea what that meant and still don't today. My daily rate of pay was a massive £2.91. Armed Forces pay is calculated daily as you are on duty 24/7, so I was being paid a whopping 12 pence an hour.

It was tough being away from home and it was here that I experienced homesickness for the first time. Feeling homesick is debilitating, and as a teenager, I found it particularly hard. You miss everything; family, pets, friends, home, possessions - everything that's familiar to you. It could hit you at any time, day or night, and would make you feel anything from just sad to physically sick. The effects could last from just a few moments to hours, bad stints could stretch into days. For people like myself everything had changed all at once, it's a lot to deal with particularly when you don't enjoy and have no control over many of the changes. From a total of around 70 recruits who started, we must have lost around 15% of the course, most of which was a direct result of homesickness.

I have always enjoyed physical exercise, but you have a different attitude towards it when someone turfs you out of your bed early in the morning and tells you that you must go running. Sharing one dormitory room and ablutions with 15 other people is a meaningful change all of its own. On top of this, making your own bed, cleaning toilets, bathrooms and communal areas to an extremely high standard before presenting them for a variable independent inspection is tough. If anything is not up to standard, it can result in a few late nights. The directing staff are not your parents and they are certainly not your friends, but they have a job to do - and boy, do they enjoy their job. Doing your own laundry, ironing and polishing shoes, pushed some people over the top. Throw in some academics and studying for tests, then you have some idea of the 16-hour or so daily routine. Several of these tasks like ironing had to be learnt very quickly or you would be put under review by the directing staff. The good news for me was that I was not the only one struggling with a number of these tasks. Others seemed to be having a much harder time than me in dealing with this strict disciplined environment. Even some of the older guys on the course in their mid to late twenties with families were struggling.

Seeing others struggle made me feel that I was not alone and helped me deal with my own issues better. I often found myself talking to others trying to cheer them up when I was feeling homesick and insecure myself. You make friends very quickly in this type of environment because you must trust each other and work as a team to get things done. Forcing such behaviour is by design and is particularly good in building effective teams. Being only 16 years old, I never had the luxury of drinking alcohol, which on reflection, was not a bad thing considering what I had to come to grips with. I had become good friends with Bob.

Bob was an Irishman in his early twenties, married with a young family who sported a neatly trimmed moustache which made him look older than his years. Bob was a quiet and sincere chap who shared the same interest in motorcycles as me. We helped each other throughout the six weeks, although truthfully, I probably leaned on him much more than he leaned on me. I treated him more like a big brother and I can still vividly remember him some forty years later. These *'forced friendships'* was a natural by-product of the tough disciplined regime, as was remembering your directing staff names. Bob and I would be on the same A-Tech-P course at RAF Halton, Aylesbury, London, which started a week after graduating our recruit course.

I graduated from Swinderby at 10:30am on Wednesday 2nd March 1977 with mum and dad in attendance. It would be the first of only two occasions that both mum and dad would see me in my *'best blue'* RAF dress uniform before dad's premature death in August 1978. The second time would be at my graduation at RAF Halton in October 1977. Both were proud days for my parents. There are few better moments in life than seeing your own children graduate in a profession they have chosen themselves. It would be over 30 years later that I would experience similar feelings at my own children's graduations. Swinderby seemed a long six weeks but there was no doubt that the life lessons I learnt in that short time, prepared me not just for my RAF career, but for the rest of my personal and professional life.

My professional training was just nine months at RAF Halton. The course was titled Aircraft Propulsion Direct 12 (APD 12). The training was different and new. Training to technician standard in nine months and in one go was new to the RAF and I was on the twelfth iteration of this training. The course itself was designed for experienced students not school leavers, but the RAF had quotas to fill and a school leaver with the right academics like me helped fill that quota. This was not the career path I had chosen. As mentioned previously, it was my intention to become a diesel fitter and the RAF had vacancies in the trade of General Technician Mechanical, who amongst other things, covered diesel engines. The recruitment staff did a great job talking up the sophisticated training I would receive on modern gas turbine engines fitted to the front line aircraft. It would be much more exciting physically working on these aircraft than just being around them. This was way beyond my expectations. I had no idea. My motivation to become a propulsion technician was now sky high.

The domestic environment at RAF Halton was a little more relaxed, you took the lessons from recruit course and applied them; simple. The academics and vocational training were challenging at times and I had to call on all my limited technical experience from working on bikes and cars throughout the course as well as my CSE grades for the academics. The good news was homesickness seemed no longer a problem. The academics demanded all my focus. Most weekends were free for me to either travel home or more likely study for an exam the following week. I graduated on 27 October 1977 as a Propulsion Technician in the rank of Junior Technician. The rank insignia was a four-bladed propeller that was worn on the arm of your uniform and shoulder epaulets on your shirt and pullover. The promotion also came with a healthy pay rise which would increase again in December once I had reached 17 ½ years old; this was official adulthood in the RAF.

Once we knew that we were going to graduate from RAF Halton, everyone on the course was excited about where they would be posted. I don't remember having a choice other than the fact I didn't want to go back to Wales. I was hoping for somewhere else, anywhere in the UK. Well it just wasn't to be. I was posted to RAF Brawdy and, for a moment, I was excited about the prospect of Scotland until I found out that RAF Brawdy was in fact in Wales. West Wales to be precise, and an area where we had holidayed as a family a couple of times when I was in school. I was posted to Hunter Rectification Flight at the Number 1 Tactical Weapons Unit, which was responsible for the rectification of some 60+ Hawker Hunter Aircraft.

RAF Brawdy like most Air Bases was in the middle of nowhere and had previously been a Royal Naval Air Station before it was handed over to the RAF in 1974 after the closure of RAF Chivenor in Devon. The Hunter was a great aircraft to look at and pilots loved to fly it. I absolutely loved working on the jets. It was better than my initial dream job of working on diesel engines. I served at RAF Brawdy from November 1977 until February 1983 and there is no doubt that during those five years Nigel grew from a boy to a man - albeit a childish boy and into a really immature man.

Although I have lots of great memories of my time at Brawdy, some of which are described in this book. It would be a place where I would also experience three noteworthy events; all of them bad. First, dad would die a premature death on 7th August 1978, exactly two months after my 18th birthday. Secondly, I would be involved in an extremely serious and life-threatening motorcycle accident on 27th March 1980, and thirdly, I would find myself under a medical discharge from the RAF just a few years into a career I thought would last a lifetime. On top of this, mum would slip into what I now understand to have been a depressive state, being left to look after my 10-year-old sister

Me leaning on a Hunter 230 Gallon Drop Tank, RAF Brawdy, Wales, 1979

with little cash from dad's death and potentially now she would have to look after her damaged son who was about to get discharged from the RAF. In the middle of all this, my brother married the girl next door from Cross Keys (the one whom mum never really warmed too) and that marriage would start falling apart eventually resulting in my brother returning home to live. All this happened in the space of a few years and on the back of a couple of traumatic house moves. In less than two years after graduation into a professional career my life would become very uncertain. I would find myself facing tough life and career changing decisions, and I was still only a teenager.

I worked shifts for the whole five years at Brawdy. There were two shifts: days (with earlies) and nights. The day shift (earlies) would start at 6am or an hour before the first programmed flight of the day which ever came first. We would prepare all the serviceable aircraft for the day's flying programme and remain on the flight line fixing snags (technical problems) after each flight. The early shift would finish around 2pm. We would just be a skeleton trade crew assisting the Flight Line crews who would be doing the daily servicing of the aircraft.

A normal day shift would start at 8am and finish at 5pm and would involve heavy rectification like engine changes, fuel tank faults and major component changes. Any aircraft fault that required the use of the hangar and major ground support equipment or any fault that could not be fixed on the flight line was the responsibility of the regular day shift. The day shift also relieved the early shift on the flight line at 2pm. The night shift would arrive around 4:30pm to take over from the day shift and finish off the day's flying programme before generating enough serviceable aircraft for the following day's activities. There were about 60 to 80 people on Hunter Rectification Flight that was made up of various trades and ranks. We had a great close-knit team and many of my friends from that era are still friends today, thanks to social media.

I learnt a lot about alcohol in my early days, more about controlling my intake than the science of understanding how it affects the body. Alcohol was the cause of my severing the tip of my little finger on my right hand. Apparently, pretend sword fencing whilst drunk, with garden implements taken from the beer garden of a pub as weapons is not a great idea. When your mate is swinging a defensive shovel and you attack him with a garden rake, such a skirmish can lead to an accident (who would have thought). Coming out of the pub on 15th February 1979 in Haverfordwest, I hit the side of the shovel with my right hand, I completely missed my mate with the rake. A quick trip in the ambulance and several stitches later the two parts of the finger were reunited. The accident report said that I fell on broken glass. After all, who would believe the shovel and rake story.

Falling asleep in a night club with your mouth open inviting people to drop their cigarette butts into your mouth was also an alcohol related event. I can confirm that filter cigarette butts really don't taste that nice even when you are drunk. Understanding alcohol and its effects on your own body takes time and it is not until you overstep your tolerance limit that you then understand exactly what your limit is; shame you can't remember afterwards. Holding down excessive alcohol can also be a problem. I can confirm that the trim in a Ford Cortina Mk3 can make you vomit if you have had too much to drink. Vinyl trim smells horrible but at least it is easier to clean than cloth. Car door handles, and mechanical window winders are especially difficult to find in a car when you are vomiting violently, and your eyes are watering. Even when you sit quietly, minding your own business, on the garden wall of your mate's house in Stranraer, Scotland, during Hogmanay celebrations you can fall foul of excessive alcohol. In this case it was my inability to respond in Scottish and move quickly enough when a drunken Scotsman walked by, asked me something that was unintelligible and then subsequently punched me in the face just because I looked at him with a sense of *'what the fuck did you just say - Jock.'* In fact, I may have said those exact words. The whole event was over in 10 seconds or less and resulted in my rolling backwards off the wall, out of sight and into the prickly rose bushes. I had disappeared as quickly as a tin soldier at a fun fair rifle range. The lesson here was that alcohol clearly has a disconnect function between one's ability to think and speak at the same time.

It was quite common during the late 70s early 80s to drink during the day, particularly at lunchtime. There were many people who did this but two people I remember, who were on my shift, could drink a lot of beer – day or night. I was still learning. These guys were perhaps two of the quietest people I knew and just happened to be aircraft electricians. To this day I am not sure if drinking was part of their professional training. During a night shift, it was not unusual to go down to the local town of Haverfordwest for early lunch and to have a few beers before you went to work that evening. Not a great idea I know, and I am not proud of what we did in those days, but the fact is that we did, and it was fun, at the time. I really believed that this was part of the culture of being in the RAF; everyone seemed to be doing it. How these guys drove back to base safely after a drinking session downtown, remains a mystery to me.

An early finish on a night shift also resulted in beer drinking. This was a cycle we went through every two weeks or so as we switched from day to night shift. Only on one occasion do I remember being a little drunk and falling asleep on the hangar floor with a pump action screwdriver in my hand. I was tasked with removing access panels for an engine change. Of course, the boys looked after me but not before they tied my shoelaces together attaching me to the undercarriage lifting jack. Luckily there was no social media in those days, otherwise my picture would have been all over the place. I hasten to add that things like this happened to everyone at one time or another, but we all looked out for each other and it was always done in good spirit.

If you made a mistake or did something stupid and endangered someone or something, there was immediate justice. You would get a physical smack around the head or you would be taken behind the hangar and pushed/slapped around a bit. You were left in no doubt that you had done something you shouldn't have. I am not condoning physical violence, but there was something about this kind of justice. Firstly, it was immediate, you knew about it, there was no doubt in your mind why it was happening. Secondly, it was dealt with and you moved on. Thirdly, it was never held against you, the only people who knew about it were those who were involved. Finally, and most importantly, you were very unlikely to make the same error/mistake again. Overall, they were good times for sure and on reflection it was just part of my adult learning and growing up.

Sunday night was disco night at the Roch Gate Motel, about five miles away from RAF Brawdy, heading towards Haverfordwest. The motel was a popular venue for the locals and the lads from RAF Brawdy. A lot of single lads met their better halves at this venue. I know this because I used to go out with the sister of one who did. What made this venue so popular was its proximity to the Base and it was on the route of the RAF shuttle bus, so you could have free transport there and back - perfect. It was on one of these nights, late summer 1978 that me and one of my mates missed the last bus back. We decided to hang around outside the motel and wait to see if anyone was coming back from Haverfordwest in their car and hitch a lift with them.

Sure enough, one of the lads from camp, who was a driver by trade, stopped and offered us a lift in his bright red Ford, Cortina, 1600E. The car already had about 6 people in it who were clearly drunk and was a mixture of males and females. The driver was sober and without even thinking said to us, '*get in the boot- there is plenty of room.*' My mate immediately rolled into the boot but there was no room for me. My mate was also a little larger than me and I really didn't fancy locking myself in the boot of the car with him. Mates or no mates. I decided that walking was a poor option at that time of night. I was wearing an old tee shirt, a warm tartan clad jacket and badly fitting trousers. It was the age of Punk, so I used to get a lot of my disco clothes from the charity shop. I was not alone, a lot of punks did. I looked quite cool - or so I thought. To most people I was probably just a normal scruffy looking teenager. I don't know why, but I suggested that riding on the outside of the car might work. Then, as quick as a flash, I spread eagled myself across the bonnet of his car holding onto the rain gutter and resting my foot against the wing mounted mirror.

He drove off slowly and all was good, but it soon became clear that I was not going to make the five miles or so back to base. As the speed went up, my eyes were watering, and my hands were getting cold. I had started to lose the feeling in my fingertips, so my grip on the rain gutter was becoming tenuous. We had got less than halfway back to camp and were approaching a tight, slow speed chicane at Newgale bridge when I noticed some powerful headlights coming down the hill towards us. As the car slowed on the tight right-hand turn, I let go of the rain gutter allowing the natural lateral forces to roll me across the bonnet and off the car. The result was a hard landing on to the tarmac followed by a few body rolls before coming to rest in a complete wasted heap on the side of the road. The lad driving kept going because we both correctly assumed that it was a police car approaching - and it was. The police stopped, checked that I was ok before speeding off after the over loaded Cortina. I think the police believed they had just witnessed a hit and run. What they saw was me rolling over the bonnet of the car. They never would have thought for one moment that I had been riding spread-eagled on the front of the car since Roch Gate Motel. Who would believe that story? I was grazed and bruised but was fine. I was also drunk which clearly helped. My punk clothing took a bit of a battering being scraped across the ground, so now it was looking even better than it did before.

Newgale hill is a killer to walk up, period. When you are drunk, I swear the bloody thing turns into a Mount Everest. The hill has some steep inclines, and even the flatter portions are extreme, but these small plateaus at least allow you to get your breath back before you tackle the next stage of the climb. The hill is the best part of 1/2 mile long, but it seems to go on forever and you can be almost sober by the time you reach the top. Even the old RAF petrol shuttle buses returning from Haverfordwest would struggle. If you were sat in the front of the bus at night time, you could see the exhaust manifold begin to glow as the engine screamed in first gear for the hill to end. It was marginally quicker than walking.

I started to walk up Newgale hill back to base and had made it a fair way up when I saw the same headlights coming towards me a second time. I knew for sure it was the police this time. Shit! Quick as a flash, and without thinking the idea through fully, I did the only honourable thing I could do and threw myself over the edge of the road rather than get arrested. I closed my eyes as I dived and then found myself tumbling uncontrollably over rocks and through some pretty prickly wild gauze bushes and stinging nettles, eventually coming to rest about 30 feet from the road. Once I had stopped tumbling, I opened my eyes and looked up to the road. I remember thinking that the clear sky and stars looked very much like the inside of the Roch Gate Motel disco room. Then reality kicked in. I was hurting all over from the rocks, thorns and stings inflicted by the wild shrubbery I had bulldozed on my way down the hill. I was also bleeding from both my hands and my left leg. I must have looked like a plucked hedgehog as I had thorns and clumps of wild bush stuck all over my clothing and in my hair. I looked up to the road and into a couple of powerful flashlights, the coned beams were flickering through the moving bushes I had just flattened. Behind the lights were the silhouettes of two policemen, one shouted *'bloody idiot'* and some other things which I couldn't quite make out. I thought better than to ask him to repeat it. I immediately shouted back telling them I was ok. I waved a bloody hand to them at the same time so they could see I was alive and could move. The flashlight beams then did a bit of a dance around the area where I was for a few seconds before they were extinguished, and it all went dark. I heard the consecutive clunks of the police car doors which was quickly followed by a screeching of rubber on black top. That was my cue. I had been left to my own devices to get my sorry arse back to camp. I couldn't believe it. The relief of not being arrested and detained numbed the adrenalin rush which was quickly substituted by the pain I was in. Thankfully, they never caught up with the Cortina.

Overall, a good result. I managed to climb back onto the road, my trousers and jacket augmented with blood stains which just added to the genuine punk theme. My tee shirt doubled up as a bandage. I got myself back to barracks, sorted myself out and made it into work the following morning. We would of course do it all again next week – minus the riding on the bonnet of cars of course. That was something if you ever do, you do only once in your life. It was such a stupid thing to do. The alcohol of course completely impairing my judgement. As was then, and today, I consider myself to have been extremely lucky that night. I was remarkably close to becoming an alcohol statistic. Was it fun, well yes, but the fun had already turned into something more serious the moment I rolled off the car. Had we been travelling at speed or I had rolled off the car and into a post or a hard object, hitting my head, the outcome could have literally changed in a heartbeat. Instead, I could put the episode down to character building and joke about it.

I was on night shift on Monday 7th August 1978 when I got the phone call from my soon to be sister-in-law telling me that dad had just died. He had suffered a heart attack whilst driving my brother's Ford Capri back from the local pub. My mother was the only passenger. The death certificate said he had died from asphyxia through inhalation of vomitus and that he had myocardial Ischaemia and coronary artery occlusion. The verdict being natural causes; what a horrible verdict. There is nothing natural about a 48-year-old man dying of these things. He was pronounced dead on arrival at the hospital.

The crash was low speed, no-one else was involved and mum was unhurt. I remember a few things about the moment I took the call. First, my future sister-in-law seemed pleased to be the person to tell me that my dad had just passed away. I don't know what it was, perhaps it was my overreaction to the news, but it didn't seem right to me. It niggled me why it wasn't my brother or mother telling me this awful news. I am sure that my mother would have had something to say. Perhaps some people enjoy telling others bad news. Secondly, I felt I needed to get back to work and finish off what I was doing before I could get my head around what I had just been told. This was shock, for sure. I had only just turned 18 and dad was gone. I remember thinking about all sorts of things on the bike ride back home to Cwmfelinfach the following day; few were thoughts of dad no longer being around, I didn't even want to think about it and was hoping that the ride would go on forever. Blocking shit out of your mind is one of the great things you can do when riding a motorcycle. However, the reality of the situation came crashing down on me when I pulled up outside our house in Arthur Street, Cwmfelinfach. Seeing mum crying at the front door to meet me, made my heart sink. I felt cold and numb throughout my whole body, my heart was broken, and the enormity of our shared loss took hold. We never said a word, just hugged and cried together on the doorstep.

The build up to the funeral, the funeral itself, and the aftermath remain to this day a complete blur. I have no recollection of dad's funeral whatsoever. Dad always wanted to be cremated. His funeral was at the Croesyceiliog (cross-he kele-og) crematorium, Cwmbran, Gwent. His ashes are buried in the crematorium gardens and his name is in the book of remembrance. It was just four years earlier that we (dad, mum and I) had visited the same crematorium during an *'open day'* to see how the cremation process was conducted. It sounds a little morbid, but it was an interesting tour. I remember dad being absolutely fascinated by the process. The tour took us from coffin acceptance from the funeral service through to the secure and private room where all the remains were stored. Individual gas furnaces and raking mechanisms were used for the cremations with the remains being placed into what looked like huge top loading tumble dryers. These crushers were simply stainless-steel drums hosting a couple of granite spheres that looked like cannon balls. These balls would tumble in the circulating drum crushing the remains into dust. The dust was then collected, bagged and tagged and placed in the secure room awaiting burial or collection. The secure room was the only part of the process we were not allowed to view; for privacy reasons. The entire process was slick and efficient and went to great lengths to ensure that ashes didn't get mixed up. It was not morbid at all.

We also learnt that cremations do not take place on foggy days. Fog prevents the smoke rising into the atmosphere. It is not good publicity to have the smell of cremations hanging around at ground level. We were also told that fat people cremate much quicker than skinny folk due to the intense heat generated by burning body fat. Some of the cremations have small black particles in amongst the grey remains. These black bits are the only remains from the burning of the wooden coffin. Well, we were all sold on the process and that's exactly what happened to dad. Mum would go through the same process in the same place many years later. Indeed, at the end of my days, that is also the process I want for my body. Unless there are parts that can be recycled, the exception being my eyes. I will be taking those with me. For some reason, I have a real phobia about anyone or anything messing with my eyes. If there is an afterlife, I want to make sure I can see. The fact that they would have probably recycled my kidneys, liver, heart or any other good organ after my death seems a little academic, I know. Please, just leave my eyes alone. For the cremation itself, I don't mind where it takes place and will leave it up to my wife and kids to decide what happens afterwards with my ashes but having some of them being scattered or buried back home in Wales is a comforting thought.

I do remember the wider family coming together at the funeral and vaguely recall my mother not being happy with several of dad's relatives, but that was nothing new. Mum was always in conflict with dad's family in some way. Dad was gone, and I had lost a key mentor and one of my best *'grown up'* friends.

Reflecting on dad's passing, I realise it is difficult to say what it is that you miss about your father not being around. You deal with things in your own way when you don't have his wisdom and humour to call on in life's situations. I was just 18 years old, a teenager and thought I was bullet proof, I was also just at the age where dad and I were becoming great mates, and I really needed him to be around. I missed him terribly. On my birthday in 2018 I was ten years older than dad when he died. I have lived almost all my adult life without his guidance, support and great sense of humour. It is a little sad that I have never once thought, when confronted with life's challenges, what would dad have done here? I have acted on my own intuition as I never had his wisdom to guide me during the years where I could have done with him being there. I have also been starved of the opportunity to share life's pleasures with him, like having children of my own, travel and of course that great British pleasure of sharing a cold beer and just talking shit in a pub all night.

After dads passing, I always thought that if I ever had children, I want to be around for them as long as possible. I want to be able to help them when they need help and to offer guidance and wisdom when they have life decisions to make or just be there for them in a supporting role. I guess I want to be all the things to my children I would have hoped dad would have wished to be for me. I would be fortunate in 1986 to marry into a great family and inherit a wonderful father-in-law and grandfather to my children. He filled a huge part of the void that dad had left in my life over many years before his untimely passing with cancer in 1999.

Don't parents say some strange things when you are a kid. And as a kid, you don't always appreciate what it is that you have been told, you just remember it. These things get recalled at various times throughout your life and you wonder what the hell was mum, or dad talking about at that time. For example, mum would always tell me that bad things happen in threes. So, when a bad thing happened to me as a kid, I was in a constant state of worry waiting for the other two to occur. What mum failed to tell me was that the other two occurrences didn't necessarily have to happen to me, they could happen to anyone we knew. I'm not sure that even armed with this additional knowledge it would have helped. It merely meant that when bad things happened to people you knew it was only a matter of time before bad things were going to happen to you.

How I ever got through my adolescent years without worrying to death by believing in this kind of parental philosophy is still one of life's great mysteries to me. Nonetheless, isn't it funny what you remember from what your parents tell you. When you become a parent yourself, you often forget the simple fact that children have the choice to remember whatever they want. You have no control over what they remember or how they remember it. Many skewed facts and statements you throw at your children in general conversation when they are young, can come up to bite you on the arse many years down the line. Just like this one did for my mother. I guess it was inevitable that two further bad events were going to happen after dads passing – and of course they did, and they were both about to happen to me.

Losing a family member in death is right up there at the top of the list of worst things that can happen. It is only afterwards, on reflection, that these life events have the potential to be one of your greatest learning opportunities. Just like learning from mistakes. The grieving process is painful and is something we all experience at some stage in our life. We are forced to deal with our own feelings and emotions along with those of others.

We make promises to ourselves to change things or behaviours in our own lives or do certain things at certain times after going through this process.

The same is true of other events like serious accidents, illnesses, or events where people have not died but are in some way incapacitated or their life has changed significantly from an incident. It is the learning that takes place subsequently that can change you; hopefully for the better. At the time of writing, there had been two major traumatic experiences in my life. One changed me physically and forever and would happen in less than a year after dads passing. The second would change me in quite a different way and would happen over 26 years later. The first traumatic event I was about to experience was actually the second incident in mums *'Triad of Disasters'* after dad's premature death the previous August. The third episode of mum's trio of doom would come within a year of the second. Dad's death and my trauma were out of my control, but I had influence over the third occasion in mum's philosophy, and I would put my heart and soul into changing mindsets and decisions that were being made on my behalf.

Chapter 5
Career Pause

My Pride & Joy, Yamaha XS650, Cwmfelinfach, Wales, 1980

I was heading home from RAF Brawdy for a long weekend on the afternoon of Thursday 27th March 1980 on my brand-new, three-month-old, Yamaha XS650 motorcycle. I was not feeling great, perhaps even a little flu like. The weather was cold and a little drizzly and I could feel the dampness of the air fill my lungs even through the cloth scarf I had wrapped around my neck and mouth. My waxed jacket and trousers were fairly good at keeping shower rain out but were bloody useless at keeping me warm. I was about two thirds the way home when I attempted to pass an articulated lorry (truck) on a single carriage highway; the A465 near a place called Glyn Neath in South Wales. I was just rear of the driver's cab when the whole unit rapidly swerved out to overtake a car he had been following. I had no chance. There was no indication, no looking, no warning, nothing. Instinctively, I hit both brakes hard and managed to drop right back to the rear boogie of the trailer before the unit contacted my left shoulder sticking to my jacket like a powerful fridge magnet. The road was so narrow and the pavement so high that it was impossible to mount the kerb and break away from the lorry. Both the bike and I were trapped - there was nowhere to go.

After what seemed like an eternity, it was physics that made the next move. The bike had started to tilt to the right and aided by gravity started to take us both underneath the lorry. I realised that I no longer had control of the steering and correctly sensed that this moment was not going to end well. As the bike slipped gracefully under the spinning rubber of the rear wheels, I didn't have a whole lot of time to think about my next move, so I literally let go and ejected myself in the opposite direction falling unceremoniously onto the kerb. I made initial contact with the ground with my back before momentum threw me awkwardly along the pavement like a clumsily thrown bowling ball. My kinetic energy from the 50mph or so I was travelling, took me some way down the pavement and my rapidly rotating field of vision of gravel, hedgerow, grey sky repeated itself several times over before I finally came to rest in the hedgerow on the side of the road. From this ground zero vantage point I watched the bike elegantly spin on its side making its way into the middle of the road. Even with my helmet on, I could hear the horrible scraping noise of the black top on the exposed metal of the exhaust, fuel tank and handlebars, each part seemed to be jostling for the biggest spark show. The lorry continued to complete its overtaking manoeuvre without a care in the world, disappearing into the distance as if nothing had happened. The whole event was all over in just a matter of seconds, but it would turn out to be life changing seconds for me.

I was to learn later from the police that the container/trailer had made it to Scotland, almost 700 miles away before it was tracked down as the *'other vehicle'*. From impact with the lorry to lying on the side of the road, could not have been longer than 10 to 15 seconds, yet it all seemed to have happened in slow motion and is burnt that way into my long-term memory. You cannot forget something like that. The injuries and subsequent disabilities I carry today because of the crash are not a constant reminder of the accident, they have just become part of who I am. I fell awkwardly on the kerb and landed on my pelvis and back. The impact broke them both, severing the sciatic nerve on my left side. My pelvis actually snapped, the force of the impact disrupting it forward also on my left side. The subsequent tumble broke my right leg, tore some flesh from my left thigh, broke an undefined number of ribs, caused additional damage to my back whilst triggering a whole load of other injuries to my internal organs. I was taken to Glyn Neath Hospital and that is where I stayed until released on 23rd May. One of the more interesting moments of this episode was watching the unconventional and rapid arrival of the ambulance. It first swerved to avoid hitting people who were in the middle of the road simply trying to clear up the mess the bike had made, before finally screeching to a stop within a few feet from where I was laying. I swear to God, I thought the ambulance was going to run over me. Under mum's philosophy that could easily have been number two of three terrible things, but to have two out of three things happen within an hour of each other, that would have been shit bad luck.

The car behind the lorry, a Mini, which was the car that I had just passed, was driven by a doctor who was keen to stop the lorry. His wife, who was his passenger, insisted that they stop immediately to help me - so they did. They both comforted me before the crazy ambulance guys took over. My crash helmet, a fibreglass Griffin full face, took a hammering as I was transiting down the pavement and without a doubt saved my pretty face as the chin piece of the helmet had been worn away considerably. I was in no doubt that it had saved my life. I was also wearing a full complement of clothing; jeans, waxed trousers and jacket and even a pair of nylon tights. Tights were great for stuffing with newspaper to keep your knees and legs warm. They all helped save my body in a small way. Armour protection was not that common in bike gear in the 1970s, maybe that would have saved my back. In any case I was alive. I had a guardian angel looking over me that day because the accident should not have been survivable. Not only did I survive, I had the delightful pleasure of remaining fully conscious throughout. I think my being young played a major part in my survival; a fact I would learn to be partly true during a later hospital visit.

The bike was a write off and so was I at that time. After they cut away all my clothing, I was spread out on a stainless-steel gurney, naked, cold, shivering and in shock with no pain relief. There were injuries all over my body and the touch of the cold steel gurney on those broken areas was intense. The vast array of sterile surgical equipment, alcohol swabs and disinfectant were jostling for my sense of smell, whilst the bustling of hospital staff running around me in the shadows of the intense lights was completely overwhelming my eyes. It was a feeling and image that will stay with me for the rest of my life. If I had been presented with a button to press that said, *'die peacefully and be free of pain'*, I would have pressed it without hesitation. The adrenaline had worn off completely and the pain seemed to be emanating from all over my body with each broken area taking turns in telling my brain that it was hurting more than any other part. There was so much wrong with me they completely missed a broken left leg. It was like a paparazzi frenzy as they took what seemed like hundreds of photos (x-rays) as quickly as they could. I felt like a circus freak displaying all my unusual charms to the world. I didn't care one bit that I was naked, I just wanted it to be over and the pain to end. Once the initial gurney frenzy was over, only then did they start to treat me and give me something for the pain. The first thing I remember after the gurney experience was waking up to the noise of what seemed like an electric drill. It was a device that the doctors used to tap the traction pin through my leg just below the knee. The pin would be used to support the weights required to straighten my pelvis and back. They didn't know at that time that the leg they were drilling was in fact the broken one.

I was on some powerful drugs by now, so I couldn't feel the pain, but I do remember on waking seeing flesh and blood twirling around the rotating traction pin like a red onion stuck to a food mixer blade with a badly fitting lid. Blood was splashing all over me, the table and the doctors' gown, all this was happening in slow motion. The doctor did not stop drilling even when he realised, I was awake. The drug trip was intense. I was flying high through the air on my own over a castle holding onto a piece of string that was connected to the castle tower. It was a beautiful day and I swear I could feel the sun burning my skin and the cool breeze blowing on my face. I would wake up fully from this drug induced heaven suspended in a hospital bed with just my head and right foot in contact with the bed. Blood and something else plugged into my right arm and a sling and some monitors plugged into the left.

Me & My Modified XS650, Cwmfelinfach, Wales, 1980

I was in intensive care for a few days with bleeps and flashing lights on small monitors demanding attention every time they changed their visual or audible routine. All those thoughts of flu like symptoms had magically disappeared. After five pints of someone else's blood and a few days' rest under some powerful pain killers, I was finally moved out of intensive care and into the normal orthopaedic ward to begin my recovery.

As mum could not drive, she was dependent on public transport or other family members to drive her. As a result, mum would pitch up at all sorts of various times. Work mates also visited when they could. These visits were a trauma at first, I just didn't want to see anyone at all. Seeing mum so upset to see me in this broken state just made things worse. She was still grieving the loss of dad and now here she was thinking she could lose her son too. It didn't help that my dad's mum came with her on a few occasions and all my nan wanted to do was talk about what was wrong with the other patients in the ward, less so about me. That's family for you.

During the first few weeks of my hospitalisation, I was left wondering what the hell had happened to me and I worried about what the future would now look like. You have a lot of time to think about these kinds of things when you can do little else. My physical pain was at times unbearable. I dreaded being lowered out of the pelvic sling. The pain was so intense throughout my whole body when I was lowered onto the bed, it was impossible to identify what hurt the most. The feeling of your legs spreading out from your body and not having control is as strange as it was painful. After about three to four weeks I could feel that things were beginning to heal and settle down. I would focus my thoughts on those small incremental progressions of feeling better and often score my pain at certain times of the day and compare those with the day before. Those small improvements acted like a catalyst in my mind for further healing to take place.

Hospitals can be a dreadfully depressing place if you are ill. However, if you are not ill, but just broken, it can be a fun place to hang out. The orthopaedic ward is full of broken people – nobody is ill. The difference between broken and ill is that there is a real community atmosphere in the broken ward, and you can have a laugh and joke about life and of course the event that put you in there. Everyone has a story to tell and you know everyone is going to go home eventually. That is not a given in the other surgical or other trauma wards where people really are ill.

The daily lowering out of the pelvic sling for personal cleaning was not something I enjoyed; it was an extremely painful experience. I had a sheep skin cloth rested over my private parts, no underwear, or pyjamas. The washing of my private parts was not the most enjoyable thing at first, I was badly bruised and battered in that area and had a catheter fitted, but the smoothing action of the washing would often result in my getting an erection, which with the increased blood flow, could be quite painful, much to the amusement of the nurses. That was until one day it didn't hurt. I managed to feign pain for a little while afterwards. I considered it one of those small luxuries I had for being in hospital.

As much as the nurses cared for me, they did neglect my left foot which was propped hard against a foot drop plate to prevent shrinkage of my Achilles' tendon. The weights hanging off my traction pin for my back and pelvis were never adjusted for my weight loss and I was losing around one pound of body weight each day. This meant that the pressure on my foot was increasing and without the proper nursing care on my foot, I ended up with a massive pressure sore on my left heel that would take the rest of the year to fix. In fact, the sore was so big even after months of treatment, it needed surgery to close it up fully.

Although I was losing weight daily, I didn't poop for several weeks due to dehydration, shock, pain medication and immobility. This became a major problem. To be fair, the hospital tried many techniques to make me poop. It started with some orange syrup and tablets, progressed to enema's and then an attempt to undertake some manual extraction. Unfortunately, it was not one of the nice delicate female nurses with tiny hands and thin fingers that was assigned to attempt this procedure, but a big hairy arsed male nurse with hands the size of snow shovels and fingers like hotdog buns. I thought my days of intense pain were over until I underwent this procedure. I have never experienced anything like it or since. Using just hot water and a pair of latex rubber gloves he tried to extract weeks old poop out of my arse.

After about 20 minutes of being subjected to this procedure, he had some success. I cried with pain as it hurt so much, so when he said he had some success, I couldn't wait to see what he had pulled out of me. Imagine my disappointment when I was expecting to see a house brick or something of equivalent size resting in the bed. I looked around to see a small black, almost perfectly round stone like object on a dry nappy surrounded by dark red droplets of my blood. It was no bigger than the size of a garden pea. I couldn't believe it, I was devastated. I insisted no more manual extraction, I was not designed that way. If they needed to get something out of the mine shaft, they had to come up with some other ideas. As luck would have it, something had shifted because of this induced trauma. The nurses were able to get some other liquid stuff up my bottom to soften the waste that was trapped. Combined with the syrup and tablets, things were about to change….and they did; big time.

Ken was the patient in the bed opposite me in the ward. A gentleman in his late 60s early 70s who was recovering from a car accident. Ken had been a passenger in a car that his wife was driving, and he had been thrown from the car. His wife was allegedly hysterical at the crash site as she was calling for her husband, but no one could see him, so they thought she was just in shock as she was trapped in the car. Poor Ken was unconscious in the hedgerow. The special thing about Ken was that he only had one leg, the left one. He had lost his right leg in the war I believe, or it could have been due to his wife's poor driving record. It was so funny to hear the story of the ambulance men searching for Ken and then finding him legless as his false leg had become separated from him in the car accident. That required an additional search. We all had funny stories to tell in the ward including the chap who had lost all his fingers when they dropped a steel plate on the top of a dumpster skip whilst he was hanging on to it. I remember seeing the result of his surgery. He looked like something out of a Frankenstein movie. Healthy looking hands but all his fingers were black and swollen and the stitching attaching his fingers to his hands looked like it had been done by the three blind mice. He was remarkably upbeat about the whole thing even though it looked as if only two of his ten fingers would be functional.

It was late into the night when my stomach started to make grumbling noises and I just knew something was about to happen soon, and my guess was that it was not going to be pretty. The ward was in darkness apart from a few random reading lights that had been left on throughout the ward and everyone was asleep. The night shift staff were on duty but there was nobody in the ward office. Ken had recently woken up and was reading, I could see his silhouette moving against the backdrop of his reading lamp. I propped myself up in my sling and whispered across to Ken to call the staff as I was about to let go of something in my stomach. My normal method of getting attention during the day was to call out, but I didn't want to do that and wake everybody up. None of the bed buzzers worked in the ward. Ken had complications with his injuries and had a special little bell on his bedside table that he could tinkle to attract the staff at night. I thought he could use that bell to get the staff to come to me. Ken immediately took up the challenge recognising the urgency of the situation as we had been joking that same day about my lack of bowel movements. I heard the soft tone of Ken's voice calling *'nurse, nurse'* followed by the tinkle of his little bedside bell.

The *'whatever'* in my tummy was getting more vocal by the minute and the urgency in my voice for Ken to get the nurse got more desperate. Ken's response was to raise his soft tone a little and to tinkle the bell a little longer than previously. This went on a few more times, but no nursing staff appeared. Then without any more warning or input by me, my bottom just let out an almighty burp and released a tidal wave of semi liquid black waste. I could feel a void being created in my stomach as it all started to flow out. Then without warning, my colon had turned into a machine gun that was being fed by some kind of automatic belt driven ammunition dispenser on steroids, auto pulsing every few seconds, pumping out more of this disgusting black gooey waste. I had no control over what was happening, the pulses kept coming and the waste kept flowing. If my arse was a volcano, this was the equivalent of a colonic eruption. The black mass of shit was slowly consuming the white skin of my inner thighs as it dipped down heading for my stomach.

The smell was intense, I swear there was a smog that had started to surround my arse. Very quickly my pelvic sling was filling up with this gooey disgusting mess. In between retching from the smell, I was pleading to Ken to get the nurse. Ken upped his game and began rattling his bell with some gusto. It is worth mentioning here that Ken's bell was smaller than the smallest hotel reception bell you have ever seen, but Ken was trying his best to squeeze maximum decibel's out of it; all to no avail. No nursing staff to be seen. With the pelvic sling now full and a third of my torso covered, the flow continued along the path of least resistance which just happened to be the dip in my abdomen stretching up towards my neck. The rapid evacuation of my colon had caused an internal void making a natural channel for the waste. I started to panic as I imagined the waste making a complete body loop by re-entering my stomach through my mouth and nose. I was stretching my neck as much as I could both as a preventative measure for re-entry whilst also trying to get my nose away from the intense smell of this tsunami of shit. Ken, sensing my fate from the stench, which had reached his part of the ward, went into panic mode and decided to take things into his own hands and go get the night staff himself.

I remember the scene vividly, Ken's bedsheet flying up passed his bedside light, Ken sitting upright just for a second before disappearing from sight completely. A second later there was one almighty crash. Ken had fallen out of his bed. In the panic, Ken forgot to attach his false right leg, and in desperation of his fate hung tightly onto his bedsheet that neatly swept away the bedside light, water jug, fruit bowl and everything else that was on his bedside table. The crash of Ken hitting the floor and the smashing of glass and plastic had the desired effect and the nurses came running out of the darkness to sort poor Ken, who, God bless him, tried his best to explain to the nurses that it was me who needed attention and not him. Anyway, we both eventually got sorted that night. I had a late-night, all over bed bath for the first time since the accident. The emptying of the colon was a significant event in my recovery, I now felt my body was ready to heal. I still had the catheter fitted but felt that I could start to take control of my arse once more and didn't need to worry about what I was eating and drinking.

The orthopaedic ward was on the ground floor of the hospital and, at that time, the hospital was undergoing maintenance on the outside so there were workmen near hospital walls and windows. The window curtains and netting were old and ineffective, so it was easy to see what was going on inside the ward from the outside. I could now poop in bed by pulling myself up out of the pelvic sling on the overhead bed ring and do my pooping into a dry nappy on the bed. I was not allowed to use a bed pan all the time I was in the pelvic sling because it would put pressure onto my broken pelvis and hips. If my aiming was off and I missed the nappy, I would just flick the poop off the bedsheet and onto the pad with my right foot. Once I received a round of applause from the workmen who clearly thought this was cool entertainment. That's the thing in hospital, you don't really concern yourself about how you look, you just do what you gotta do.

I was discharged from hospital on 23rd May 1980, so was at home for my 20th birthday on 7th June. I had to wear my sister-in-law's trousers as none of my clothes fitted me. I had lost over 50lb in 57 days. Now the hard work would begin. I was on crutches, wore a foot brace for my left foot drop, nursed a serious pressure sore that needed daily treatment on my left heel and was depressed. Going from hospital to home was hard. I went back to RAF Brawdy before going back into the RAF hospital at Wroughton on 30th June 1980 for treatment of my pressure sore. After two weeks, they decided to send me to the hospital at RAF Halton on 13th July 1980 for plastic surgery to close up my pressure sore. The doctor had decided that the options were to have plastic surgery and a skin graft or just pinch the two sides of the open wound together and stitch it up.

In good old RAF fashion, the quicker and cheaper option was chosen; they would just stitch it up. I was happy with that decision. The operation on 15th August 1980 was a success and I eventually entered rehabilitation at the Military Rehabilitation Centre at Chessington, London, on 16th September 1980. This intense physical rehabilitation was exactly what I needed. However, my progress was slow, and I was finding it extremely hard both physically and mentally. The army doctor was not impressed with my progress and made a recommendation for my medical discharge. I was absolutely devastated, I knew I was not recovering at the rate I should have been, but it was not all physical. I was broken mentally and getting more and more depressed.

I remember literally pleading with the doctor at Chessington to give me some private time at home, so I could work on my own recovery/rehabilitation. After all, I had suffered a traumatic accident and had come straight out of hospital after months of bed ridden treatment and had been dependent on other people, into a strict physical regime that had little to no sympathy for me and my condition. Life had changed significantly, and I needed to come to terms with everything that had happened and what was going on at home. I was wrestling with my insurance and a court case that was not going in my favour.

The insurance episode was a huge lesson in life for me. I only had 3rd party insurance for the bike. Not comprehensive. Accident cover for myself and the bike was not part of the policy. If you can't afford to buy a bike/vehicle outright, make sure you can at least afford fully comprehensive insurance. It is a game changer in these circumstances. Indeed, the insurance battles from the accident would not be settled until two weeks before I was about to marry a girl I hadn't even met yet. The criminal court case was not proven, all the evidence we had was characterised as circumstantial, time and place stuff. Apart from some scuff marks, there was nothing else the police could produce linking the trailer which they believed had hit me, to the driver. The defence lawyer was good, maintaining that there were thousands of these lorries and trailers on the road and without hard evidence, we could not prove without reasonable doubt that the police had found the right lorry and driver.

Subsequent advice from a barrister suggested that we only had a 50% chance of winning a civil case and that would cost money up front to pay for counsel. That of course would never happen these days. They would be falling over themselves to help me for a percentage of the claim. In the end, it was the Motor Insurance Bureau, a neutral non-profit company who compensates people for injuries sustained where insurance did not cover them (like hit and run) that paid me a small compensation for my injuries; that money effectively paid for the bike with some money left over for mum. Mum was still grieving dads passing and I needed daily care from her at home. My RAF career was close to being terminated just two years into it. Life was looking pretty dire at just 20 years of age.

I must have told a convincing story at Chessington as the doctor agreed to suspend the medical review board decision for three weeks, giving me time at home to sort myself out. I would need to return to Chessington for a second time to complete my rehabilitation, which I did. I was discharged on 23rd October 1980 and returned to work under regular medical reviews every few months.

The first couple of days at home after my first stint at Chessington were horrible. I was a complete mess. I cried all the time, my mum cried, we cried together. I had two contrasting choices; curl up into a ball, feel sorry for myself and stay at home with mum and do nothing or get myself out there and back on track. The easy route was of course to do nothing and that was a thoughtful consideration for me at the time. I was depressed. I thought of nothing else and was just feeling sorry for myself. Why me? It's not fair. It's not my fault. The injustice of it all. All negative thoughts, which just breed even more negative thoughts. Depression pulls you in this direction, it's like a virus in you and it takes a lot of inner strength to pull yourself out of this depressive state. There is an absolute need to do this because the alternatives of going deeper into a more severe depressive state are not good, particularly if your body is broken. Sadly, pulling yourself out of this circle of negativity does not happen overnight. However, the decision to do something different does. Not so much an epiphany in my case, more a tipping of the scales in favour of considering the other option.

    I have heard many first-hand inspirational stories of people experiencing something similar after major trauma in their life. I guess this is my story unfolding here. It is no different in principle to what others have done, but this is what happened to me. What followed the day I decided to consider the better alternative was the first day that my attitude changed, and my outlook took on a positive posture. I would now look forward to the future a little bit more every day. This change in attitude slowly grew into a real determination to make a difference, as I started to experience a more positive outlook whilst feeling small incremental and positive changes in my physical and mental recovery. The sun was always going to be shining from now on and even when it's not, I would always look at the positive of that, thinking that it won't be so hot outside today when I go out training.

I bought myself a second-hand bicycle. I couldn't walk much without crutches or sticks and I needed to build up my leg muscles as well as exercise and build up my core body strength. Cycling was good for everything, and I enjoy cycling, so it was a no brainer as a method to get myself fit. Getting on and off a bike was a real challenge for me. Ultimately, I could fall off when I stopped, but I needed assistance to get on the bike in the first place. My sister Jayne was an immense help here. I cycled every day and built up my time in the saddle a little more each time, to the extent that by the end of the three weeks I could walk with the aid of a walking stick. This would be a great advantage to me when I returned to Chessington. I worked so hard every day at Chessington I was exhausted by the evening. I remember that I was either working out, having treatment, working out in the occupational therapy class in my spare time or sleeping. It is fair to say that I hated the place, but it was an awesome environment to rehabilitate. The food was high protein and excellent quality, which was terrific as every little bit helps during the recovery process.

Many of the military patients at Chessington were victims of the IRA bombings that were taking place in the UK during the 70s and 80s. Missing limbs was the most common disability. Most mornings we would start the day with the bums and tums class. We would all sit in the main hall (about 60 of us) and dance to Abba music whilst sitting on our arses on the cold wooden floor. Fun to partake and entertaining to watch. On Thursday evening, there would be a disco colloquially known as the 'Crips Disc'. Imagine people dancing with missing limbs, in wheelchairs', on crutches and everything else in between. The whole place looked like a bar scene in the Star Wars movie. Fights were commonplace and crutches, walking sticks and indeed wheelchairs became effective weapons of choice.

Thankfully, due to my hard work, I was only at Chessington for two weeks instead of a month. When I left, I could walk unassisted, albeit not the most elegant gait in the world, but I could walk. Even the doctor was impressed by my rate of progress second time around. I couldn't bring myself to tell him that I hated the place. I just took the compliment and left. I was given a temporary three-month medical category to return to work. This would be reviewed every three months for a maximum of two years and then a permanent medical category would be given. During the first three months I would need to continue with regular physiotherapy in between work shifts.

I had failed my Corporals promotion exam just before my accident. I had another chance to sit the exam whilst I was in the Neath hospital and my Flight Commander and Squadron Warrant Officer made the trip down from RAF Brawdy to see me. They had arranged for me to take the exam from my hospital bed. I could not write as my left hand was strapped, so the Officer would ask the questions and the Warrant Officer would write my answers down. It must have been comical to watch as everyone in the ward stayed deadly silent for the duration of the exam, and everyone was looking at me with some enthusiastic egging on between questions. The Flight Commander would ask the question and then even before I had the chance to answer, *'Taff'* the Warrant Officer would jump in and tell me the answer up front or direct me towards what my response should be. The Flight Commander got pissy with Taff every single time he helped me. They would argue as if they were my parents the whole time they were there. Taff would repeat *'the boy knows this stuff, he just needs some guidance'*, and the Flight Commander would insist that I had to answer the question on my own with no help and that he (Taff) was there merely as the note taker. I argued that I knew all the answers anyway, just that Taff could put it into words better than I could.

I got notification that I had passed my Corporals exam sometime after I had returned to work from Chessington. Yet, my medical category remained temporary, and was still below the standard required for promotion. I knew the doctor at RAF Brawdy pretty well as I had spent a fair bit of time with him over the period. He was a pragmatic person who didn't seem to be bothered about the details of the Air Force medical boarding process. I thought I could convince him to medically upgrade me if I had some local management support. Promotion would automatically happen as I had been cleared; it was just my medical category holding me back. Also, I had a career aspiration to be promoted to Corporal before I turned 21 years old.

I asked Taff, the Warrant Officer, if he would give me a recommendation or at least provide a verbal statement to the medical staff to say that my work was unaffected by my medical condition and I could fulfil the full range of duties expected of me. Moreover, I had recently done a squadron deployment to RAF Wattisham, as they needed people qualified to tow aircraft, and I was one of the few qualified to tow. Taff knew that I was trying to manipulate/influence the doctor but made no attempt to stop me. Taff was a great role model and would protect and support his airmen if you worked hard for the squadron. Even if you were in the wrong, he would support and help you. He had a knack of making you feel like one of his favourites and he was the kind of chap you felt privileged to work for. It was a win-win situation. It was good military leadership.

I made the medical appointment and clearly Taff the Warrant Officer did have words with the doctor and the medical team. The Squadron Leader doctor signed my medical category unchallenged and wrote me up as fully fit for all duties. Not only did he upgrade my medical category, it was a permanent upgrade from a recommendation by the Wing Commander surgeon who would correct my foot drop later in the year. I wasn't expecting a permanent upgrade, I could have kissed him. My review came into effect on 19th March 1981 and I was promoted to Corporal the same day. I was 20 years old. The medical category didn't last long, a different Medical Officer at Brawdy reviewed my injuries on 17th September 1981 and he perceived my medical situation *'as a somewhat complicated problem'*. He recommended my case be reviewed at the Orthopaedic Conference at RAF Wroughton on 23rd October 1981. His assessment was of course correct. My knee and instability in my left leg continued to be a major issue and my foot brace for my drop foot kept breaking causing a loose article hazard around aircraft. I had got used to all this of course, but clearly, I was becoming a medical nuisance, so they felt obliged to downgrade me once again. It was fair enough, the medical upgrade helped me reach a personal career milestone of being promoted to Corporal before I turned 21, so I was happy with that. This further downgrading and review could only result in a better outcome if I needed more treatment. Overall, I was feeling I had turned a corner on my career and life. I was ready to face anything. I really felt as if I had overcome the hardest part, nothing was going to stop me now.

It was during my short stint at the RAF Halton hospital in July 1980, whilst having my pressure sore closed, that I met a genuinely inspirational person who unwittingly taught me the benefits of positive thought whatever your condition or set of circumstances. I didn't realise the extent of his influence at the time, but I certainly felt that I was a better person from knowing him. His name was Bill.

Although Bill was a little older than me, he was still only 23 years old, married and recently his wife had given birth to their baby daughter. Bill was a Senior Aircraftsman (SAC) RAF Regiment Gunner by trade. For those who knew guys in the RAF Regiment you knew they were made of pretty tough stuff. Bill was no different. Bill had crashed into a tree on his Triumph motorcycle in Germany. The fibreglass fuel tank exploded leaving him with severe burns to his body. His legs had been amputated below the knee and the top half of his legs were withered and useless and so was one of his arms. He continued to have saline baths every day and had lost count how many operations he had been through. But he always had a smile on his face and was always up for a laugh. For the short time I was with him in hospital, we had become good mates. I only had one opportunity to take Bill out in his wheelchair during my time there and I messed it up. In a big, but funny way.

The operation on my heel was straight forward and had been a success, but now I needed to get myself a different pair of trainers to fit my recently shaped left foot and newly modified foot calliper. Up to this point I had to buy two different sizes of shoe to fit my feet. There was a local shoe shop about a half mile away down the hill from the hospital and the staff gave me a temporary chit to leave the hospital grounds to go shopping. I convinced the nurses that by pushing Bill in the wheelchair would give me stability as I was supposed to be partially non-weight bearing on my heel for a few more days. At the same time, it would offer Bill some much needed fresh air. It was summer and it turned out to be a cracker of a day. Not a cloud in the sky, with rising temperatures throughout the morning. Reluctantly, they agreed, but made it clear to me that I needed to be back around 3pm for Bill's bath time. Easy, I estimated we would be back around lunch time, what I failed to factor into the adventure was Bill's plans.

We set off around 9:30am and had my new trainers all sorted by 11am, easy. Bill had hardly been outside much and had always had a plan in his mind to go for a beer with me before I left. Bill had not been allowed a drink in hospital and had drank hardly anything at all since the accident. I initially said no, but then thought one drink won't hurt, right….. Wrong. I think we only had two drinks, well maybe three. Not much I thought. We left the pub around 1pm. What I had failed to factor into this scenario was the warm weather, my tiredness, Bills inability to process alcohol, and the fact that I had to push him back up the hill with a bad foot. Bill was fast asleep not long after we set off from the pub and was slouched in his chair holding on to my new training shoes. I got really close to the hospital ward but was exhausted. I couldn't get Bill and the wheelchair up the steps. I decided to move Bill and leave him in the shade of a tree with the brakes on whilst I go inside and get the staff to come and help me. Unfortunately, I ended up slouched over my bed and fell asleep without telling anyone about poor Bill.

I was woken up by the ward nurse shaking me furiously and ranting on about the trouble I had caused and the fact that the Nursing Officer was on the war path. It appeared that a hospital guest had found Bill under a tree, still asleep in his chair, gripping some new bright yellow training shoes. The guest was wondering how the hell he had got there with only one arm and why he was clutching a pair of brand-new trainers when he didn't have any legs. Both Bill and I found ourselves grounded because of this episode and Bill insisted that he take the brunt of the blame for the incident. I thought to myself then, if someone like this can accept life as he is, and still enjoy life's little moments and share a laugh, and then take responsibility for something that was not his fault, then I had nothing to complain about. In life, there is always someone who is worse off than yourself and it doesn't hurt to reflect on your own situation and be thankful for what you have. Concentrating on what you don't have is not a healthy way to look at things and doesn't help you or others around you. Seeing what a motorcycle accident did to Bill, gave me cause for reflection on whether I would continue motorcycling after my accident, so I dabbled with three-wheeler cars for a while. These *'death traps'* were popular in the UK at that time. Not trikes but fully enclosed cars; two wheels at the rear and one at the front. You could drive these things on a motorcycle licence. They were not classified as a car because they didn't have four wheels and were under a certain weight category. On the inside they looked and drove just like a car; they even had a reverse gear. In many ways, these vehicles (let's call them vehicles) were considered more dangerous than motorcycles. They were extremely unstable at speed and during windy conditions. Cornering could be exhilarating too. In short, they were fun things to drive and I really enjoyed my time owning them. However, they were no match for a motorcycle. Both my three wheeled vehicles were Reliant Regal Vans. Reliant also made a 3000cc Scimitar car at the time which was one of the fastest cars on the road in the late 70s and early 80s. The Regal (as was the Scimitar) was an all fibreglass body construction. The regal had a 700cc engine but there was so little weight in these things (less

Reliant Regal, The Plastic Pig or Resin Rocket, Cwmfelinfach. Wales. 1980

than 1000lbs) they would accelerate quickly, and you could cruise between 60 and 70mph if the conditions were favourable.

Only once did I tip mine over in a small ditch on the back roads of RAF Brawdy. I overcompensated on a corner and even at relatively slow speed, it went over. Clearly, I wasn't going slow enough. I think these cars should have been fitted with a clinometer as going from three wheels to two happened quite quickly, and if you did nothing about it, going from two wheels into a capsize condition would happen even quicker. For the one spill I had, I must have had 50 or more close calls. No real damage, just a few scrapes to the car and a red face for me. It was so light I just climbed out the rear door of the van and pushed it upright again.

Three wheels led me invariable into four wheels. In fact, I bought my first legal car, a Vauxhall Viva, before I even had a car licence. I would drive the Viva into Haverfordwest from Brawdy to have a driving lesson in the driving school's car. I never declared to my driving instructor how I got to his lesson and to be fair he never asked, even though I would meet him in the car park where I had parked my car. I only had three full lessons and passed my test first time at 9:45am on Thursday 19th February 1981. I had my third lesson just prior to the test and legally drove my car for the first time when I drove it back to camp afterwards. I put my success down to the experience I had gained driving three wheelers and of course I had been driving

1st Car, Vauxhall Viva, Cwmfelinfach, Wales, 1980

David Brown tractors for almost three years and towing aircraft. Nobody even noticed I had been driving with a gammy leg.

Fixing aircraft, ground running jet engines, towing aircraft and leading small teams at home and on detachment was such fun as a 21-year-old. I loved my job, my career and my life. Clearly, things were physically different for me since the accident, but it never deterred me from doing the things I wanted to do. In computer terms, it was as if my life had been rebooted (no pun intended reference footwear) and had re-started in safe mode. Everything worked fine but I had to be mindful of some of my physical limitations; not to stop me doing things, just needing sometimes to proceed with caution. I would thank my hospital buddy Bill, for the attitudinal stuff. I noticed positive things continued to happen with positive thoughts, but it would be an element of luck that would see my physical progress take a step change (another unintended pun) for the better. I would meet a doctor in October 1981, who would recommend an operation that would literally change my life.

Every year in the UK, a group of orthopaedic surgeons would gather at one venue, normally a hospital ward, to study and review up to a dozen unique or unusual orthopaedic cases. On 23rd October 1981 it was the turn of RAF Wroughton, near Swindon. The RAF Wing Commander doctor that had been overseeing my case in consultation with the new Medical Officer at RAF Brawdy thought it would be a great idea for me to attend the seminar. I would be one of his specialist cases. How could I refuse. After all I had nothing to lose and felt that I was repaying a favour for the time the Wing Commander had given me a positive recommendation that resulted in my promotion. On the day of the review, myself and another half a dozen other patients were admitted to Wroughton hospital.

A group of around eight orthopaedic surgeons all wearing neatly pressed white lab coats gathered with precision around each bed space in turn. Once in place, the Wing Commander introduced the patient and described the gory medical details that had made theirs an interesting case. Discussions then ensued about progress, treatment and future therapy strategies before the group moved onto the next bed space. I was the second patient they discussed. Once they had moved on, we were free to leave.

After they had discussed my case and had moved off, I was getting my things together ready to leave, when one of the surgeons in the group asked if I could stay a little longer; he wanted to talk to me. He returned to my bed space about 30 minutes later, introduced himself again, and began asking me detailed questions about the accident, the trauma I had suffered and the difficulties I had with my recovery. His interest was piqued in my case as he had significant experience being the orthopaedic surgeon at the Isle of Man TT Motorcycle races over several years. He told me that he had only seen injuries like mine twice before. Both were motorcycle accidents, and both were during TT races and sadly, both patients had died from their injuries. He was curious how I had survived mine.

His parting words to me was that I should consider myself a *'lucky young man'* to have survived such trauma. He said that his fellow doctors agreed that there was little to no chance of further neurological improvement for my drop foot, but they also believed that I was a good patient for an operation that could correct it. His final words to me were along the lines of; *'someone must have been looking out for you on that day'*. Those comments resonated with me and I immediately thought of my father looking over me from someplace in the afterlife and wondered if indeed there was some substance to his words.

Mum took some solace that maybe dad had, somehow, influenced the accident outcome. The story made her smile. It made me smile too and was quite comforting in its own way. I am not a strong religious person, but I do believe in there being some reason for us being here. Whether you believe in this kind of stuff or not, it felt pretty good to think that the day of my accident was not my day to die. The result of the medical review was that the group of doctors recommended to the Wing Commander that because I was so young, I was a prime candidate for a tendon transfer to correct my drop foot. It would be this operation that would significantly change my life.

I was to be admitted on Wednesday 2nd December 1981 to have the operation. Unfortunately, I had an infection, a snotty cold, and was discharged only to be readmitted on the 16th. On readmission, the Wing Commander surgeon was over booked, so I was sent home a second time. I was admitted for a third time on 20th December for an operation the following day. Third time lucky. Well it was Christmas, so the likelihood of another discharge at this holiday time was quite high. After all, I was not ill, so would be the first to be knocked off any operation list. Based on this uninformed thinking, I decided to risk it and drive myself to the hospital. The first attempt I had used public transport and my brother drove me the second time. If I was going to be bumped a third time at least I had my car locally to get myself home. This would turn out to be a bad idea.

Prior to my operation, I had received three different foot braces for my drop foot. The first one was extremely painful to wear and consisted of a large spring held to my leg via a Velcro strap and a hard-plastic foot plate that would hold my foot at a 90-degree angle to my leg. I needed a larger shoe size for my left foot to wear this thing. When walking it would flex at the ankle allowing my leg and foot to move with my walking action and then flick my foot up towards 90 degrees when I raised my left foot off the ground. I hated wearing the thing, it was heavy, and it looked hideous. However, it was robust and would last much longer than the other two braces I had.

The second and third braces were both one-piece moulded plastic braces that were shaped to my leg and foot. They were much more comfortable to wear but they could not withstand the constant flexing at the ankle and therefore would crack and fail. I lost count how many times I had to repair them with rivets and small aluminium plates. It would be these repairs that resulted in my being taken off certain aircraft work as they were considered a loose article. I had become a walking FOD (Foreign Object Damage) hazard. The thought of having an operation to correct my foot drop enabling me to walk normally without a foot brace was an exciting prospect, and of course it would allow me to work on aircraft unrestricted and do other things like play sports.

Post Foot Drop Operation, Christmas, Wroughton Hospital, England, 1981

The Wing Commander had never done this operation before and he asked me if he could video the procedure. '*Sure, no problem, providing I can see it too*" I joked. So, it was to be, on Christmas Day 1981, I would be propped up in my hospital bed at RAF Wroughton watching my operation on video tape with a visiting Father Christmas.

The operation was a success and it was a little strange to see myself on the operating table being cut up and pushed around like a rag doll. A non-walking plaster was applied to my left leg from just below the knee to my toes. The plan was to have it removed after three weeks to remove the stitches before fitting a second cast for a further three weeks. Thereafter, I would have to learn to walk again. So, another stint at RAF Chessington Rehabilitation Centre was on the cards. I really didn't want to go back to Chessington, so I worked extra hard on my recovery and the hard work paid off. I was reviewed on 15th February 1982 where it was decided that a further stint at Chessington wasn't required and I could return to work fit for all duties except marching, parades, and General Service training; I thought what a bonus, no more marching.

It would be almost a year later, 24th February 1983 that the Wing Commander suggested that his recommended post operation assessment had been harsh, and I had recovered well enough to fulfil a full range of duties. So, he upgraded my medical category and made it permanent. I was so excited that my career was now fully back on track. I considered myself to be extremely fortunate to have had such support from family, friends in work and the medical branch of the RAF. I have no doubt that my youth was a key player in my physical recovery, but it was my attitude and love of my job and career that got me through mentally. The only downside of being fully fit meant that the RAF believed I was fit enough to do marching and parades.

The operation to correct my drop foot consisted of cutting the Achilles' tendon in a Z shape, stretching it, raising the foot so it would be at right angles to the leg at the ankle, then stitching it back together. At the same time, disconnecting the Tibialis Posterior Tendon (the tendon that pulls your foot in towards your other foot) at the lower end of the tendon before pulling it out of the foot and re-attaching it to the instep. Please do not try this at home. Although armed with a Leatherman pocket knife, pair of scissors and a stapler you could give it a bash. The result meant that when I pulled my foot inwards, it would pull the foot up. Yep, that's exactly how it works and it's quite weird. Even today it seems weird.

The actual movement is quite small, but the tendon does hold the foot at right angles allowing me to walk without a foot brace. I had to re-educate my brain to pull my foot in when I wanted to pull it up. This process was key in allowing me to walk without tripping over. It was not easy at first and took some serious physiotherapy and walking in front of mirrors to retrain my brain. Some would argue that I have never mastered walking again. I would agree with that. I certainly have a unique gait and once I had mastered how to walk, it was not long before I could jog. If people thought my walk was odd, they hadn't seen me run.

Unfortunately, I had to avoid contact sports because of my weak knee. After exercise, the knee had a habit of relaxing and could somehow disconnect from my lower leg. When it happened, the pain was intense, and I learnt that by whacking my lower leg just below the kneecap, the knee itself would click back into place. I needed to learn a new sport that would keep me fit and strengthen my knee. So, I learnt to play Squash.

What I never anticipated after the operation was the need to have a non-walking plaster fitted to my left leg. This would pose a bit of a problem because I drove myself to the hospital in my car. My car was a manual Ford Escort, RS2000. This car was a partially rally spec prepared, was a big step up from the Vauxhall Viva and was fitted with a few extras, one of which was a competition clutch. The clutch pedal required twice the downward pressure of a normal clutch from your left foot and it operated like an on/off switch. Not operated correctly, you would either stall the car or with excessive use of the throttle it would shoot off like a startled rabbit. There was a small tolerance band in between, and it took some getting used to.

On discharge from the hospital, I assured the staff that my brother was picking me up. I was getting around on non-weight bearing crutches so was not allowed to leave the hospital grounds on my own. I convinced them to let me go into the car park so I could look for my brother; I assured them I would be back if he wasn't there. They agreed. When I thought no-one was looking, I climbed into my car, threw my crutches and backpack onto the back seat and started to drive myself home. I had made it just a few miles down the road before the clutch pedal went straight through the plaster and into my foot. Holy shit – what do I do now? And, it had started to snow. Shit. I didn't feel any pain as the base of my foot was not the focus of the operation. Luckily, the plaster over the top of the foot had stayed intact so the pressure of the clutch pedal was just pushing my foot upwards into the top of the cast. This was not a good look just two days after the plaster had been fitted.

Ford Escort RS2000 & Plaster Cast, Newport, Wales, 1982

I did think about going back to the hospital but that would just get me into trouble. The hospital staff would keep me in longer and then I really would have to get my brother to come and pick me up. Bugger it. I decided to continue to drive all the way home. By the time I got there, the plaster was completely trashed on the bottom of my cast and was in pieces all over the floor of the car. I was worried because I had felt no pain and thought that perhaps the tendons had become detached. I could feel the skin on the bottom of my foot pulling from the clutch pedal action, but it was too late to worry about it now. I was home. To make the cast look a little better, I cut a piece of aluminium plate and strapped it to my foot with duct tape to prevent the plaster from completely falling apart. The modification worked a treat and enabled me to continue to drive my car. Not a smart decision on reflection, but I was 21 years old and that's how a 21 year old thinks. I had a knackered foot that's all; I wasn't ill. My foot was knackered before, and it didn't stop me driving then.

I reported back to the hospital a few days later escorted by my brother. I admitted that the plaster had got wet and had softened. They would have been horrified if I had told them the complete truth. There was nothing to be gained by declaring my stupidity, I knew I should not have driven home. Clearly, I had a lot more faith in the strength of the plaster, but that faith was founded on absolutely nothing. The hospital replaced the plaster cast and my brother drove me home where I immediately refitted the aluminium plate. Another splendid example of doing stupid things when you are young and needing to tell a few wee tales along the way. I never told mum or the doctors what I did, what would that achieve? Einstein once said, *'anyone who has never made a mistake has never tried anything new'*. Well, I think fitting an aluminium plate to a non-walking plaster after my mistake was genius.

A combination of luck and youth overlaid with hard work and determination got my life and career back on track. I had managed to get through teenagerhood by the skin of my teeth. You would have thought that as I entered my twenties, life would become a little calmer, more focussed and I would find it plain sailing. But no. Clearly, I had more to learn. Sometimes in life you must overstep the mark to know exactly where the mark is.

Chapter 6
Pushing the Boundaries

Early in the new year of 1981, a few months prior to my motorcycle accident, I had a couple of opportunities. The first of which was being considered for aircrew training. Unfortunately, this option was taken from me before I had time to get excited about it. I continued to suffer from bad seasonal allergies (hay fever); these conditions were a medical showstopper for aircrew at that time which resulted in my application being terminated. The second opportunity was not so much dependent on my medical condition, more on my professional performance. Here I had a real opportunity to steer the direction of my career rather than leave it to the RAF to decide. I was getting incredibly good reports from my superiors and had been identified as a potential tradesman to work on the *"Queens Flight"* at RAF Benson, Oxfordshire, England.

The Queens Flight was a unique organisation within the RAF that transported the Queen, members of the Royal Family and senior members of Parliament around the world. It operated independently with a handful of specialist and very well (perhaps overly) maintained aircraft. For me, it was a fantastic opportunity as a young junior technician to experience another aspect of the RAF and perhaps travel the world. Along with several others of my rank and trade, I was called forward for an interview. The hangar set up was like the best car showroom you have ever visited. Everything was immaculate and looked brand new. The hangar floor was polished, all the equipment had its own place in the hangar, and everyone was immaculately presented. It was quite different from the crow ridden, windy and often freezing conditions of the RAF Brawdy environment. Nobody was wearing oil soaked and tatty coveralls. I was impressed and was eager to work there, it was a different world.

I was notified within days of returning to work that I had been selected as *'first reserve'* for one of the positions. I was so excited of the prospect of working on the Queens aircraft and the posting to England. I got notification of the intent to post me whilst I was in hospital, just a couple of weeks after my accident, I was gutted. It seemed like someone was rubbing salt into my wounds (no pun intended). I have no doubt that my career would have taken a vastly different path had I not had my motorcycle accident. Not better, simply different. The fact was, I couldn't accept the job, I was in hospital and they needed the position filled immediately. Although massively disappointed at the time, I had other things going on in my life that were of greater priority. Ultimately, I understood that the decision was never really mine to make in the end. My medical condition had made the decision for me.

In helping me come to terms with this disappointment, I realised that in life there are many things outside of your control. This particular career opportunity had ceased to become an option for me the moment I had crashed. So much had changed as a result of that brief moment in time. Acceptance of the situation is neither easy nor quick. It was tough. Equally, I don't have any regrets about this period, nor do I wonder about what might have been. I still consider it a privilege to have been selected for Queens Flight and I knew that more, but different opportunities would come my way one day. Those are the thoughts you cling to; those are the thoughts that get you moving forward. Nevertheless, you can't sprinkle glitter on a turd and call it a gift. It was shit news that I really didn't want to hear at a particularly low point in my life.

One of the best things that came out of my motorcycle accident was my decision to learn to drive. Although motorcycles were my preferred mode of transport, I really needed an alternative to get myself around and cars were much cheaper to buy and run than motorcycles. A main advantage of having two wheels before four was that I knew all the hazards of the road (apart from passing articulated lorries on two lane roads) and overall, I believe it has made me a much better driver. The Ford Escort, RS 2000 was an awesome car and had the performance of a middle weight sports motorcycle, but in the two years or so that I owned it, I went through two engines, a gearbox, several alternators, numerous sets of tyres and a few exhausts. The engine needed to be tuned and carbs synchronised every 3 months or so. It was quite honestly, a money pit.

It was whilst the engine was out one time that we had notification that we were deploying on TACEVAL (Tactical Evaluation) to the RAF base at Coningsby. Our Hawker Hunter aircraft were going to be used in providing Close Air Support for the Air Defence Phantom Squadrons. I had already committed to drive from Brawdy with three other guys on the team but needed a car. I looked around locally and bought a cheap Mk II 1300 Ford Cortina with a jacked up rear end. The car was a shed (shed = slang for a car being in poor condition) but cost me next to nothing to buy. Arranging insurance was a quick phone call and I was covered. The Cortina had a MOT (Motoring Organisation Test) but was not taxed for the road. I decided that I would take my tax disc off the RS2000 and stick it on the Cortina. Easy. Except of course it is illegal to do so, but people do it all the time and don't get caught - right.

We arrived at RAF Coningsby around midday on the Sunday and decided that we would pop into the seaside town of Skegness for a look around before we booked ourselves into camp accommodation. Everything was going well until around 3pm when we decided to head back to camp. I reversed out of the car park and didn't see the policemen in my limited view through the back window and bumped into him. Not hard, but you don't hit a policeman whilst driving a car without some kind of re-percussion. Bugger! The policeman and his colleague were all over the car checking it out and of course it was all legal except for the tax disc in the windscreen. Anyway, I was arrested, had a free ride to the police station in a police car, got stripped of my belt and shoes and was locked in a police cell for five hours whilst they checked out my story of the RS2000 being off the road. The boys were left behind in the car park and had to find their own way back to camp. The car was impounded and our detachment supervisor, the Flight Sergeant, had to come and bail me out of police custody later that evening.

Ford Cortina MKII, Cwmfelinfach, Wales, 1982

Not a great start to the detachment. I was in big, big shit, so volunteered for all the extra duties whilst we were on the detachment. That was the least I could do. That was also the very first time I had visited Skegness. So many memories – few of them good. The second time I visited Skegness was four weeks later, when I made a personal appearance in the Magistrates Court. The magistrate, who was a genuinely nice lady in her fifties, was extremely sympathetic to my story. I played the military commitment card hard and urgency of the situation, defence of the Nation etc, etc, followed by a dramatic heartfelt apology for my stupid behaviour. It worked. She took it all in, smiled at me for being such a grown up about the whole affair and I walked away with just a fifty pound fine. I was absolutely over the moon and could have kissed her. Somehow my civil arrest and the subsequent charge never found their way on to my RAF record. That was just pure luck. The takeaway lesson from this episode was simple. *'You make a mistake; you take responsibility for it – no excuses'*. If you have the chance to put your mitigations (not excuses) forward, then do so with heartfelt sincerity and let others judge you.

I didn't hesitate to take ownership; I had let myself and the team down big time. I should have told the Flight Sergeant before the detachment that I could not take my car, but I successfully sorted it out myself and, I guess, my luck just ran out. Would I have done something differently today? Simply, yes. I would never be caught out like this again juggling cars. As I was a young single lad with money, the only real solution to prevent a recurrence was to buy more cars. Not that I needed an excuse to buy another car but having two cars full time would help. I had the appetite for something quick, but wanted a bit more comfort and reliability, so I bought a nice Triumph 2500cc pi (F(p)uel Injection) car. The police used a version of this car, so I bought a white one thinking I would never get stopped by the police – and it worked, I never got stopped once driving this car. I only kept it for a few months and then flicked it on to a work mate (for a significantly reduced price). I learnt from this short-lived experience that cars were not my forte, they were just money pits. I also realised that I was shite at managing my own money. I needed to address both these issues if I wanted to save for the future. I was in my 20s. Who in their 20s thinks seriously about their financial future?

Having a full car licence and being over 21 years old allowed me to rent vehicles which got me thinking. Many of my mates were single lads. Most of us had moved out of barracks and were now living in the local community. Well, not exactly the local community, mainly old derelict farmhouses with extortionate rent, little to no heating and miles away from civilization. I suggested that we get together every now and again and have a long weekend away; bank (public) holidays being the perfect opportunity. I could hire a Ford transit van, take some sleeping bags so we can stop wherever we decided to party. Just go somewhere and experience life outside of West Wales. The idea took off big time and I had a full van before I knew it. I wanted a minimum of six and a maximum of eight and the first adventure would be a trip north to Blackpool. You certainly get to know people and their habits reasonably quickly living in the back of a van for a couple of days.

Triumph 2500, Me & RS2000 Outside Lyster Barrack Block, RAF Brawdy, Wales, 1982

We had a great time and it was a huge success. And of course, just as importantly, it was a cheap weekend; apart from the beer. The second adventure took us to Rhyl, North Wales. This was a day longer than the Blackpool trip and was probably an extra day too long. Living on cheap fast food and beer for four days and three nights, partying late into the night for each of the nights and all sleeping together in a small transit van took its toll on most of us, and the van. Nevertheless, once again we had a great time – what we could remember of the trip. The third and, as it turned out, the last adventure was not so uneventful. I had decided that we had been north enough, so we needed to travel east, giving the city of Bristol the benefit of our company and our hard-earned military pay. Once again, the van was fully booked, and, as was normal, I would drive into Haverfordwest, pick up the van, drive back to RAF Brawdy, load up the van with sleeping bags, snacks and beer and away we would go. Except this time there was a problem with the van. It wasn't ready. I had to wait almost two hours for it to be returned and then cleaned and prepared before I could take it. I got back to camp to pick up the lads much later than they were expecting, over two hours later. Sadly, they were in control of the beer and you can drink a fair bit of beer in two hours.

The boys were already in great spirits (pun intended) having drunk a few beers by the time I had arrived back. But it didn't take them long once we got on the road to get drunk. Even before we had left the camp boundaries, there was loud music, singing, farting, laughing and all sorts of stuff going on in the back. I think everyone got a little deafer with each beer they drank as the noise was increasing by the mile. I lost count how many times I had to stop the van for people wanting to take a piss. In the end, I found myself stopping every 20 minutes or so and kicking everyone out for a pee whether they needed it or not. I thought we were never going to get to Bristol. When we eventually got onto the motorway, the pee stops got fewer as the roads got smoother and much straighter.

As we were approaching the Severn bridge, heading into England, there was no stopping, and it had gotten a little quieter in the van at this stage. I decided to press on. The music playing in the background was interrupted by the occasional fart and giggle, but most of them were either sleeping or just chilling out as was my front passenger and navigator Russ. Whilst crossing the Severn Bridge, Russ woke up making some strange noises, one of which sounded like a cat spitting up a hairball. He was going to be sick......bloody hell. *'open the fricking window Russ, quickly'*, I shouted. Russ's hand eye coordination and realisation that he was sitting in the passenger seat of a transit van was not quite as sharp as his vomiting. Russ managed to get the window open a little for the second load of vomit and what did make it outside was quickly blown back onto the side of the van or was splattered into his window. The stench was disgusting, and the residual that never even made it outside was blown all over his side of the cockpit in the van. The noise of Russ's cat impersonations and his cyclic retching coupled with the stench of his beer ridden vomit woke those who were sleeping. One of which was Richard. Richard was well over 6-foot-tall and weighed around 220 lbs. Richard was the BFG (Big Friendly Giant).

Richard awoke from his beer induced coma desperate for a pee and before I could say *'what the fuck are you doing Richard'*, the rear doors of the van swung open and Richard was already pissing out the back. Thinking he would fall out the van and be killed by the impact and the following traffic running over him, I touched the brakes momentarily and the sight of Richard hurtling backwards, holding his penis spraying his piss over everyone and everything including our sleeping bags and spare clothes is a vision that will stay with me for the rest of my life. The rear doors slammed shut on the van and we continued over the bridge. We eventually arrived in Bristol and everything was either stinking of Richard's piss, Russ's vomit or a cocktail of both. It most certainly did not smell like your Giorgio Armani Pour Homme Eau de Toilette Travel Spray and we had not even been out on the town yet.

We parked the van close to Bristol town centre, covered ourselves in whatever toiletries we had brought with us and hit the town. When we eventually got back in the early hours of the morning the van was still stinking of piss and vomit and the contents of Russ's stomach gracefully adorned the side of the van like some psychedelic business motif. To make the night complete we were visited whilst sleeping in the van by the local Bristol City police. I did all the talking as I had the ignition keys and I explained to the police, in my best pretend to be sober voice, what we were doing and where we had come from. It was obvious that we had been drinking - a lot! I assured them we were all sleeping in the van – nobody was driving for at least another day. We would be sightseeing tomorrow.

Luckily, there was no issue at all with the police, in fact they were great blokes, very understanding and looked in on us several times throughout the night. I don't think the police would react in quite the same way if we were to do this again today. Seven young lads pissed up and sleeping in the back of a transit van in the middle of Bristol. We had such a laugh, and in my defence, we were young and naïve.

Just before I left Brawdy, I was fortunate enough to be introduced to Royalty, none other than HRH (His Royal Highness) Prince Charles, The Prince of Wales, at a luncheon on 9th December 1982. I was sent a letter signed by the Station Commander detailing the *'do's and don'ts'* of the lunch, dress code and protocols for meeting HRH. Prince Charles was also an honorary Air Commodore to RAF Brawdy and he was paying one of his programmed visits to the base and it was his desire to meet with base personnel over a buffet lunch at the Sergeants Mess. During these lunches, which are of course orchestrated and planned to the nearest second, groups of select people from around the base stand around and generally make small talk, nibbling on small bite size titbits and drinking gin and tonics, wine or a tipple of their choice. Everything stops of course in your group when HRH comes to meet you.

Just to set the scene, at this lunch there were 10 groups and each group had between eight and 10 people. Each group was made up of a cross selection of people from around the base. One person was nominated the group leader who would introduce each member of the group individually to HRH. HRH would then speak to one or two people in the group before moving onto the next group. We were supposed to let HRH lead the conversation and we were told not to introduce controversial topics ourselves or to *'hog'* the Prince in conversation. We needed to be in place at least 30 minutes before his planned arrival time of 12:30pm.

There was a collection of officers, officers' wives, senior civilian executives, Senior NCO's, and of course a few airmen. One of which was yours truly, Corporal Sainsbury. I was in Group 7. As a 22-year-old Corporal who was a single lad living off base and having to feed himself, the thought of free food and drink in the Sergeants Mess was not something you wanted to miss. HRH would not be interested in me (I thought), there were far more important people there than I, so I could drink and eat to my heart's content. Unfortunately (fortunately for me) HRH was late; almost an hour late and you can drink a lot of G&T in that time when they are free. When HRH finally arrived, I was rosy cheeked, relaxed and having a good time. When he eventually got to Group 7, our group leader introduced us all and then the Prince decided he would speak to me. I was the most junior of the group by far and I looked it too. I joked that I had been drinking free G&T for over an hour and was grateful for his being late. I informed the Prince that I had probably drunk his quota too. I think we spoke about something else as well, but I don't remember what. I do remember the group leader and his wife not being that impressed, but it made the Prince smile, so everyone smiled; that's how it worked. HRH moved on to Group 8, I ate some more food, had another drink, and politely made my excuses as soon as people had started to leave. I honestly thought that there would be a message waiting for me to go and see the Warrant Officer when I got back to work. As a minimum I was expecting some etiquette training, or even a quick reprimand, but there was nothing. I doubt the lunch was as memorable to HRH as it was for me.

My five years at RAF Brawdy had been a rollercoaster of emotions, but overall, they had been an absolute blast. I really did grow up in so many ways. I had been through a hell of a lot for a 22-year-old. A few personal relationships, the family trauma of losing my father, the motorcycle accident and everything to do with that including the insurance, my on/off/on career and of course my physical recovery. I had bought and sold numerous cars, three wheelers and motorcycles and had been arrested (twice). My second arrest (after the Skegness episode) was for breaking a child's swing in a playground. I was on a local motorcycle rally and we had stopped for lunch. Whilst eating fish and chips I decided to rest my weary arse on a playground swing and it immediately broke in two and I fell on the floor scattering my fish and chips everywhere. It was all a big mistake. The swing was very old and clearly defective – that was my only defence. It was a terrible defence and would not hold up in court. I was over 14 years old and should not have been anywhere near a child's playground, let alone sitting on one of the swings. I was arrested in work, the police tracked me down from my number plate on my motorcycle. After some discussion with the police and my supervisors they decided that if I paid the village 50 pounds to replace the swing, I would not have to go to court. I paid up immediately. Once again, I was lucky. Like the

Skegness incident, this episode somehow never found its way onto my RAF record of service.

Hunter Rectification Flight, RAF Brawdy, had been a fantastic first posting, but like all good things, it was about to come to an end. I felt I had become professionally competent as an aircraft tradesman. At the back end of 1982, I was one of the longest in post at five years. The RAF needed people to set up a third line, depot level maintenance organisation at RAF St Athan, South Wales and all the people who had been in post the longest from around all the different bases would be used to fill the manpower establishment. Few people wanted to be posted to RAF St Athan, hence the policy of creaming off the longest in post from around the RAF bases, which included me. I was posted to the Tornado Engine Accessories, 9 Squadron, RAF St Athan. I could not believe it. I had been born and bred in Wales, joined the RAF to move away from home, got posted to RAF Brawdy - in Wales, and then posted a second time to the very base that had inspired me to join the RAF - in Wales. This was the closest base to mum, so I was effectively going home. I was absolutely gutted. My hope of a RAF career that would involve travel and seeing the world was taking me back to the very place I worked hard to get away from.

Chapter 7
Dreams, Duty and Decisions

Packing up your life, downsizing and getting rid of stuff, saying goodbye to friends, moving to a new area and starting a new job is all part of the lifestyle/adventure of being in the military. The process, although simple and defined, is one that you never really get used to. It is easier said than done. Sure, you become very efficient at doing it, but there is always an amount of trauma associated with each move and the trauma is different each time as your life changes along the way. It does not get any easier that's for sure. It is difficult to explain to those who have not moved around much, but it is all part of serving in the military. You just accept it and get on with it; stressful as it is. The move to a new job, which may or may not result in a physical move to a new location, is necessary for your own development and quite often is done to meet the needs of the organisation. It was the latter that drove my move to RAF St Athan. I certainly would not have chosen to go there myself. I was incredibly happy at Brawdy and now I was going to move even closer to home. It is worth mentioning here that home in this context was the place (village) where mum lived and most of my school friends still live, not the actual house that I was going to live in.

Once a posting is confirmed, acceptance comes quite quickly and before you know it, you are looking forward to the challenges of the new job and the exciting prospect of being on a new base. You very quickly move on from where you were and start to look towards the next chapter of your career and the professional and personal opportunities that come with it. Once moved to the new location, you become very adept at adjusting and quickly settling into the new living and working environment. In work, people are much the same as before, military. Military people know what it's like and they make the move and transition so much easier. The part of resettling into the new work environment does seem to get easier with experience, but the family aspect can cause complications.

Although I had a couple of girlfriends during my time in West Wales, I was still hard-core single. I had lived in barracks and off site rented accommodation at Brawdy. I wanted to live in rented accommodation at St Athan as soon as I could. Barracks just did not do it for me anymore. As you grow up in the military, you become even more independent and you feel that living in barracks is a bit of a restriction on your lifestyle. Barracks are secure, usually located on base and close to your place of work. The first step in independence is normally moving out of barracks. I was grateful for the RAF providing barrack accommodation as it was cheap, you didn't need transport and the Mess Hall (canteen) always had food available for you, within the restriction of published mealtimes. The food, in the main, was particularly good. In fact, when I lived in a four-man barrack room, I shared the room with three chefs. We always had free food available, they were fun guys and worked shifts, so we were never all there at the same time. When I got promoted to Corporal, I was forced against my will to move into a single man room. I was gutted that I had to move out, partly because of the availability of decent food but mainly because I missed the company of my chef roommates.

I had not been at St Athan long before I moved into rented accommodation with a few work mates in the local town of Llantwit Major. It would be the girlfriend of one of the guys that I moved in with, that would introduce me to my wife, Diane. I did not know it at the time, but I would spend the next five years of my career at RAF St Athan. This posting would, like RAF Brawdy, bring about significant changes in my personal life and a change in my career trajectory.

I arrived at 9 Squadron, St Athan on 28th February 1983. The squadron was a new unit established during the early 80s to service and maintain a range of mechanical components fitted to the fleet of Tornado aircraft. The Tornado entered active service just three years earlier. Along with industry, 9 Squadron would provide front line support to the aircraft squadrons both at home and overseas and the numerous component and engine servicing bays located at Tornado operating bases. I was employed on the engine accessories, auxiliary power units and gearbox line. Due to 9 Squadron being a new unit, several of us undertook *'one off'* manufacturing courses on the components we were repairing, and it would be our job to train others *'on the job'* as they were posted into the squadron. As the Tornado aircraft was a three-nation development project between the UK, Germany and Italy, I was lucky enough to do courses in all three countries. At last, I was travelling overseas. Additionally, through conducting these courses, I quickly realised that teaching others was something that I not only enjoyed but discovered that I was pretty good at as well. This skill set would play a major role in one of my later career choices.

The first of the overseas courses ran from 22nd October until 02nd November 1984 and took place in Somma Lombardo, Italy (north west of Milan). I was required to work alongside an Italian technician who couldn't speak a word of English whilst I couldn't speak a single word of Italian. Somehow, we managed to get through the training successfully using nothing more than hand gestures, smiles, nods of yes and no and much laughter. Incredible really when you think that we were working on very technical components. Me and my mate Bob, who was also my supervisor at the time, found a nice little pizza place close to our hotel where we could eat pizzas and drink red wine in the evening after work. We became friendly with the restaurant owner who allowed me to make my own pizzas in the evening, which just encouraged us to use the place even more. A diet based on only pizza and red wine played havoc with my intestines, resulting in my constant farting during the day whilst working alongside my Italian counterpart. My bottom burps clearly made an impact on the Italians as it was mentioned on my leaving certificate. I learnt a little piece of Italian; *'çativo vento'* which literally means *'tis an ill wind that blows nobody good'*, a very posh Italian phrase for a fart. I learnt this phrase very quickly as my Italian trainer used it every day – sometimes several times a day. Little did I know then, but I would use this exact same phase in June 1987 whilst holidaying in Kenya with my wife, Diane.

We were having a safari day during our three-week holiday in Kenya. The safari site was about an hour away by air from our hotel in Malindi, Kenya. The aircraft was a small twin engine, six-seater Cessna type aircraft. We shared the flight with an Italian family consisting of the father, mother and their early teenage daughter. The aircraft was cramped. The father was six-foot-something tall, was very fit and covered in an impressive array of Italian bling; he looked like *'The Don'*. His wife and daughter were equally attired with a vast array of bling and Italian designer clothes. They looked like they were special guests at a Hollywood awards ceremony rather than a family about to go on a hot and dusty safari.

The night before the flight, I had a meal of maize and fish in the hotel and it was not sitting well in my tummy. Diane was sat in the back behind me along with the Italian family. I was sitting next to the pilot in the co-pilots seat. The take off and transit to the safari site was uneventful, but as we made our approach to the landing site, which was nothing more than a grass strip that had been cleared between the wild bush, it became evident that we could not land. Several groups of animals were grazing on the grass and were scattered both on and around the landing strip. The pilot was quite used to this intrusion and as there was no one on the ground at that time, he explained to us his technique for clearing the site. To get the animals off the strip, he would make several quick, low level passes directly above the animals to scare them away. To get to low level (about 50 feet) he would put the aircraft into a steep decent followed by a moderately quick pull up, maximising the engine and aircraft noise as he did so. Clearly thinking he was a military pilot, in a single seat aircraft, he executed these manoeuvres with gusto and without really considering the impact such a manoeuvre would have on his passengers and my percolating stomach.

    I held on as long as I could but the rapid changes in altitude resulted in what can only be described as an almighty audible applaud of relaxed sphincter muscles followed by the rapid flooding of colon gas into the cockpit. I was not worried about the noise so much as we were all wearing headsets. Sadly, we were not wearing oxygen masks. The smell of stale fish and maize having been permeating in my stomach all night was so intense the pilot had to open both small side windows in the cockpit and make the obligatory hands signals to me that simply said *'what the fuck was that, what is that smell?'* in a broad Kenyan accent with a British twang. Unfortunately, his opening of the windows just forced the smell into the rear of the cabin where Diane and the Italian family were seated. The Italian family were not coping well with the motion of flying so when their sense of smell was overloaded with the rapid deployment of colon gas, there was always going to be a response. The daughter went first and unceremoniously threw up. The mum just about held it together and the dad was clearly furious with me. It's not as if I could blame it on anyone else in the aircraft or hope that the air conditioning system could take it away. All I could do was give them a nervous sorry looking smile. I didn't know how to say sorry in Italian but at least I could explain to them in their own language what had happened. I repeated *'çativo vento'* several times in a soft voice hoping that they would accept my unconventional apology. I think the dad would have punched my lights out had he not been preoccupied with trying to console his family from my colon gas cabin invasion. I thought to myself at that time, those two weeks in Italy, learning a little bit of the local language had not been wasted. I was grateful for the opportunity to practise my Italian. You never know in life when you are going to call on your experience – however outlandish that experience may be.

There were only a handful of us new guys posted into the small section on 9 Squadron, apart from the manufacturers courses we would undertake, our initial tasks included setting up the workbenches, building up the tool kits, specialist tooling, writing the publications and commissioning the testing cells. The whole package was in preparation for the work that was about to arrive at our front door. The specialist training we had undertaken was expensive, and, as a result, we had all been *'screened'* in our post for a minimum of five years. Screening was a word used by the RAF Personnel Department to prevent people being routinely posted. This screening effectively gave you some stability in the same place for an extended time whether you liked it or not. Supposedly, the organisation would not penalise your career for being stuck in one place. I benefited from this policy having been selected for promotion to Sergeant. I completed my General Service Training on 22nd May1985. I was just 24 years old and still under my posting *'screened'* time, so I remained in the same section but was made a line supervisor. I was proud of my career achievements considering what I had been through just a few years earlier.

With a willingness to listen, learn and a little ambition it is surprising what you can achieve, and in my experience, it is a great recipe for a successful career. I had been at St Athan just two years, was promoted to sergeant and had a bright future ahead of me. Being a Senior Non-Commissioned Officer (SNCO) comes with quite a bit of additional responsibility and an expectation that you know what you're talking about – all the time. Bob was not only one of the best role model SNCOs I knew, but we became great friends and remain so today. He was my unofficial mentor and wrote the Foreword for this book. Bob enabled me to make the successful transition from corporal to sergeant. He himself would also be promoted in this environment and I have extremely fond memories of our time working together. Bob made work both rewarding and fun and allowed me to pursue my extracurricular activities and training without payback. Payback in terms of working overtime for missed time at work.

The squadron was also a technically challenging environment attracting many senior visitors from around the RAF. It was during one of these visits that I followed Bob around wanting to learn from the *'Jedi Master'*. How does a young SNCO handle senior people and answer their questions? Bob was always courteous and relaxed during these visits and had an answer for everything even if he didn't really know what he was talking about. Listening to him, I knew that some of the information he was giving out was absolute bullshit, he was making some of this stuff up. I never corrected him of course but challenged him afterwards. He admitted he didn't know some of the answers but made the judgment call that it really didn't matter if his response was not 100% correct. He pointed out that what was important to these people is that the organisation is in safe and capable hands with competent SNCOs. The lesson he was teaching me was that '*If you look in control, you are in control*'. Effectively, if you talk confidently to people, they will believe you. It was sound advice and I have remembered his words on many occasions when I have found myself in similar circumstances. Bullshit can baffle brains, but you must carry it off with conviction. Bob could certainly do that, and do it consistently.

Every RAF base has duty staff which generally look after the guardroom after working hours. The guardroom is one of the few buildings that is manned 24/7 and is the place where all visitors arrive, building keys are held and the armoury and fire alarms are replicated. The set up at St Athan was no different. During the normal working day, the dedicated guardroom staff deal with everything. Out of normal working hours, the guardroom would be manned with the Orderly Sergeant (Ord Sgt), Orderly Corporal (Ord Cpl) and Duty Airman. The Orderly Officer would be on base but generally would remain in the Officers Mess being called upon as required. There were also several specialist people that were on standby at home and could be called in as required, like the duty armourer, workshop technician and duty driver. The guardroom staff would activate these people.

My first Ord Sgt duty at St Athan fell on a Friday. There was not much to do during a weekday, the Ord Sgt would be the one to take over the guardroom from the permanent day staff around 4pm and hand it back at 8am the following morning. On a weekend, the Ord Sgt would hand it over to the oncoming Ord Sgt. But, this Friday in late 1985 was a bit different, and it would not be a good day to be a member of the duty staff. A large bomber aircraft and another aircraft had landed earlier in the day and needed close security, so the RAF Police team were a little pre-occupied with this task.

The weather was unsettled. It was windy and raining, a normal miserable day for South Wales and the evening was not going to be much better. I took over from the guardroom staff on the appointed hour (around 4pm) with the two other duty staff; the Duty Airman and the Ord Cpl. The Duty Airman was there to help with the issue and return of keys, selling of meal tickets for the mess and other duties the Ord Sgt seen fit to give him/her. The Ord Cpl had set security duties and needed to conduct regular security checks over the base and would be gone for an hour or so during one of these checks. Also, during my handover, the guardroom staff explained to me that I had a prisoner who was under close arrest awaiting trial.

The guardroom building was fitted out with a couple of prisoner cells. These cells would be used to detain arrested drunks or to accommodate people under close arrest. My prisoner for the night had stolen equipment from a tool franchise and was awaiting Courts Martial. The guardroom staff explained that he had been under close arrest for nearly two weeks and was no trouble whatsoever. He would help with guardroom duties as required and he also made a nice pot of tea apparently. Really.

The first few hours of duty went by without a hitch, but the weather had deteriorated significantly and then all hell broke loose. The Ord Cpl was already out on his rounds when lightning struck an electrical transformer and took out the electrical power on the married quarters and over half the base including the guardroom and Armoury. We switched over onto emergency power immediately. The armoury, which had all its alarms replicated in the guardroom was going berserk. The different coloured lights and various noises would have been okay on their own, but we were under emergency lighting and it looked like we were in the middle of a loud disco. Within a minute the phones had started to ring, and the Duty Airman and the prisoner were doing their best to deal with all the incoming calls whilst I was trying to sort the power outage, silence the alarms and contact the Orderly Officer for some help.

The Orderly Officer was, of course, no-where to be found. The officers mess were not answering any of the numbers I had listed in my duty book, and there was no response to the pager. One-way pagers were a common device issued to duty personnel alerting them to get to a phone and call in. It was a simple small wireless telecommunications device about the size of a matchbox, capable of receiving and displaying a small alphanumeric message.

After about 30 minutes, I managed to track down the armourers to sort the armoury alarms, but the incoming calls were not letting up. The Duty Airman had a young wife and new-born baby at home in married quarters. His wife rang in and was terribly upset and anxious about being alone in the dark. The Duty Airman asked if he could go and comfort and support his distraught wife. I let him go with specific instructions to come straight back, we needed him here in the guardroom. Yet, deep down, I knew I wouldn't see him anytime soon.

I could not track down the Ord Cpl, so this left me and the prisoner in the guardroom. I managed to identify the electricity company who dispatched a technician immediately. He arrived at the guardroom about an hour or so after the blackout. He told me that he suspected it was a transformer across the airfield, but he didn't know how to get to it - it was dark. The RAF Police were unavailable (looking after the visiting bomber aircraft) so all I had was myself and the prisoner under close arrest. I had no idea where the defective transformer was, but the prisoner suggested it was close to his old place of work and he could take the electrician straight to it.

The rain continued to pour down and the phone calls kept coming. Now I had a dilemma and needed to decide what I was going to do. After wrestling with my conflicting thoughts, I decided that I would let the prisoner go with the electrician to fix the transformer, but with strict instructions to both that they must return to the guardroom once the problem was sorted. *'No problem Sarge'* the prisoner said – *'you have my word'*. So, off the prisoner went into the night with the electrician in his van. As I watched them drive off towards the airfield, rain pouring down I remember seeing the van lights slowly disappearing into the night. I sat there with my head in my hands wondering what the fuck I had just done. Not only had I released a prisoner under close arrest, I had also given him a set of wheels as a getaway. I was now alone in the guardroom on a shitty Friday night in the dark. My career was surely over this time at just 25 years old. I should start writing my defence in preparation for my upcoming Courts Martial.

The next 30 to 40 minutes seem like an age but then the lights came back on, the armoury alarms were silenced, the Ord Cpl had returned, and the rain had eased significantly, but I was still down two people. The Duty Airman rang in and asked if he could stay at home with his wife for a few more hours but the prisoner was still at large. Should I ring the police? I decided no, they never came to the guardroom during the blackout so what's the point? I instead chose to worry like hell thinking about my own Courts Martial. It would be another 30 minutes before the prisoner showed up and about 10 minutes before I had decided that I was going to ring the civil police. I didn't know whether to hit him or hug him. I was so relieved to see him. The prodigal son had returned home and suddenly, my career was back on track. Nobody needed to know.

His reason for being late was that the rain had eased so he decided to walk the two miles back to the guardroom instead of having a lift from the electrician. I pondered on what to write in the activity diary for that Friday night, but decided in the end that there was no point in documenting everything that had happened other than I complained about the lack of accessibility to the Orderly Officer in a crisis. For all the rules and regulations we had, there was no guidance for the set of circumstances I found myself in that night. I had to act on my own initiative and in the end, I did what I thought was the right thing to do. If that meant getting into trouble, then so be it. There was a greater good. I felt pretty sure that anyone else faced with a similar set of circumstances would have acted in much the same way. I would not do anything differently today which indicates to me, that even at 25, I had started to recognise the benefit and power of wisdom and good judgement in doing the right thing. In the end, I simply did what I needed to do.

I did many guardroom orderly duties over the years. Other than releasing a prisoner as the Ord Sgt, the only other noteworthy event happened whilst I was Ord Cpl on a Saturday night whilst in charge of the guardroom at RAF Brawdy. Brawdy was also the home of a detachment of US Navy Seabees, the construction workforce of the US Navy. For some reason, I don't remember the Seabees being very well liked by many on the base even though they built a ten-pin bowling alley and contributed in many other ways to base activities and its infrastructure. Perhaps one of the reasons they were disliked was their inability to look right whilst pulling out of their Naval facility which was located about halfway down Brawdy straight. Brawdy straight was the name given to the piece of road that stretched from the camp exit to the first major intersection and was about a mile long. This piece of road was great for motorcyclist but sadly several of them, including a good friend of mine, were hospitalized by American motorist pulling out of the facility and failing to look right.

This particular Saturday night, the Americans were having some kind of party on base and clearly there were other things being passed around other than alcohol. In the early hours of the morning, a Senior Aircraftman entered the guardroom dressed in a tightly fitting Basque wearing full facial make up, stockings and high heels. He looked as if he had just come from a rocky horror show. I don't know what had happened to his facial make-up, but he had either been in a fight or had put lipstick on with a toilet brush. His drunkenness did not seem to be due to alcohol alone, the smell of smoke from his body was not from cigarettes. Although surprised to see him come into the guardroom, I felt my initial reaction was reasonable, appropriate, and blunt: *"Get the shit out of here and go to bed before the RAF police catch you"*. I don't remember how many times I said that or variations of the same thing, but each time I did, he would reply *"please arrest me - please arrest me"*. The man was bat shit crazy, and was clearly on something, this was not just alcohol talking.

As a Corporal, I had the powers to arrest and charge although I had no idea how to do it. Most technical corporals have no idea – that's why the RAF Police exist. And hey, we have all been in situations and made bad choices wishing that someone could have guided us to a different place - right. Well, this was me trying to do my bit for this fella, but he was having none of it. Secondly, I did recognise the chap under the makeup and tried my best to get him to leave before the RAF police arrived, but he was not budging and just insisted he be arrested. In the end, I had to oblige.

I rang the RAF Police and they were on site within seconds when I told them what I had standing in front of me. The RAF Policeman must have thought it was his birthday. The RAF Police dream of arresting people like this, it was a gift from heaven to him to see this chap under some kind of influence other than alcohol and dressed up like a semi-professional transvestite. This was a Courts Martial case for sure. The guy was duly arrested and placed in the cell within the guardroom, and I had the privilege of his company for the remainder of my shift. I never did find out what happened to my visitor, but in those days, drug related offences would have been an instant dismissal from the Service. The dressing up part, well, that may have actually worked in mitigation for him.

One of the extracurricular activities I got involved with at St Athan was playing in a band. Just down the road from 9 Squadron was the oxygen servicing bay. One of the guys that worked there was a fellow Corporal, Mick. Somehow Mick found out that I been posted in and owned a keyboard. I did, it was my Siel Cruise synthesizer, a state-of-the-art keyboard I was lucky to purchase from the money gifted to me on the passing of my Aunty Edna. Aunt Edna used to be a schoolteacher, and I thought she would approve of my spending it on a musical instrument, something I could enjoy and learn to play. Mick approached me in work one day asking if I would like to join his band. Mick had recently sacked the rhythm guitarist and he thought a keyboard would be a good replacement allowing expansion of the band repertoire of songs. I declared to Mick immediately that I couldn't really play the keyboard to that standard and I could not read a note of music. I just enjoyed making different sounds and lots of noise. My only audience up until then had been the crows that lived in the roof of Number 7 Hangar at RAF Brawdy where I used to practice on a weekend. That didn't put Mick off and he convinced me to give it a go at one of his band practices.

I plucked up the courage and attended one of the practices where Mick taught me to play my very first song called *'Hymn'* by Barclay James Harvest. Actually, what he taught me was the chord of E. My very first band experience was playing and holding the E chord adjusting the waveform on the selected synth sound making it sound like I was playing several different chords. Nevertheless, I was hooked. I bought another keyboard shortly after, a Roland Juno 6, and for around six weeks I practiced every night playing basic chords and all the songs that the band played. A simple lesson in life here, if you want to learn and improve a skill quickly, get mixed up with people who are better than yourself. I had owned my keyboard for over three years and had not really progressed passed understanding an octave and the difference between the black and white keys. I considered myself a well below average keyboard player, but in just six weeks my skill level had increased exponentially. I even surprised myself. Mick not only taught me how to play chords, but how chords are constructed and the different elements that make up a song. I probably learnt around 25 songs altogether and if the songs had just three chords like C, F & G or A, D & E then I could learn them pretty quickly. I was incredibly nervous at the first couple of band practices, so you can imagine that I was almost shitting myself the first time I played for real in front of an audience at our local pub.

The *'Fisher Bridge Inn'*, was our local pub. Colloquially known as the FBI. The female manager, Kirsty, would allow us to play there every Thursday night for free. We were called Zuma - after the famous 1975 album from Neil

Band Practice, RAF St Athan Social Club, Wales, 1984

Young and Crazy Horse. We used that name when we played in the pubs, but our (professional) club name was Stilletto. I have no idea where that name came from, but it was a good club band name. In the pub, we would place a bucket in front of the band where people could throw their money in. It was nothing like my childhood dream of playing onstage in front of thousands, but hey, it was a start.

On my debut, I managed to get through the first few songs unscathed and then my confidence grew, and I loved every minute of it – it was addictive. I never got over stage nerves – ever, but that never stopped me from playing either. Every gig I played I suffered from anxiety and could not really relax until I had the first few songs under my belt. That anxiety could last the whole set at the paying venue. A set would typically last between 45 minutes to an hour. Nerves and adrenaline = shaky hands, shaky hands are not good when playing a keyboard or any instrument come to that.

To reduce the nerves whilst playing I would always have a copy of the words of the song on a bit of paper with the chords written above the words and the synthesizer settings for that song. I put them into plastic sleeves and filed them into a book and it all looked very professional in 1983. I still play like that today at home and still have most of my original songs sheets. I would learn over 100 songs in my time in the band and have almost doubled that since.

Mick was both the lead guitarist and lead singer and was a real talent. Mick introduced me to alternative music and artists. Neil Young was one of his inspirations (hence the name Zuma) as were the Eagles, Stones, Clapton, etc and lots of other artists like Barclay James Harvest who, by the way, I had never heard of. Mick opened my mind to music and to this day I can still play *'House of the Rising Sun'* by the Animals and Bob Dylan's *'Knocking on Heavens Door'* on guitar and keyboard without any prompts as I must have played those songs a thousand times or more.

Mick was also the typical lead singer of a rock band. He smoked, drank and dabbled in other things over the time I was with the band (1983-86). Mick also wrote his own songs and to this day I love playing those songs. Nobody knows them of course because Mick never became famous outside our sphere of influence. However, we did have our own local followers and we loved playing those songs to people who recognised them. Perhaps the most famous one for us was a song called "Nuclear Age". This was a great song Mick wrote about the cold war and the Nuclear standoff. It had a huge lead break in the middle of the song where we could all do our own solos, and depending on the gig, we could make it go on forever or knock it on the head pretty quickly if no-one liked it. We were lucky to get to record three of Mick's songs in a professional recording Studio in Cardiff over one weekend. Another great experience. I still have those recordings somewhere in my mass of old cassette tapes.

Our drummer, another Nigel, was another great guy with a passion for playing music. A real gentle guy until you pissed him off. His temper was invited out one night and he got so angry he threw one of his precious drums at a committee member of the club we were playing at. The committee member told us they didn't want us to play any more songs that night. We had only just started our first set which is usually gentle country and western style stuff as a warm up so nothing bizarre or loud. The tactic of social clubs stopping bands playing was a common scam in those days. It only happened to us once, but if a club doesn't think you are an appropriate act for their paying audience, under the contract, they can pay you off before you finish the third or fourth song of the first set. It was the closest we had come to a real pub brawl – it was awesome.

The payoff was nothing more than a few pounds each for petrol.

Our bass player was a classic bass player; big frame, straight face, big moustache but a real gentle giant, another terrific bloke called Dave. No rock star behaviour from him - I thought. We had stopped in a lay-by on the way to a gig one night and he said he just wanted a quick toilet stop. He seemed to be taking ages, so I walked up to his car only to find him taking a dump between the open left-hand side front and rear doors of his car. Nice one Dave – classic rock star behaviour. He immediately became a member of my Rock Star Hall of Fame. I considered myself the 'C' Grade semi-professional, well-behaved member of the band, because I couldn't ad-lib as good as the others. I was just a novice in rock star terms compared to them. I was also in a new and meaningful relationship with my girlfriend (soon to be wife), Diane. I never felt inclined to misbehave. I was clearly maturing.

Mick wrote some brilliant ballads and the words would always tell a story of an incident or event that had happened in Mick's life. And there was a lot going on. Mick taught me the real meaning of lyrics and he was a master of his art as well as being a gifted guitar player. Sadly, Mick passed away in 2015 aged just 54. I owe a lot to Mick and the boys in the band. We had so much fun and every gig was memorable in one way or the other. The band enabled me to live my childhood dream - not quite on the scale of bands like Queen and the Rolling Stones, but the feeling I got when on stage would have been no different if we had played Wembley Stadium. Playing in the pubs was great fun and my favourite, but that didn't pay much, if anything at all. But it was free play for us. We could play whatever we wanted which was mainly our own songs and popular rock songs of the time. We also used the opportunity to practice a few new songs. Everyone was chilled out in the local pubs, nobody knew that we were practicing at times, they just enjoyed the music and we enjoyed playing for them.

In contrast, playing as a professional outfit in the Working Men's Clubs and other private venues over the weekend was a much more lucrative proposition but that meant a lot of hard work, travel, and some extremely late nights. For the two and a half years I spent in the band, I didn't have much of a life outside as practice and playing was a huge commitment. A typical week would be practice on Tuesday, play Thursday in the pub then play the clubs on Friday, Saturday and Sunday. The clubs were mostly arranged through our agent and we would get paid on the night by cheque. Once we got the cheque, we would sign the back of it and cash it in behind the bar. Mr M. Mouse and Mr D. Duck were often signatures on the back of the cheque so that we could not be financially tracked as a person or as a member of a band. We would pay our agent separately therefore avoid any connection to financial institutions. Once again, this was something Mick took care of. He lived for his music and looked after the members of his band.

I didn't have a bad voice then, and I have the same awful voice today. Mick was always trying to encourage me to sing. I could sing but found it difficult to play and sing at the same time. Multitasking does not come naturally to me. I could either sing or play. I accept that I am not a natural musician nor singer, so doing both at the same time was always going to be a challenge. I did sing a few harmonies on a few songs. I then took it upon myself to sing a cover version of a song called 'Moonlight Shadow'. A Mike Oldfield song sung by a female, Maggie Reilly. Perhaps not the best song to go solo on. I think Mick liked the lead guitar solo which is why the song ended up on our set list. We had to drop a few octaves from the original for me to sing it. I used to get so nervous that I would sing to

Diane in the car on the way to the venue but sing out of tune to lighten the mood and to calm me down. That turned out to be a bad idea. One night (luckily in the pub), I could not sing the song in the correct key. I remember Mick looking at me in disgust and he said, *'What the fuck are you doing?'* That was it, that was my singing career over. I never sang again in the band. I just concentrated on the music. The singing would be confined to home use only.

There were many memorable nights with the band, but two events stick in my mind. The first event took place in a workingmen's club somewhere in the Welsh valleys. We were playing the second set of songs and there was a ballad towards the end of the set where I had little to play. There were a lot of people dancing, so I got down from the stage and ended up dancing with this lady who must have been in her early sixties. She was keen to smooch with me and we danced for a little while and then she whispered in my ear; *'you can have me if you want to.', 'Really.'* I said, *'thank you'*. *"Yes, I have not had it for a while, so you might have to chip the crust off first when you get down there'*. There was no reply to that other than - I need to get back up on stage now…. Although not quite the rock star image I had dreamt about, it did bring a huge smile to my face and was a reminder of the huge amount of fun it was to be part of a band.

The other event was a private gig on a farm near Cowbridge, South Wales, on a Saturday night. We didn't even get there till around 1:30am as we had just played a gig in a local club in Llantrisant, a few miles down the road. The farm had been occupied for the whole weekend by some motorcycle group from Somerset and the West Country. There were a couple hundred people there including many locals. I remember on arrival at the farm driveway, there was just one local policeman making sure no one was leaving the farm. This was not a good omen. His other job that night was to make sure that people going into the farm, knew exactly what they were going into. I was shitting myself. I could hear music from the main road and as we drove the half mile or so up to the barn where we were to play, the heavy metal type music was getting really loud. Mick had arranged this gig of course, and it would be a cash deal. We were to get several hundred pounds for this gig plus beer and whatever else you wanted. It was pretty clear what the anything else was. I actually felt like my life was in real danger and I was hoping we would all change our minds and just leave and go home. No such luck.

We were met by some of the toughest looking bikers I have ever met in my life, but they were really nice to us - thank God. We were shown to the back of the barn where we were to set up and then they left us to get on with it. My eyes were everywhere, I have never experienced so many drunk and drugged up people in my whole life. The air was rich with fumes of all sorts of different smells either being smoked or burnt. My senses were working overtime. I was reminded of when I accidentally sniffed glue fumes and got a bit of a high with my brother and mother when we were sticking hardboard wall boards within a confined space at mum's house. Spending several hours in this environment would be a similar scenario, I would be in danger of getting high on secondary dope smoke or whatever it was they were burning. I observed people injecting drugs, popping pills and all sorts of shenanigans going on. I have a vivid memory of one couple in a semi naked embrace who looked like they were shagging (or trying to), whilst rolling around in cow shit and hay by the side of a milking barn near the car park. All this was going on before we had even started to play.

The DJ had been playing for about five hours before we arrived and had done a fantastic job getting the crowd ready for us. It was bloody manic. I didn't want to think about what would have happened to us if they didn't like what we were about to play. I was genuinely scared. When we did start to play, we just made sure that the first song was popular and loud, very, very loud. My amp was set on 10. I had never played on 10, and I would have ramped it up to 20 if I had such a setting on the volume knob. I just wanted us to be loud. Loud would work with this audience. First song was *'Jumping Jack Flash'* by the Stones. How appropriate. It worked. We rocked for around four hours. We played all sorts of songs, many a few times over. The key (no pun intended) was to play loud and fast - whatever the song. Our own rock version of John Denver's *'Country Roads'* was interesting, but we were able to pull it off. By the time we were finished, I think most people were either asleep or dead. We had been paid up front as promised, and we left the farm around 06:30am with no incident whatsoever.

The only real episode happened in the first 30 minutes of us playing, a young chap who was only half dressed, had clearly taken something and had passed out, he was laying in front of my keyboard stand. Then, suddenly, he awoke and went into a crazy dance frenzy almost knocking everything over. I had to stop playing and grab my keyboards as they were slipping off the makeshift stage and would have ended up in a pile and on top of people dancing. As I grabbed them, one of the "*Management*" witnessed what was going on, came over and punched this lad so hard in the head, he went out like a light. I thought he had put him into some sort of coma; he didn't move for ages, but he never bothered me for the rest of the night. I said a nervous *'thank you'*. How I did not physically shit myself in the first hour is a mystery to me. Nevertheless, as a band, we were awesome. It was a fantastic night of music and the crowd loved us. On reflection, it was probably one of the best gigs we had done and for a variety of different reasons. I certainly went through a full range of emotions that night. I finally got home smiling around 08:00am Sunday morning thinking that was one hellofa weekend, and one I would never forget. Putting yourself outside your comfort zone can be daunting. I was well outside my comfort zone that night, but the rewards were well worth it. I was never totally confident playing in the band, but that night was a massive confidence boost for me and had the long-term effect of reducing my anxiety. If I could play under these circumstances, I could play anywhere.

By 1985 the relationship with my girlfriend, Diane, was getting serious. We were falling in love with each other and I had decided to propose once she had returned from a big girlie holiday with her friends. My life was about to change course from the one I was currently on. I felt that I needed to change, and the timing felt right too. It was clear to me that I could not pursue a professional RAF career, get married and continue in the band. Something had to give. I had such a memorable experience with the band, and it had been an awesome two and a half years, but I was never going to be a professional musician; I knew that. It was time for me to let it go and move on.

In the 1980s it was common for newly promoted sergeants to do a stint behind the bar of the sergeants' mess. Not just help, but actually run the bar as a business for two weeks at a time. I did my first stint early on in my promotion and found it to be enlightening. It was a great way to get yourself accustomed to mess traditions, whilst meeting many other SNCO's and Warrant Officers who also worked on the base. St Athan had some 4,000 military personnel on active duty at the time and there were two SNCO messes. At a guess, each mess would have had upward of over 400 members in each, so you were kept busy during lunchtime and the evening. Luckily not everyone would turn up at the same time. Tips were good too, and at the end of the two weeks you needed to reconcile the stock book with your takings. All the cash taken that was over and above sold stock was yours. It was a fantastic way to earn extra cash. If there was a function during your tenure it was quite easy to make several hundred pounds' in profit and tips.

Mess Bar duty was real work and you would not be required at your normal place of work during those two weeks. Effectively you would live in the mess for the whole period. The practice stopped during the mid to late eighties along with the widespread practice of lunchtime drinking. I didn't expect this duty to influence my career, but it did big time. When you work behind a bar, you see and hear things that you don't necessarily witness when you are there socializing. You also see a different side to people you thought you knew. I witnessed some sad people whose life revolved around the SNCO's Mess Bar, their work, and little else. I would often see the same people at lunchtime as I would in the evening. They tended to be much older SNCO's, in their forties mainly, many of which were bitter and twisted about how they had been treated over the years by the RAF and its officers. Some had become pretty grumpy individuals. Perhaps missed opportunities, unrealistic aspirations or just maybe they were naturally miserable people, I never knew, and I really didn't want to engage with them to find out.

Unwittingly, these negative people played a major part in my next career move. I was 25 years old. I did not want to find myself in the same position as these people when I reached my forties. I thought deep and hard about my professional future and what it may hold. In parallel to this, I also found myself being overly critical of the leadership being shown by several of the commissioned officers that were running the squadron where I worked. I honestly believed that I could do a better job than some of these people, many of which I considered to be bordering on incompetent. Saying I was going to do something about it was one thing, doing it would be another. I didn't know it at the time, but it would take me almost four years' hard graft to raise my game, and to prove my point; but prove it I would. In doing so, I would achieve another career milestone.

I met Diane, by pure chance. I had offered to drive my flat mate Sam, Sam's girlfriend Elaine, Diane, and Diane's other friend Cheryl to a night club in Cardiff one Saturday night. Diane was the fun one to be around and we really hit it off from the moment we met. I invited Diane to come and see me play in the band, at a local fancy dress gig. The rock star image clearly won her over and after two years of courting and band gigging, we were married on 31st March 1986 in Diane's hometown of Barry. I was 25 and Diane just 21 years old. We grew as a couple and Diane was always incredibly supportive of me, my career and the professional opportunities I had along the way. Diane's parents and siblings were also very supportive of my career, and I quickly became part of this very close-knit family.

Diane and Me at our First Band Gig, Wales, 1983

This whole of family support thing was critical to me. However, I did have serious concerns about succeeding in the officer commissioning process, particularly the physical aspects of the training. On the other hand, I didn't see myself remaining as a SNCO for the rest of my career, not after my bar duty experience. I wanted to stay in the RAF, I knew I had more to offer in terms of a professional career. As mentioned previously, I had experienced poor leadership qualities in several officers that ran our squadron, and quite honestly, I got fed up of talking about their odd behaviour and poor decision making. The officers were often the topic of conversation in our SNCO crew room because of the stupid things they had done or were proposing. The criticism from my fellow SNCO's could be quite brutal, and I found myself emulating similar views. I remember thinking to myself, I can't just continue to be critical of these people, I needed to do something about it or shut up. I passionately believed that I could do at least as good a job as them, maybe even better with some training. Those thoughts alone drove me to progress my career in that direction and it was a sound career decision; the timing in my life was right, and I was doing it all for the right reasons. I would become a commissioned officer.

I needed to get a professional qualification at a higher level and Diane would be key in coaching me along the way. Diane was far more academic savvy than me, and she was key in getting me through my GCSE (O Level) in English Language. Without this basic English qualification, I was going nowhere with my commissioning goal. Diane also taught me exam tricks and writing techniques for revision of the other technical subjects I would study at college. At work, Bob my supervisor, allowed me to take day release from my duties so I could study at the local college in Barry. After three years of college study on an Ordinary National Certificate (ONC) course in Mechanical and Production Engineering, I got myself academically qualified for becoming an engineer officer. I had been working hard all this time on my physical fitness too, and eventually passed the physical tests required to enter the commissioning process. I found the physical aspect much tougher than the academics. All I needed to do now was pass the leadership and cognitive tests involved in the officer selection process at RAF Biggin Hill. There was only so much preparation you could do for those tests, so I was on my own. I must have impressed the selection team because I passed first time in early 1988. Everything was now in place for my career to switch lanes. Time to hand in my non-commissioned status for a Queens Commission.

Chapter 8
Switching Lanes

Me & Tiger, No1 Aberyswyth Crescent, Barry, Wales, 1984

I was already living in my own house when Diane and I got married. It was a small two-bedroom end-of-terraced house at the bottom of a steep hill in Barry, South Wales. I was living there with *'Tiger'*, my cat, who would be the family cat for the next 18 years. I should have done more homework on buying houses because the house was not in the greatest or safest part of Barry. It was not until I moved into the house that I realised my end of terrace location was an ideal pissing stop for those nice people on their way home from the pub. If emptying your bladder was an Olympic sport, the training ground was the side of my house. Most drunks thought it was a good idea to piss on my property before making the trek up the steep hill. My small back garden provided these drunken idiots with a dumping ground for that last beer bottle. So, I provided them with the complete service. For those idiots who were feeling brave and adventurous, the drainpipe from the roof to the pavement was an ideal prop for them to show off their mountain climbing skills. Unfortunately, moulded PVC plastic is not strong enough to hold these drunken adventurers, so the drainpipe would detach itself well before they could put their second dirty foot mark on the side of the whitewashed house. I trust that those who tried this futile adventurous act fell and seriously hurt themselves, perhaps even falling on their own half empty beer bottles.

My father-in-law was a builder and he had serious concerns about the structural integrity of the house. I took his advice seriously and gave up living in Barry and took the opportunity to move into public accommodation (married quarters) at RAF St Athan. We stayed there before buying our very first house in Llantwit Major, not that far from the rental house I moved out of just a few years earlier. After the experience in Barry, I swore I would never buy a house again without some impartial professional advice. I had bought the Barry house on a bit of a whim (it looked nice inside) and I had been lucky to flick the house on quickly without too much drama. It could have been an awfully expensive mistake. I was lucky and had learnt a major lesson. I was shit at handling money for buying cars and motorcycles, I didn't need to make the same mistake with houses.

16 Wren Road was our very first married quarter and the only one we lived in at RAF St Athan. All the streets on the married quarters had names of birds so when you were drunk all you had to do was remember a bird's name. Eagles, Bullfinches, Wagtails, Partridges, Kingfishers and Woodpeckers surrounded us. Married quarters living was quite an experience, and one that set such low standards for housing we were never going to be disappointed again. Cold damp houses with storage heating systems that were so inefficient it could empty your bank account and overload the national grid at the same time, and you still needed to put a thick jersey on.

On taking over the house, which is called a *'March in'*, the carpets had been cleaned. However, the water they had used to clean them remained soaked into the carpet, it was as if the house had been flooded. It absolutely stank. Not a great introduction to our married quarter life. During the winter months, we were given instructions by the RAF to open the attic space and let all the expensive heat from the storage heaters go into the roof space to prevent the water pipes from freezing and bursting. In fact, the RAF threatened to charge people who didn't do this if they suffered a burst pipe. Not sure how enforceable that would be nowadays, but they were the strict rules we had to live by if we wanted to occupy public accommodation in the mid 1980s.

We had the added benefit of occupying an end of terrace house, which was a magnet for uninvited house guests. Mr and Mrs Rat and family could climb through our outer wall and get into our attic space through the air gap between the internal and external wall. After all, it was nice and warm up in the attic. We could hear them running around and nibbling through whatever was up there. The local rat catcher pitched up one day in a suit and tie with a briefcase full of different poisons. He looked like an insurance salesman, but I guess when your business is catching and killing rats, you probably want to look as professional as possible.

After a comprehensive study of the rat shit that had been left around the attic space, and a damage assessment of the attic trauma the rat had caused, he concluded that the rats were in fact just one rat and it was quite a small one. The thought of even one rat in the attic is bad enough, it didn't really matter how big the bloody thing was. I did ask whether he could tell if the single rat had invited any of his friends and had held a party up there at some time, because the noise at night sounded like an army of rats partying hard with steel toe capped boots. He assured us it was just the one. The poison he laid would make the rat very thirsty. The idea being that the rat would leave the attic space in search of water. The rat would not have to go far if there was a burst pipe of course, but invariably they would leave the house, find water and drink. After drinking, the rat's body swells enormously as if it had binged on fast food for a week and eventually kills the rat by heart attack or some other organ failure. He assured us that the body swelling and dying bit happens before returning to the warm confines of the attic. The rat man pointed out that his strategy would work because the swelling happens almost immediately after drinking. Even if the rat did try to return it would get stuck between the walls. Great! We would then have a dead rat as wall insulation. His plan worked well, and the noises went away soon after. But this kind of entertainment we could do without, so it was not a difficult decision to move into our first proper house at 9 Wimbourne Close, Llantwit Major. This would quickly become the first family home. Soon the two of us would become three.

First Family Owned Home, 9 Wimbourne Close, Llantwit Major, Wales, 1988

We found out that we were expecting our first child, Daniel, in the first quarter of 1988. Dan was due to make an appearance around late September time but arrived on 3rd October 1988. I had just successfully gone through the officer selection process at RAF Biggin Hill in March 1988 and was now ready to enter officer training that year. The RAF was considerate and fair to us once they knew we had a baby on the way and left the decision to us as to which officer training course I should join.

The first opportunity to enter training would be August 1988, but that would mean I would miss the arrival of Dan. The other choice would be sometime soon after Dan was born.

I knew that the first six weeks of officer training was extremely physical, and with my bad leg in winter (after Dan's arrival) that was always going to carry a serious risk of physical failure. I did not want to do the 18 weeks of officer training twice. The summer entry on the other hand, would still be just as physical but the warmer weather would be much more favourable for someone like me with a weak leg and a left foot prone to infections. We decided that the summer course would afford the best opportunity for my physical success, but it did mean that I was highly unlikely to make Dan's arrival unless it was on a weekend. It was not an easy choice. We were lucky that we still lived close to Diane's family, they would support us whilst I was away and be there for whenever Daniel decided to enter the world. Although tough, it was the right decision made for the right reasons. I so wanted to be there for Daniel's arrival, and it played on my mind right up to the day he was born, which just happened to be on a Monday.

I had joined No 113 IOTC (Initial Officer Training Course) in August 1988 at Royal Air Force College Cranwell, Lincolnshire. We were in the middle of a deployed exercise when I got a call to go and see my Flight Commander. He informed me that I had just become a dad. A healthy baby boy and both mother and child were doing well. I cried. The relief that everything went well, and both Diane and Daniel were doing fine was a relief. The feeling of happiness of becoming a dad for the very first time was completely overwhelming. That contented feeling quickly turned into a feeling of guilt. I felt that I really should have been there to support my family even though we had talked about it extensively beforehand and had made our decision. These mixed emotions made me realise that we had done the hard bit and had made this sacrifice for the sake of my career. There was absolutely no bloody way I was going to fail this course after this. I was already motivated to succeed, the arrival of Dan just made me focus harder. Fortunately, even the directing staff were human and on the recommendation of the Padre, allowed me a little time off to go home to see my new family.

The news that I had been given a 48-hour pass was awesome and totally unexpected. I was then, and remain now and forever, proud of becoming a dad and I couldn't wait to get home to see Diane and Daniel. The emotions of seeing, for the first time, your own flesh and blood is incredible. It is extremely hard to describe in words seeing this new human being, a person that you help make, breathing and looking at you whilst lying totally helpless in your arms. To put it into perspective, becoming a parent goes down as the greatest achievement and feeling I have ever experienced in my life. I was then, and always will be, proud of having children. It was an amazing moment seeing Daniel for the first time with Diane in our very own home. Just being with my new family for a few hours, just the three of us – was perfect. I cried again. I would cry a lot over the coming days, but they would be tears of immense joy and happiness. There is no greater gift than the gift of life.

Looking Slim, Back to Cranwell, Ford Sierra XR4i, Llantwit Maior. Wales. 1988

I returned to the exercise with a renewed enthusiasm and determination to complete the physical and leadership aspect of the course. However, in the last few days of the exercise I did some damage to my weak left foot which needed medical treatment. I masked the damage by taking numerous painkillers and anti-inflammatory drugs to get me through. I knew the medics would pull me off the exercise if they examined my foot and that would just result in my being held over and re-coursed. I was so close and there was absolutely no way I was going to get myself removed before the end of this phase of the training. I just sucked it up and kept my boots on for the remainder of the exercise. My foot was literally a stinking mess at the end, I needed anti-biotics and ended up wearing oversize training shoes for much of the academic phase because my foot was so infected and swollen.

I had made it through the physical aspects of the course. It was so satisfying to successfully complete this physical aspect of the training with no dispensations. I did better than some of the more able people on the course. The fitness training was so intense for me during these first six weeks that I could consume several *'Mars Bars'* and many other high protein and fatty snacks between meals, and the weight would still fall off me. That weight loss ended abruptly during the academic phase. It would not be until the end of the course and on the receipt of a congratulatory letter from my senior commander, that the concerns of the directing staff and medical team came out. They all had serious doubts from my medical history that I would be able to complete the physical aspects of the training. Such news just made the success even sweeter.

My walking and marching never improved during officer training and during the practice sessions for the graduation parade, I was simply Mr Music Man. I was responsible for stopping and starting the recorded marching band music over the public address system whilst everyone was outside in all weathers practising for the graduation parade. I would be sat in the comfort of the little music room in the main College Hall building simply starting and stopping the cassette tape at the appropriate time during rehearsals. I never did one parade practice. Sure, I did the marching technicalities bit, but I already knew most of them from my airman recruit training.

To graduate I physically needed to take part in the parade, that was the deal. So, on graduation day, 15th December 1988, I was placed in the middle section of one marching flight. The two guys either side of me had been given instructions to keep me in line and upright. I tended to drift left and right when marching due to my limp. I don't think anyone really noticed and the parade went off without a hitch. It was a proud moment for families, friends and us graduating officers. I wondered what dad would have thought about my achievement. I am sure he would have been proud. Our entry lost around a third of its people over the 18 weeks and Number 1 Flight (my flight), which started with eleven, graduated with the fewest of all, just three of us. The graduating photo was small, the staff making up 50% of the photograph. I graduated in the rank of Flying Officer. The rank is the second most junior rank of the commissioned branch and is usually awarded to

No 1 Flight, 113 IOTC Graduation, RAFC Cranwell, England, 1988

people like me who had previous airman experience. Graduation also meant that I could no longer revert to the non-commissioned ranks. If I didn't like my career as an officer, I would have to leave the RAF, I could not go back to be a SNCO or airman.

Diane and I celebrated our first family Christmas that year and although we were a little apprehensive about the future, we were also excited about what 1989 would bring. At the very least, we knew it would bring a major change in my RAF career and the first of many family moves.

Diane had three other siblings and her whole family were all incredibly supportive of my career achievements. Her mum and dad became my mum and dad over the years, and we would spend more family time with them than any of my own family in South Wales. It was not a conscious decision which family we spent more time with, it was just the way it was. Dan was the first of nine grandchildren on this side of the family and over the following years as our family grew, we would even plan family holidays together. That is how you felt in this family. Life was always good. Diane's dad was a hard-working self-employed builder/carpenter and a man who always put his family first. He was a man I grew to respect enormously.

I was proud to be the first son-in-law; we had such great times together as a family and my father-in-law in a way became my mentor. He treated me like his own son and taught me how to catch, gut and cook fish, and taught the kids how to plant things in the garden and blow bubbles with washing up liquid. He was a terrific grandfather period. I also went to work with him a few times, so he taught me a few tricks of his trade. A classic phrase I will always remember of his was *'measure twice, cut once'*. As a carpenter, cutting the wrong length of wood (shorter) is terminal. You can't stick it back together. I have adopted that phrase to other things in life like, check you have your passport twice before leaving for the airport. Make sure you have your keys twice before you slam the door shut. It's become learned behaviour.

He was always a man who lived in the moment and it was difficult not to live in the moment with him. I didn't recognise this as a life skill at the time, I just thought it was the FIL (Father-In-Law) factor. It was some years later that I learnt to recognise this living in the *'now'* moment, as a competence and one I have yet to master. I always enjoy the moment but savouring the moment for everything that it gives you, takes the experience to another level. All too often we look towards the next moment, acting like a tourist who has been given 30 seconds to get off the bus to take a photograph of a sunset. We have the memory (photo) but we can't savour the experience in 30 seconds. Savouring the moment and watching the sun set completely and having the photograph purely as a memory jogger is something quite different.

My first job after graduating from officer training would be a holding position at the Ministry of Defence, London. I had been commissioned from the ranks, with the minimum academic entry requirements to be an Engineer Officer, I still needed to undertake additional academic training which, at that time, was conducted at the Royal Naval Engineering College at Manadon, Plymouth. Though, the entry would not be until later in 1989 so, in the interim, I was sent to the Ministry of Defence and into the aircraft engine support and policy department, DD Air Eng 3 (RAF) (Deputy Director Air Engineering 3). I would be there from 23rd January until 7th May 1989.

My three months in London was not without drama. In the first few weeks of my time there, I left my briefcase by the side of a rental car in the car park sparking a major security alert. This was at the height of the IRA terror campaign. There is nothing like impressing your new bosses with a security alert. They were about to start an evacuation of the area, including the 31 storey Empress State building where I worked, before my briefcase was identified as a benign threat. Thank goodness for name tags. My Cranwell name tag was on the outside of my briefcase, so it was relatively easy to track down the owner. It could have been a lot worse for me. Luckily, as a very junior Flying Officer I could claim I was young and stupid – or at least stupid, not so young at 28. It's not often you can play that card, I got off lightly with a reprimand.

It was during my time in this interim post that I also learnt about fax machines. I think we had one of the most complex copiers/fax machines in the world at that time. I never understood how the damned thing worked and would always get a fail message resulting in my having to go back to my boss or get someone else to do it for me. Clearly there was a knack to it and I didn't have it. The first time I thought I had mastered the beast, I received a confirmation of a successful send (rather than one of the many different fail notices it usually gave me) and returned to my desk feeling quite smug with my achievement. Around 15 minutes later I got a phone call from a lady who worked at Victoria Wines, a specialist wine outlet store on Oxford Street, asking me if they were the correct recipients of my fax on engine oil sampling data and approvals. Bugger! Luckily, no security breach this time, but embarrassing, nonetheless. Clearly, the commissioning process at RAF Cranwell had not only turned me in to an officer, it had made me an incompetent one. I thought I had become one of those bloody useless officers that motivated me to take a commission in the first place. It was early days for these kinds of thoughts, things could only get better.

I must admit that the commissioning process, did nothing for my self-confidence. I felt more confident going into the process than I did coming out the other end, and I know I was not the only one. I could hardly decide on what I wanted for lunch, let alone making major policy decisions as an officer. It would be some time down track, that I got back to the level of confidence I once had before commissioning. Sending successful faxes all counted towards rebuilding that professional confidence. I was to learn afterwards (anecdotally) that the commissioning process I went through was deliberately designed to break everyone down at the beginning so that they had a common baseline to rebuild/mould you as a commissioned officer throughout the remainder of the course. Whether or not that was true, it certainly matched my belief in the commissioning process. If it was true, then it was flawed. I struggled enough with the physical aspect; they didn't need to mess with my head as well.

Diane and I had already made the decision that we would move as a family with my career. We were now a one income family with a stay at home mum. That was a conscious decision we made when we decided to start a family, and that's how it would remain for a couple of years at least. We knew we were going to be involved in a lot of house moves due to my training schedule of academic postings and short productive tours. We also wanted to stay together as a family and not be subjected to separation by long distance commuting. We had already tried the long-distance commuting with my being in London and didn't like it one bit. The first full move as a family of three would be to Plymouth.

Plymouth is a city that has always been associated with the Royal Navy (RN). As the RN also fly aircraft, they too have a need to employ aeronautical engineers just like the RAF and would train their sailors at the Royal Naval Engineering College (RNEC) at Manadon, Plymouth. The RAF trained its engineers at the Department of Specialist Ground Training

(DSGT) at RAF College, Cranwell. To enter DSGT as an engineer you either had to have an engineering degree if you were a direct entrant in to the RAF or, if Commissioned from the Ranks (CFR), you had to hold the minimum of a Higher National Certificate (HNC) in an engineering discipline. Being a CFR with an Ordinary National Certificate (ONC) I still did not meet the entry requirements. To encourage more CFR's into the engineer branch, the RAF teamed up with RNEC Manadon where RAF Officers with an ONC could upskill to HNC and then re-enter RAF engineer training at Cranwell. The use of RNEC Manadon was a cost-effective way of doing this without the RAF investing in its own academic airman training school. My course was 89 AESDOC 1.

Although predominately Navy, Plymouth also had an RAF presence at RAF Mount Batten. Originally, a seaplane station operated by the Royal Naval Air Service, RNAS Cattewater. It was taken over by the RAF in 1928 and renamed RAF Mount Batten, operating flying boats. By the time we got there in 1989 its flying days were well over and many of the married quarters were vacant and run down. The RAF School of Survival continued to operate from the base and several the off base married quarters had been kept in relatively good condition. These were perfect for RAF students attending RNEC Manadon.

Our move to Plymouth in May 1989 allowed us to occupy one of the very large four-bedroom married quarters located just a few miles from RAF Mount Batten and about the same distance from RNEC Manadon. The house was almost twice the size of the one we owned in Llantwit Major. This was the first time we had lived away from close family. Fortunately, many of the people living in the houses on the married quarter site were also under training at RNEC Manadon and in a way, they became our family and we offered mutual support to each other. Our attached neighbours were in a similar situation, they also found themselves away from home with a young family. Steve was on the same officer training course as I was, so we knew each other a little from the outset. Little did we know then that the family friendship we were to share would go on to last a lifetime. Indeed, we never imagined at that time that Dan (who was less than 2 years old) would be best man at their son's wedding in 2016.

The posting to RNEC Manadon was just 10 months, running from 8th May 1989 until 22nd February 1990. During that time our course made sure we enjoyed our time with the Navy. We learnt that naval officer behaviour was a little different to that of RAF officers in the Officers Mess (Wardroom). We attended a *'Battle of Taranto'* night at the RNEC Wardroom. This historic battle took place on the night of 11–12 November 1940 during the Second World War between the British naval forces and Italian naval forces at the harbour of Taranto in the Mediterranean Sea. The battle involved the British dropping torpedoes from Fairy Swordfish biplanes into the shallow waters to destroy the Italian fleet. This activity translated into exploding cabbages being run across an extended wire line in the wardroom simulating the torpedoes. Once we were all covered in green cabbage leaves, the long-polished dining tables were cleared and pushed together to simulate an aircraft carrier landing deck. Numerous fire extinguishers were set off soaking the table tops, the water acting as a lubricant as you threw your fellow officers down the table simulating a carrier deck landing. A shit load of fun but broken bones, cuts and general injuries were sustained by the few brave souls who thought they could survive being thrown across a wet table top by some hefty human catapults. Provided the participating officers paid for or replaced everything that was broken or needed replenishing, then everything was good. The doctors could deal with the medical stuff. No questions asked. Navy sure does things differently to the RAF. That kind of behaviour in an RAF Mess could quite easily lead to Courts Martial.

We also got to experience a *'Thursday War'* which is the colloquial name given to the weekly war-fighting and damage control exercises held by Flag Officer Sea Training out of Portsmouth, some three hours' drive away from Plymouth. The Navy test vessels' readiness through a series of drills and exercises and simulated attacks by aircraft, missiles and submarines. It really does test the crew's ability to fight fire, floods, injuries and anything else that may crop up whilst underway. Unfortunately, on this Thursday (25th January 1990), the UK was about to experience one of the worst storms in years. In fact, it had its own name, It was called the *'Burns Day Storm'* and was responsible for many deaths in the UK when it hit. Some of us hoped that the day would have been cancelled, but it would take more than a violent windstorm to stop the Navy training.

Our arrival at the dockside was in the dark. It was an overcast sky and even as the dawn arrived it stayed relatively dark. We were to be hosted by the Captain and the crew of HMS Gloucester, a Type 42 Frigate. On the sea transit out to the Frigate, on the Rigid-Hulled Inflatable Boat, (RHIB) one of our team members was physically sick, such was the sea state at that time of the day and we were still in the safety of the harbour. On reaching the ship itself, which was also within the harbour walls, we had to wait for the top of the swell and then grab the climbing rope net on the side of the ship as the RHIB fell away. You had about 5 seconds or so to move further up the net before the next swell would bring the RHIB up behind you. There was no looking back once you had grabbed the rope. The only way was up. Taking one at a time, we all eventually made it on board thinking that was an exciting start to the day. Once on board, the swell was nowhere near as bad as what we had just experienced in the RHIB. That let us into a false sense of security. Things were about to get worse, a shit load worse.

We had no idea about what was going to happen or how the day would unfold. If we had, I would have stayed at home this day. We did have some indication of the extent of the weather conditions when the ships helicopter crew had already flown the helicopter onto *'terra firma'* even before we had arrived. Also, the smaller mine sweeper ships had already decided to call it a day even before the exercise got going. Clearly, the weather was going to be a little too rough for them. These were not good indicators. The Captain of HMS Gloucester had 12 young RAF Officers on board and there was no way he was going to call it a day. He would give his RAF guests a navy experience they would never forget, and he was absolutely correct.

We got underway quite quickly once we were on board, and as we entered the English Channel from the safety of the harbour, the sea state picked up significantly. From the relative comfort of the bridge, I can still remember the relaxed behaviour of the Captain, his feet up on the desk talking very casually to us as the ship rode the waves. This would be the day I discovered that I could never be a sailor. The continuous sinusoidal movement of the ship would eventually make most of us ill. At the start of the cycle, the bow of the ship would point skyward, riding up the wave like a roller coaster car going up its ratchety climb. As we reached the crest of the wave, the ship seemed to creak and linger for a second or two before accelerating into a steep dive clinically piercing the water below like a cormorant fishing.

As the ship entered the bottom of the wave and then began to level out, the forward decks dispelled the massive blanket of sea water that had engulfed everything in front of us. If the ship had been human, it would be gasping for breath. The ship then headed skywards once more. It was like we were doing the butterfly stroke. The windscreen wipers on the bridge were on rapid mode, only clearing the way ahead whilst the ship was in the climb and for the few seconds in the dive. This cycle of up (grey skies), steady (variable horizons), dive (wall of water) and recover was kind of fun for a few minutes but then it became a little scary and unsettling on the senses. The weather and sea state were getting worse and if that didn't scare us, then the sound of the capsize alarm when the ship turned broadside really relaxed my sphincter and for some reason made me hold my breath. If the ship had been hit by a giant wave on its broadside, the drills would no longer be drills, they would become real as the ship would be in danger of being toppled over. Hoping the Captain would call it a day and return to harbour after impressing his bunch of RAF officers was a pipe dream. That option was quickly taken off the table as soon as we got the message that the harbour had closed. We were now stuck in the English Channel and literally had to ride out the storm. I wasn't the only one who thought *'Holy shit – this is going to get ugly'*

We spent a little time in the aircraft hangar talking to the crew who maintain the aircraft. Looking outwards, the sight of the stern of the ship when the bow was pointing upwards was incredible if not a little frightening and disorientating. All we could see was water, there was no skyline, just a mass of water. In less than a few seconds, the water curled and grew into an aggressive tongue like wave from the turbulence created by the stern of the ship, then it simply flipped itself inwards towards us. As this tongue of water unleashed itself it consumed the flight deck quite quickly before making its way towards the hangar. The drill for this wave wash was to grab the pipes in the ceiling of the hangar, pull yourself up and let the tidal wave of water enter the hangar. You needed to remain off the ground whilst the water hit the back of the hangar and then lets itself out in a kind of licking motion just as the bow of the ship had started tackling the next wave. Once again, a lot of fun for a few minutes but over a period of around 10 hours – not so much. It becomes tiring and you start to wonder when it is all going to end. Even five minutes seems like an hour in these conditions. It takes all your energy to deal with what's going on, you just can't relax – it's exhausting. Just imagine riding the same roller coaster continuously with no respite or any idea when it was going to end. I had already been physically sick a few times after being subjected to this cycle of up, down, side to side motion with little to no reference points. I just wanted to curl up and go to sleep, it was bloody horrible.

I ended up carrying around a large black plastic bin liner that captured whatever was left in my stomach. My breakfast had already made an appearance in the first hour of the sailing. There were no sick bags left to be found anywhere in the ship after a few hours. I was so weak through throwing up, I really needed medical treatment. I was given a small tranquiliser and was sent to lie down in the wardroom after about four hours. I remember the clinometer in the ships mess hitting the stops as the ship bobbed around in the storm like a cork in a piss pot. That coupled with what seemed like the constant sound of the capsize alarm when we were turning broadside, just made the whole experience bad. I thought it would never end.

It was whilst we were in the hangar that my friend and neighbour Steve was smiling at my unfortunate situation. He was an experienced diver and had sailed many times before and was coping with the ship's movement quite well - so he thought. In fact, many of the navy seamen also fell sick during this sailing, and quite a few had been admitted into sick quarters several hours before me; I might add. Anyway, I remember talking to Steve just after a wave attack and watched his face go from pink to white to green all within a couple of seconds. He looked around for a sick bag but of course there weren't any left. All that was available was a couple of clear plastic bags that were used to protect aircraft documentation. There was no way I was giving up my bin liner, I had become quite attached to it and there was no room for his stomach as well. I have never seen a clear plastic bag fill up so quickly, it certainly took him less than two retches. The bag was bulging with puke and you could see all little bits of breakfast stuff floating around in this clouded liquid of stomach bile. It inflated quicker than a bottle filled kiddies helium balloon at the fun fair. I held this warm brown bag of stomach acid at arms-length as he set about bettering his previous record in filling a second bag and then part fill a third. It was all done with the same enthusiasm he had used on the first. It was an incredible sight to behold and if it had been filmed, it would have looked like the bedroom scene from the Exorcist.

It was getting late and dark by the time we could return to the harbour and we would learn that several people on other ships had been injured and at least one had been hospitalised. It was a day of survivability for everyone. Even when we were back on land the swaying motion had not subsided. Indeed, it would take another day or so before we would all recover from this experience. The weather remained cold, wet and windy and we were exhausted but still had a long drive back to Plymouth. Steve had taken his car and the drive home was a little subdued, we were drained. But this adventure had one more little surprise for us. We took turns driving and I drove the car for the final leg and noted to Steve that the low-level fuel light was on. *'No problem keep going Nige, we have plenty of petrol to get back'*. Famous last words. We ran out of fuel about five miles from home. It was still pissing down with rain and blowing a gale. It was the perfect shitty end to a perfectly shitty, but memorable day. I earned my sea legs but was reminded of why I had joined the RAF and not the Royal Navy.

The RAF wasted no time once we had graduated RNEC Manadon and we entered the RAF Engineer Training System at RAF Cranwell on 5th March 1990. The RAF system of engineer training at the time was a sandwich course. A five-month academic and engineer orientation course called Engineer Officer Training (EOT) Part 1. The military are not very inventive with the names of courses, but it was functional, and everyone understood it. We would call it 'Eeohtee'. On completion of EOT 1, our first operational posting would follow for around 20 months before we would return to Cranwell to complete the second part of the sandwich course. This second part was cleverly called Engineer Officer Training Part 2. Thereafter, your second and subsequent postings would be based on where the RAF needed you with some consideration for where you wanted to go and the type of job you wanted to do. Most of the Manadon Course made up the majority of course Number 31 EOT 1.

The move to Cranwell from Plymouth was an exciting move for the whole family. We were expecting the arrival of a sibling for Dan. Joshua made an appearance on 6th July 1990 at Grantham and Kesteven Hospital, Lincolnshire, right towards the end of the 1990 Football World Cup. I am convinced that his interest in football growing up and into adult life was based upon his arrival during this competition. Josh would be the only one of the family that was born outside Wales. England lost to West Germany on penalties on 4th July just before Josh arrived. West Germany went on to beat Argentina in the final. Just seven months after Josh arrived, Grantham Hospital, made National News and for a period became one of the deadliest places in Britain. It was here that one of Josh's future football team players who was only five months old at the time, narrowly escaped death. A State Enrolled Nurse turned serial killer, Beverley Allitt was convicted in May 1993 of murdering four children, attempting to murder three other children, and causing grievous bodily harm to a further six children over a period of just 59 days between February and April 1991. Josh's football teammate was one of the lucky ones. Allitt received 13 life sentences and is unlikely to ever be released from the secure hospital where she is detained.

The move to Cranwell would see the completion of my transition from the non-commissioned to the commissioned cadre of the RAF. My first productive tour as an engineer officer after EOT 1 would be some six years after my decision to switch lanes. I could have trained to become a doctor in less time. I was really motivated to cross the finish line of my transition. After this, it was time to pay the piper. All military training and exercises prepare you for war. Indeed, the training is so realistic you do nothing different during war. Nevertheless, I didn't think I would put all my professional training and the last six years of work into practice so quickly.

Chapter 9
Drinking from a Fire Hose

Our first postings came through several weeks before the end of EOT 1. Although we had an input to where and what we all wanted to do; the posting positions were pretty much already determined by others. It would be a combination of our choices, performance on the course and the recommendation of our course and personnel desk officers that would ultimately determine who went where and did what. I was posted to Engineering Wing Headquarters at RAF Bruggen, Germany. Initially thrilled at being posted overseas, but disappointed with the actual position, we discussed the posting at home from a family perspective and thought that it would be better if we stayed in the UK this time round. Josh was only a month old when we finished the course on 3rd August 1990, and we were grateful for the continued support we had from Diane's family. That support would not be available if we were to move to Germany. Luckily, one of my course mates had been posted to RAF Lyneham, Wiltshire, and would have loved to have landed the Germany posting. After a few chats, our personnel management agreed that our postings could be swapped. We would now go to RAF Lyneham and I would be Officer Commanding Aircraft Support Flight (OC ASF), start date 6th August 1990. We were thrilled at the prospect of going to an operational base and having the luxury of being close to both our families in South Wales. I was finally going to be the professional RAF Engineering Officer I had aspired to be.

RAF Lyneham was the home of the Lockheed Martin, Hercules C130 transport aircraft. At that time, the RAF had around 50 operational aircraft which included a strange looking meteorological aircraft called 'Snoopy', nicknamed because of its extended nose used for flying through adverse weather conditions, including measuring the effects of volcanic explosions and dust discharge into the atmosphere. Lyneham was an exceptionally busy air base with a lot going on during a normal day, but the week before we arrived, on 2nd August 1990, the Iraqi leader Saddam Hussein decided to invade Kuwait, thus kicking off the first Gulf War and *'Operation Granby'*. The C130 fleet would be the workhorse of the operation and would be the first to deploy for the workup, continue through sustainment, and would be the last to leave for the rundown of the operation. I would be in post throughout the whole period. The combined code name for operations leading to the build-up of troops and defence of Saudi Arabia was *'Operation Desert Shield'* (2nd August 1990 – 17th January 1991) and that turned into *'Operation Desert Storm'* (17th January 1991 – 28th February 1991) which was the combat phase. I never knew what a normal day looked like throughout my whole time at Lyneham. When I left in Jan 1992, the aircraft maintenance organisation was still recovering from the incredible amount of flying that had been conducted during Operation Granby. The operation had certainly taken its toll on both the aircraft and the people who operated and supported it. To say that I was *'drinking from a fire hose'* in my learning would be an understatement. I oversaw various second line (off aircraft) component servicing bays and external contractors, and was responsible for the painting, finishing and fabric trade; about 70 people in all. I was personally responsible for the flight's outputs and, more importantly, the welfare and morale of the people who worked there. I learnt so much about leadership and management and the difference between the two; it was unreal, and I had to learn fast.

The increase in flying rates for the aircraft during these deployments meant that we had to literally double our outputs within weeks of the start of Operation Granby. We had no guarantee of additional resources and we had to sustain these outputs for an undefined period. It was one hell of a challenge, but because it was all for real and not an exercise, everyone pulled their weight. Motivation and morale were extremely high. There is nothing like a war to generate a motivated workforce in the military. Along the way, I was rewarded on 15th December 1990, exactly a year after graduation, by promotion from Flying Officer to Flight Lieutenant. Although the promotion was automatic and based on time, I had to keep my nose clean to get it. That was a much tougher task. No longer could I use rank as inexperience for making mistakes or doing stupid things. What I did realise, was that promotion just meant that the daft things you invariably continued to do, would now be far more serious than the same ones you did as an inexperienced officer. I know this because I put it to the test during Operation Granby. Let me explain.

During the Falklands Island War of 1982, the RAF modified a four berth 1950s family caravan to fit into the back of a C130 aircraft. This VIP caravan was capable of transporting Margaret Thatcher, the British Prime Minister down to the Falkland Islands. OC ASF, yours truly, was responsible for this piece of role equipment but I had no idea what it looked like or where it was kept. When we had notification that the then Prime Minister, John Major, may want to travel into theatre to see the troops involved in the Gulf War, senior management at RAF Lyneham turned towards OC ASF and the preparation of the VIP caravan. A VIP 1950s style caravan and the back of a C130 aircraft doesn't really conjure up VIP style transport to me. It was not even fitting for the 1990s. Nevertheless, I was keen to impress my senior management with this important operational task, I drove around the base and eventually found this shitty little green derelict caravan sitting in the back of an old equipment park.

We spent about 1000GBP and around 100 man-hours refurbishing the trim and generally trying to update the internal design, making it fit for a Prime Minister. It was like sprinkling glitter on a turd. We did our best, but it still looked like a shitty old caravan. Nevertheless, it was now a clean 1950s caravan. We decided to keep the caravan warm in the hangar and at a state of operational readiness it had not reached for at least eight years. As we approached the time for the first operational mission of the caravan, we were told that the mission had been cancelled at the last minute. I wondered why.

I suspected that someone had shown the Prime Minister a photograph of the caravan and explained to him that he would be sat inside this horrible farty green box, which would itself be sat inside a noisy, smelly, slow moving propeller driven aircraft for two days. Alternatively, he could fly business class with British Airways, sip gin and tonics and be there the same day. Your choice Prime Minister. That would have been a tough call for sure. Anyway, the result was that the caravan sat in the hangar for months doing nothing other than take up space. In fact, it was never used again for its intended purpose.

It just so happened that during my time at Lyneham, I had a keen interest in building a kit car. I had visited the Lincolnshire Kit Car Show with my mate Steve, earlier in the year whilst we were on EOT 1 and was keen on building a three-wheeler car (two wheels at the front, one at the back) called a 'Kindred Spirit' by Hudson Cars, Norwich. The car was designed around using a Renault 5 as a donor car. The two-seat tandem (no doors) configuration looked very much like the racing car I drove at Silverstone. I had driven a Formula Ford racing car as part of a driving school course a few years earlier and the cramped seating position felt remarkably familiar. I thought it would be a fun car to build, but didn't realise how much of a money pit these projects can be. Also, the amount of time you spend on building them is more than double what the car manufacturer advises you. How I ever found enough time to build this car during my posting, whilst managing a busy section and bringing up a young family remains a mystery to me, but with lots of support from home and from work, it got built in the end and it looked really cool.

Kindred Spirit, RAF Lyneham, England, 1991

Being OC ASF, I had at my disposal all the facilities and resources I needed. Paint stripping, bead blasting, coatings, paint, general service tools and all sorts of engineering equipment. My mate, Kerry (another Welshman), commanded the General Engineering Flight and he kept me supplied with used general nuts, bolts washers etc. The car would stand to attention when the national anthem was played, such was the amount of military help and equipment that went into the build. The final phase of the build was to paint the various fibreglass panels in British Racing Green.

One of the painters offered to get the paint and do the job for me for a small charge. However, he needed somewhere for the panels to hang dust free for a few days, for the paint to cure. I had the perfect solution, the VIP caravan. I was the boss of this caravan after all and gave permission for the painter to hang my panels on the inside. Problem solved, or so I thought. Unfortunately, Officer Commanding Engineering Wing, a senior Wing Commander who was quite a strict disciplinarian was due to carry out an inspection of some of the bays and took it upon himself to visit the VIP caravan. Which, by the way, was not on his visit programme. He just wanted to see for himself how we had spent the 1000GBP and expended all those man-hours on the lavish C130 travel cabin. Not unreasonable, I suppose, he just never mentioned it to anyone beforehand. I was away at the time of the visit but my deputy, who was a very mature Flight Sergeant in his mid-fifties, said that the Wing Commander *'tore him another arse hole'* when he seen the fibreglass panels hanging inside our plush new caravan. To make matters worse, the painter had touched up a couple of the panels in-situ and had managed to splatter the new trimmings with British Racing Green polyurethane paint. The stench of paint and thinners in an enclosed area completely overwhelmed the Wing Commander who thought it was an explosive hazard. That little sideshow resulted in my being hauled into the Wing Commanders office in my best uniform to explain myself.

When asked about the caravan and my car panels, all I could do was apologise and say sorry – bad judgement. I took full responsibility and promised to sort things out and put it right. My admission of guilt certainly took the heat out of the reprimand and I was under no illusion that I was being reprimanded. Although, I think he was more pissed that I had never mentioned to him what I was doing and felt that he may have given me his approval (with some caveats) if I had asked him first. I didn't really know, and I didn't want to take the chance. I didn't find him the most approachable of people and his leadership style was more of instilling fear than confidence. Everyone had an opinion on his leadership style - that was mine. Also, I was the boss (so I thought) and took full responsibility for my actions and did wonder about why he was making a big deal about it. I guess I thought it was better to ask for forgiveness than to do something against his will.

I know that *'honesty is the best policy'*, but in my defence, I didn't tell any lies, I just didn't say anything. On reflection, I guess it's a fine call at the end of the day whether you say something or not. I also think that if you are an approachable and reasonable person, then people will ask for your permission beforehand, or just mention to you what they are doing in general conversation if you take a genuine interest in them. Making yourself available to your subordinates, being approachable and fair are a few core values I learnt from this little episode.

I should have done more research on building kit cars. Without the support and facilities around me at Lyneham, the build cost and time would have been prohibitive, and I would never have finished the car. I would never undertake such an ambitious project again. I sold the car not long after finishing the build as the enjoyment of driving it was not as great as I thought it would be. The challenge and attraction were all in the build and seeing it completed. I guess that's the engineer in me. It did look pretty cool and my sons Dan and Josh loved riding in it.

I also missed not having a motorbike to ride throughout this period. With a young family to support, we could not afford both. Instead, I took up the sport of hang gliding. For a short time, I was the Officer in Charge of the RAF Lyneham Hang Gliding Club so had access to the club's equipment. Unfortunately, during my hang-gliding training camp in South Wales, I spent more time scraping cow pats from my torso through crash landings than I did flying, so I decided that this sport was probably not for me. I did fly a powered hang glider as a birthday gift, but found that dangling from a very large handkerchief at 500 feet strapped into a fabric sling with an engine buzzing away behind your head did very little for my insecurities. I clearly over thought the possible negative consequences which ultimately stopped me doing this kind of activity. I had done some proper fixed wing gliding at Cranwell along with a few flights in the Bulldog and Firefly from RAF Barkston Heath. I had also accumulated around five hours in a Chipmunk aircraft whilst at Manadon and was very lucky to fly in a privately-owned Piston Provost aircraft at Lyneham. I had subconsciously decided that after these positive experiences, if I was going to get airborne, it would be in the comfort of a cockpit – preferably one with an ejection seat.

I took the kit car back to Cranwell with us when we moved and decided to sell it shortly afterwards. With the money from the sale, I bought a brand-new Yamaha XJ 600 motorcycle. I was delighted to be back on two wheels again and this bike would be a reliable second form of transport for my next posting.

It was towards the end of my time at Lyneham that the Hercules celebrated its Silver Jubilee, 25 years of RAF Service. The painters were commissioned to paint one aircraft in livery that would celebrate and be fitting of 25 years' service. In exchange, several painters and their boss (i.e. me) would travel (via Gander, Canada) to Dobbins Air Force Base, Marietta, Georgia, USA, where the aircraft was built, for a celebratory few days in the city of Atlanta – just before Christmas. This would be my first operational detachment outside of the UK and my swansong. I had no idea what to expect but would learn very quickly that the Americans really know how to throw a party. We were looked after the whole time by Lockheed Martin and made to feel very welcome. We were shown many of the sights and attractions of Atlanta – some of which were clearly not labelled as tourist destinations and were night time venues only. It must have been really hot in these places because most of the women never had any clothes on, and those who did took them off after only a short time of coming into the room. Fortunately, we could only stay in these places for about six hours because we had things to do in the morning. The only other detachment I did at Lyneham was soon after my promotion, it was a trip to Ascension Island, a tiny island you can hardly see, right in the middle of the North Atlantic, a stop off base on the way to the Falkland Islands. Our route there would be via Dakar, Senegal.

On the Ascension flight, I was charged with being the safety officer responsible for the safe delivery of a tank of Liquid Oxygen. Sitting in the back of a C130 for tens of hours watching a single pressure gauge was not a great deal of fun. If the pressure got too great and the tank vented, the emergency procedure was to open the ramp door at the back of the aircraft, release the tank locks and push it out the back into the ocean below. Fortunately, I never had to carry out the procedure, but I never volunteered to do the task a second time. It was mind numbing. Having said that, I almost never made the Ascension flight in the first place. We had a stag dinner in the Officers' Mess the night before we were leaving, and I accidently got drunk. This resulted in my missing *'wheels'* for the crew pick up as I was asleep on the floor of my married quarter having been throwing up during the night. I had the foresight to change into flying clothing when I got home as I knew it was a 5:30am pick up and I didn't want to be late. So, in my defence I was ready, I was just asleep on the toilet floor. I had been home just a few hours. A second and special run out to my married quarter (which was just outside the main camp gate) to get me, allowed me to make the flight with just minutes to spare. I was not very popular with the flight crew as I was the safety man, but all was forgiven when I bought them all beers at our night stop-over in Dakar. I would like to say that I learnt my lesson, but I would be a hypocrite to make such a statement. I have always enjoyed a little alcohol. But I have moderated my consumption with age. I have never missed a flight through alcohol consumption since, so I guess I learnt something from this experience. I was never the first person to miss *'wheels'*, and I am pretty positive that I would not have been the last. I would learn another valuable lesson about alcohol a few years down the line. Funny enough, that too would be after a recent promotion.

During the eighties, kidnapping by Islamic Jihad terrorists of journalists and others who thought the Lebanon was a wonderful place to hang out, was commonplace. One of those kidnapped was a journalist called John McCarthy. McCarthy was taken in April 1986 and was held in captivity until his release on 8th August 1991. During his time in captivity he shared a cell with the Irish writer Brian Keenan. On release, both McCarthy and Keenan were repatriated back to RAF Lyneham. In fact, John McCarthy remained at Lyneham for some time whilst he was being debriefed and medically overhauled. I would often see him having driving lessons around the base, clearly preparing himself for the outside world. He was quite a celebrity at the time, but his occupying rooms in the officers' mess along with many specialist's staff who needed to be with him, did not go down well. Several living-in aircrew members were ousted from their own rooms whilst they were away on operations. They would return to find their rooms being occupied by strangers and their personal kit being abused and, in some cases, either broken or missing. That part of the good news story never did make the press.

Mr Terry Waite was a hostage negotiator and a Special Envoy of the Archbishop of Canterbury. On 10th November 1984, Waite successfully negotiated with Gaddafi for the release of the four remaining British hostages held in the Libyan Hostage Situation. However, he himself would become a hostage when he was associated, through contact with the Americans, with the *'Irangate'* scandal. On arriving in Beirut on 12th January 1987 with the intention of negotiating with the Islamic Jihad Organization who were holding hostages, Waite was taken hostage himself on 20th January 1987 and remained in captivity for 1,763 days, the first four years of which were spent in solitary confinement being chained to a wall for 23 hours and 50 Minutes a day.

Terry Waite was finally released on 18th November 1991 and was also repatriated back to RAF Lyneham. This was huge news in the UK at that time. The Initial Press Conference was held in the hangar at RAF Lyneham next to a C130 making all the daily newspapers. Waite then made a surprise guest appearance at our Mess Dining-In dinner just a few days after his release. He spoke about his personal experience as a hostage negotiator, his faith and his thoughts on his capturers and confinement.

There was complete silence whilst he was speaking, you could have heard a pin drop. It was incredible to experience the atmosphere he created just through his presence in the room. He was a giant of a man standing over 6ft 7ins, slim for his stature with dark hair and a greying beard. He looked a little gaunt in the face and older than his 52 years, but his voice was clear and authoritative. I remember looking around the table and there was not a dry eye in the house. I have never heard such an emotional and heart felt (unscripted) speech in my life. The man was a saint. He gave me goose bumps. It was by far the most memorable formal dinner I have ever attended. I think everyone enjoys a little *'me time'* occasionally, but this was extreme. I think most people would have gone mad being subjected to such isolation. His faith was a massive advantage to him and something that never faltered throughout his time in captivity. It was the one thing that could not be taken away.

I would eventually leave Lyneham on 27th January 1992 and head back to Cranwell for Part 2 of Engineer Officer Training. I had plenty of experiences to share from my 18 months at Lyneham, as did all junior engineer officers from their first postings, so what could Part 2 teach us that we haven't already learnt?

The move back to Cranwell was our fourth move in quick succession as a family, and we had become proficient at taking down photos and packing up the family home in a day or two. We had enjoyed being closer to family but enjoyed living in Lincolnshire and was pleased to be heading back to Cranwell. The primary school had a great reputation and the community spirit within the married quarters had been the best we had experienced. We were looking forward to going back, even though we knew it would be for another short period.

There would be ten of us on course; Number 23 EOT 2. The course started on 10th February 1992, and after graduation on 19th June 1992, I would head straight onto Officers Command School at RAF Henlow, just 80 miles down the road for a month (6th-31st July 1992). This course was a mandatory staff course and an integral part of career progression for junior officers. Having me do the staff course on the back of EOT 2 meant that the family could stay at Cranwell for six months instead of five, and then we would all move together to our second posting location - wherever that may be.

The first five weeks of EOT 2 was the Management Module, a useful recap on management techniques and leadership styles that would prepare us for our next posting and indeed, the rest of our careers. The technical aspect of the course was not so enjoyable or that memorable, and several years later the sandwich system of training was ditched in favour of a single stream system, similar to what was in place before the EOT 1 and EOT 2 system. What goes around comes around, I guess.

For those who did not have a front line on-aircraft operational tour for their first job/posting, then the chances were that they would get one for their second tour. The RAF really wanted its engineer officers to be *'all-rounders'*, able to be employed in the wide range of positions the RAF had to offer. My posting to RAF Lyneham was a second line appointment i.e. not directly in charge of aircraft, so my second posting (hopefully) would be onto the front line, an aircraft operational squadron - somewhere. Once again, the postings came through a few weeks before the end of the course and I was posted to Number 4 Flying Training School, RAF Valley as the Junior Engineer Officer for Number 3 Squadron, operating 12 Hawk TMk1 and TMk1a aircraft. The squadron trained young pilots to fly fast jet aircraft and then teach them how to use the same aircraft as a weapons platform.

There were only three RAF bases in Wales; Brawdy in West Wales, St Athan in South Wales and Valley in North Wales. I would achieve the hat-trick of Welsh bases from this posting. I was not at all disappointed going back to Wales this time and thought it quite comical that being a Welshman, I would have served at all three RAF Bases in Wales and not actually asked to be posted to any of them. Sometimes the posting system works in mysterious ways. Nevertheless, I was looking forward to getting to work around aircraft once more. I commuted for a short while from Cranwell on my brand-new Yamaha XJ600 motorcycle, due to a lack of available married quarters at RAF Valley. This gave me a little time to get up and running with the cut and thrust of being around operational aircraft once more.

The Hawk aircraft is a single engine, tandem seat trainer, therefore there is always a spare seat when staff pilots are flying solo. It was forbidden to fly with a student as a passenger, and quite rightly so, some of them were absolute shockers. This 'spare seat' was not lost on me and I was keen to do as much flying as possible, so I got myself an aircrew medical and undertook hypoxia training as a passenger for fast jet flying.

Experiencing oxygen deficiency and rapid decompression in the comfort of a hypobaric chamber under medical supervision is a very safe way to find out how your body reacts. During the decompression, my bowels were free to move and there was plenty of audible warnings letting my fellow chamber mates know that my intestines were simply purging my colon. Of course, we were all farting, just that mine seemed to go on for longer. Sensing and experiencing slow oxygen starvation and the onset of hypoxia was an eye opener (no pun intended). The ability to do even the simplest of tasks quickly become difficult. It is an insidious degradation of your brain to function and the purpose of this exercise is for the individual to experience the symptoms so that you recognise the warning signs of hypoxia if it happens for real whilst flying. For me, I remember feeling all hot and flushed, but it is different for everyone, hence the need for this training. Knowing these symptoms can save your life, and of course others if you are the pilot. Once the doctor is satisfied that you have had the experience, the oxygen levels are increased back to normal. I could feel a headache almost immediately, which is quite normal as your blood gets enriched with oxygen quite quickly.

I flew 32 sorties in the Hawk over my two years and was fortunate to fly all over the UK and in parts of France. One of my first flights was taking part in the Battle of Britain flypast on 11th September 1992. This was an incredible experience and I felt really honoured to be flying amongst different aircraft types on such a special occasion. Conducting full flight tests was a favourite, we would operate the aircraft at the limits of its safe design in about an hour. It takes a little while to get there, but the view from 45,000 feet is spectacular. It is completely black when you look up, and the view out the front or to the side show cases the curvature of the earth (sorry flat earthers). We never flew far from the base to conduct these tests, and at that altitude the isle of Anglesey is clearly visible as is much of the Welsh coastline.

Gently throttling back the engine at that altitude, there is a sense of calmness and the aircraft seems to be just hanging there in space. There is no sense of speed and apart from the normal buzzing of the electrics and air conditioning system, it is quite peaceful. You can hear yourself breathing, and with the rubber oxygen mask toggled down on your face, the smell of rubber took me back to my early visits to the dentist, where they would put a mask over your face, tell you to pretend you were a pilot, then force nitrous oxide into your lungs before working on your teeth. The outside air temperature sits at a cool -56C (-70F); the temperature remains a constant from around 37,000 feet up to 65,000 feet. Although a sub-sonic aircraft, Mach.88 in normal flight, in a dive the Hawk can get supersonic. The gradual pull back on the control column to positive +8G not only tests the aircraft but tests the strength of your neck muscles to keep your head up. The anti-g suit does its bit by inflating and squeezing your thighs, thus preventing the blood draining from your body. That is quite fun to experience. However, flying inverted and bunting momentarily to negative -3G is horrendous. It is like jumping into a swimming pool from hight, feet first and the water forces itself up your nose and into your head and wants to make your eyes pop out. You can grey out under positive G, hence the anti-g suit, but there is no preventative flying clothing to stop you getting red out.

Some of the best memories from the cockpit were flying at 250 feet and at 420knots (480mph) through my homeland of Wales (around the Mach loop) and through the Scottish Highlands and Lochs. Travelling at 8 miles a minute, you cannot afford to get lost. Even a 15 second distraction can put you off track by two miles. Dropping 9kg practice bombs and firing the centre mounted 30mm Aden cannon whilst strafing the live firing range was an amazing feeling, mentally challenging and a shit load of fun. Flying in a formation of 26 Hawk aircraft making a '75' in the sky in July 1993 was another incredible experience. The formation was for the RAF Fairford Air Show, to celebrate the 75th anniversary of the RAF. The significance of the event made it a proud and memorable flyover.

Landing in heavy rain, cross winds and patchy fog during a grey day at an unfamiliar airfield is not much fun when you are flying in a small jet, being tossed around like a cork in a piss pot unable to focus on anything outside the cockpit is scary. It is during these times I really got to appreciate how good RAF pilots are, how well they can fly on instruments and how much self-confidence and faith they have in their own abilities. They also put a considerable amount of trust in the groundcrews ability to make sure the aircraft is airworthy. Things can go wrong very quickly during normal flight, but in adverse conditions it can get bat shit crazy and you must keep your cool. It was during experiences like this, I realised that I never would have been able to fly fast jet aircraft for a career. I just don't have the mental aptitude to assimilate everything that's going on in such a short space of time to make good and calculated decisions. These are great life learning opportunities too. Knowing your weaknesses is just as important as knowing your strengths. Seeing others perform in these circumstances simply earns my respect.

I witnessed something going wrong for a pilot from the comfort of my office one sunny afternoon. One of the staff pilots (on another Hawk squadron) was practicing a *'turnback'* manoeuvre. The turnback was a simulated engine failure after take-off requiring the pilot to throttle back the engine before tightly turning the aircraft through 180 degrees to land back on the runway. He got it wrong and was forced to eject over the airfield. I heard the loud bang of the ejection, looked out the window to see the rocket pack on the bottom of the seat accelerating the pilot and his seat skyward out through the shattered canopy of the cockpit. I watched the ejection seat fall away leaving the pilot gently swaying back and forth on the end of his parachute just like a kiddie's action man doll slowly returning to earth. He landed with nothing more than a bump and a roll to break his fall. The aircraft had turned slightly to the right before smashing into the ground and bursting into a large fireball about 100 feet or so away from where the pilot was just about to come down. It was all over in 20 seconds.

The pilot was lucky to get away with cuts and bruises. His decision to eject would have been made in a second. That's how quickly things can go wrong. This was not the first time we had lost an aircraft conducting this manoeuvre. But it was one of the last. The *'turnback'* was kept for the simulator only.

Back to the 75th anniversary formation flight, on Saturday, 24th July 1993, we were forming up to do our first flypast of the weekend and were told to go into a holding pattern several miles out from the run-in line where we would fly directly over the airfield. It is quite difficult to hold so many aircraft in close formation and

Tiger Meet (Hawk Ground Crew), Hawk XX226, Cambrai, France, 1993

then go into a holding pattern. It was a manoeuvre that was never practiced, and we were held off for some time before we were given the all clear to re-join the main display. The reason for the hold was that a pair of Russian Mig-29 fighters were doing their display and collided mid-air and crashed. Fortunately, no one was hurt. Even the pilots landed safely after ejection. A photographer captured the moment of collision with a series of photographs. One of these photographs won the best photo award of 1993.

On 1st October 1992, Number 3 Flying Training Squadron (FTS) took the badge and Squadron Standard of 74 Squadron from the Phantom FGR2 aircraft. The Phantoms were being retired from service at RAF Wattisham. Number 74 Squadron dates back to 1st July 1917 when it flew Avro 504's in the Royal Flying Corps and through the years have been disbanded and reformed with different aircraft types. Number 74 Squadron is also a famous *'Tiger'* squadron because of the aggressive spirit shown by its pilots. Allowing Number 3 FTS Hawks to take the standard enabled the squadron to reform as a reserve fighter squadron allowing both the history and the association to remain active. One of our Hawks (XX226) was painted jet black with a huge tiger head on each side of the tail. It looked very impressive and I was fortunate to fly in the aircraft from Valley back to Cranwell to hand over my married quarter on 15th October 1992. The 40-minute flight was much quicker and much more enjoyable than the normal four-hour drive.

Being a Tiger squadron, we could now attend *'Tiger Meets'* and meet up with other military Tiger squadrons from around the world. Over period 21-24 May 1993, I was lucky to take a detachment to the Mini Tiger Meet at the French Air Force Base Cambrai, near Paris. There were two memorable events on this detachment, neither of which had anything to do with flying. One, I beat a German Officer in the wine drinking competition, and two; I witnessed someone shit themselves whilst in a drunken slumber. The drinking competition rules were straight forward. It was a sprint to drink a full bottle of wine; easy. Nothing to be proud of now, but at the time I was king and found fame for a few moments.

The second memorable event, the parking of a curly python, aka the shitting event, was something quite incredible. I had never in my life experienced anyone showing such a lack of body control whilst still in a deep sleep and have no desire to ever see such an event again. I was sharing a room with one of our pilots who was a good mate of mine. He got absolutely hammered (drunk) one evening at a social event and decided he needed to go to the toilet in the middle of the night. Completely naked, he got up and made his way to the door. That was as far as he got. He must have thought, that was far enough as he then decided to lay down, adopt the foetal position and point his arse towards the corner of the door opening. As I watched his stumbling around and then settle on the floor, I thought it was all over; clearly it was not. He made a slight groaning noise before I heard a gentle crackling sound, the audible warning that a *'Richard the Third'* (turd) makes as it squeezes itself out of your arse. I couldn't bloody believe it. He was giving birth to this turd whilst sleeping. They spent the night next to each other; both fast asleep on the carpet. It was just gross, absolutely gross. I agreed that I wouldn't tell a soul about the events of that night and I have kept my word until now. But I would never share his name. That will always remain a secret, he is still a mate. I was holding up the adage that what happens on detachment, stays on detachment.

We held a reciprocal Mini Tiger Meet at RAF Valley over the period 2-10 May 1994. Drinking complete bottles of wine would not be part of the entertainment here – thankfully. Neither would crapping whilst drunk and sleeping on the floor.

I also had the opportunity to travel to the USA with six of the squadron pilots including our American exchange officer. A cultural week in the USA visiting West Point, Army Military Academy and sightseeing around New York City whilst staying with our exchange officer's family was special. Whenever I went away with the squadron, I was always the impress holder – the money man. I controlled the allowances and decided what was public funding and what was not. It was me who had to account for the spending and justify to the accounting staff on our return to base.

The currency on detachment was always called the BLAT. Didn't matter where you were going, the currency was always the BLAT, it stood for Breakfast, Lunch And Tea. The daily food allowances. It's akin to Zulu time. Zulu time is the universal 'same' time anywhere in the world - no time zones. It was during this USA detachment that we were making lots of friends in a bar when we inadvertently ran up a bar bill of $1100 ($900ish + tip). How the hell that happened I don't really know to this day. It didn't matter, I had to deal with it. It was a difficult sell when we got home to justify it as public *'representational'* spending. In fact, it was even more difficult at the time because I only had $900 on me in cash and of course we had to put the tip on top of that. I did not have refined diplomatic skills at that juncture of my career, rather I used a selection of superlatives and hand gestures; it was the best I could muster. Luckily, we had bar staff who understood our English predicament of not tipping and bouncers who were open to negotiation. Needless to say, we left there with empty wallets - or rather my wallet was empty.

Thanks to all the guys I flew with at RAF Valley. I had an incredible two years on the Squadron. One of the most interesting, but scariest flying experience I had, was operating the aircraft in *'ground effect'* over water. This requires flying the aircraft at around 20 feet from the surface. It is difficult to judge your height, but you can feel the ground effect when you are at the correct altitude. It looked more like five feet to me, and I could clearly see below the surface of the water. It was almost a hypnotic feeling as the horizontal wall of water raced under the aircraft as we skimmed across the surface at around 400 mph. The jet blast from the small turbofan Adour engine, turned the water into a huge aerosol like spray cone in our wake - I could see it clearly in the cockpit mirrors. The aircraft felt like it was floating due to the increased lift, and decreased aerodynamic drag on the wings, caused by flying so low. I had learnt about the physics of *'ground effect'* in training and how birds use it to save energy. To fly so low and fast was an incredible and privileged experience, but I have no desire to do it again. We had briefed the manoeuvre before we took off, and I was so excited about the experience, but within seconds of us dropping down to such a low level, I had had enough. Thoughts of fun and excitement quickly turned to fear when I realised how close we were to the water. Another reason why I would not have made a particularly good pilot and now I had even more respect for RAF aircrew.

Military aviation is quite different to its civilian counterpart. Apart from the flying and the mission set, the biggest difference is that the military regulates itself. It is its own airworthiness authority and by default it is responsible for investigating its own accidents. It can call on experts like accident investigators, aviation psychologists and other specialist groups, but the process is all military - including any disciplinary (legal) actions. On the afternoon of 26 August 1993, a Chipmunk TMk 10 training aircraft crashed at RAF St Athan shortly after take-off. The Chipmunk is a tandem seat, single engine (piston) primary training aircraft that has been around since the 1940s. Sadly, the pilot was killed. The passenger survived but received major injuries. A Board of Inquiry was immediately convened by the Air Officer Commanding. The Board consisted of a President, an aircrew member and me as the aircraft engineering member. I was chosen for two reasons. Firstly, I was already part of training command by being at RAF Valley, therefore I would directly report to the same Air Officer who convened the Board, and secondly, I was the only engineer they could find who had Chipmunk experience. I wondered how 5 hours flying in a Chipmunk aircraft qualified me but that seemed enough, there really was nobody else (apparently).

I had no technical experience whatsoever on the aircraft type and had not even trained on piston engines. Nevertheless, I was flown down to St Athan in a Hawk to meet up with the other two board members: the president and the aircrew member. On attending the crash site, I will never forget the sight of the twisted aircraft wreckage, the smell of human flesh and the sight of splattered body parts and blood throughout the cockpit. It was a stark reminder to me that when either not handled correctly or through a technical failure, flying even in the most benign of aircraft like a Chipmunk, can have disastrous and fatal consequences. Other than witnessing the ejection from a Hawk at RAF Valley, this was the third time I had experience of visiting a crash site.

My first crash site was a Hunter aircraft that had suffered an engine failure and had crashed into a field near Carmarthen, Dyfed, Wales. The two pilots ejected safely. At the crash site I had to dig myself under the aircraft and then climb underneath one of the wings to get a fuel sample for the Board of Inquiry. The crashed Hunter was almost intact and was nothing like the scene of the Chipmunk. I learnt so much about aircraft investigation and Human Factors from the Chipmunk accident. Indeed, Human Factors would become a major topic of study for me over my career such was the influence this accident investigation had on me.

Human factors being defined as the study of how humans behave physically and psychologically in relation to environments, products or services; in this case, how they behave in and around aircraft.

I worked very closely with the aviation psychologist who had been assigned to us for the duration of the investigation. The causal factors of the accident had quickly focussed on the pilot. Delving into the state of a dead person's mind and untangling the why's and wherefores of their decision making became a fascination to me. I would go on to teach and lecture on Human Factors as a direct result of my own experience from this, and a second aircraft accident that I would investigate in less than three years' time. This second crash also turned out to be another significant Human Factors investigation, but from an aircraft maintenance perspective.

Crashed Hunter, Tail Number 82 (XL593), Carmarthen, Wales, 1982

Diane was working as a pre-school teacher with her friend, who just happened to be my boss's wife, at the station playgroup. Being surrounded by kids all day and there not being a lot to do at RAF Valley in the evenings, the paternal instincts become overwhelming. We had decided early in our marriage that we would try for three children and a third baby now would grow up with the boys. In fact, Diane would have liked another two children but settled for one more. So, it was no surprise that Diane fell pregnant with our daughter, Sian, in the summer of 1993. Of all the achievements at Valley this would be our greatest and make our family complete. Sian made an appearance at Ysbyty Gwynedd Hospital, Bangor, North Wales on 8th March 1994 just five months before we were about to move again. We were over the moon that we had been blessed with three healthy children, and now it was time to consider some permanent family planning.

The RAF did vasectomies for free, so we applied on 8th September 1994 whilst we were back at Cranwell, but the waiting list was so long we decided we would go private. Also, I was to hear a few horror stories of things going wrong in RAF hospitals. There was a story of a vasectomy patient who glanced at his notes on the way to the operation theatre only to find out he was about to have an operation on his varicose veins. The mix up occurred because he had the same first and last name as someone else in the hospital at that time. Imagine the other poor person who went in for varicose veins. His post operation pain would have been a bit of a surprise. Folklore or not, it helped sway the decision to go private. Going private also meant that it could be done quickly, and they would use a different procedure to the RAF that required a local anaesthetic instead of a general. I cancelled the RAF operation on 22nd September and would go private in Boston, Lincolnshire, just down the road from where we lived.

We found a practice who would do it and I was asked to bring two things. My wife, Diane, so we could both be counselled prior to the procedure, and a tight-fitting pair of underpants for afterwards. I was ok with everything and we were content that this is what we both wanted. That was until I got undressed, laid on the gurney and then they whipped my meat and two veg through a hole in the dark green operating sheet. I immediately started to hyperventilate when I felt the heat of the powerful operation lamp on the family jewels. I could feel my nuts wanting to rapidly withdraw back through the sheet and hide somewhere in my groin. It was as if they knew exactly what was about to happen.

I was awake throughout the whole procedure and watched everything whilst wearing nothing but an operation gown and a cold sweat. I now had a real experience of the old cliché *'you will just feel a small prick Mr Sainsbury'* just prior to the first of two local injections into either side of my ball sack. After a few minutes waiting for the local to take effect, the doctor then massaged each testicle in turn, made a small incision at the base of my penis and then with what looked like an elaborate crocheting needle, hooked out a very long, thin white tube. It was several inches long and then I watched him burn a length of the tube (without cutting it or burning it through completely) with what I thought was a homemade soldering iron before he tucked it back into the testicle for safe keeping. I can still remember the smell of the tubes burning and the small cloud of smoke coming up from the tip of the soldering iron into the beam of the operating lamp. It was looking like he was cooking up a BBQ down there, we just needed to be holding a few beers and telling each other rude man jokes to make the scene complete. I chatted incessantly to the doctor throughout the procedure, this was more to calm my nerves and cause a little distraction from what was really happening to me than any casual conversation a patient may have with his doctor. By the time he had got around to finding the tube on the other side, I was quite relaxed, and, in my mind, it was just as if I was watching the procedure being done on someone else.

Other than the small prick, I hardly felt a thing. I think my nerves were kept at bay by my constant talking. Once both the tubes were burnt and safely tucked away in the carry sack, a few strips of tape across the incisions and the job was done. I put my underpants on very tightly as instructed, as I had this horrible thought that everything was going to fall out into a messy heap on the floor when I stood up. Flash to bang was quick and the whole procedure was over in about 15 minutes. The ride home was gentle and gave me time to calm down and allow the local to wear off. After supplying three samples of hand generated nut juice over a couple of months, we finally got the all clear that the operation had been a success.

We had an active music club at RAF Valley, and I took over as the Officer In Charge for a while as the club went through a bit of a resurgence. Many people played instruments on the base and we had formed a band called the Valley Blues. There were 15 of us in the band (most of the time) and we were from all over the base. Included were the Station Commander (Bass), the Padre (Trumpet), the Hawk display pilot (Drums), a few other aircrew, some administrators and myself as the token engineer. We had a few guitars, a brass section, keyboards, a lead singer and a small group of female backing singers. We only played on base and our big gig was the Hangar Dance on 2nd April 1993 to celebrate the 75th Anniversary of the RAF. It was an awesome night and we had some great reviews. Admittedly, people were drunk when they gave the reviews, and a few of the better reviews came from band members themselves, but they all count.

The tour at RAF Valley would come to an end on 22nd August 1994. I was now approaching my mid-thirties, our family was complete and we were enjoying the lifestyle the RAF was providing us. We had been fortunate to move around within the UK, but not be too far from our families in South Wales. I had found my vocation and was settling in nicely to my new career as a commissioned engineer officer. It had been one hell of a journey up to now. I had seen and done things in my professional and personal life that I never thought were possible as a busted and depressed 19-year-old. My itch to travel had been scratched with deployments to Europe, Africa and the USA. I certainly felt very privileged and proud of my achievements but recognised that it had not been a solo effort. The love and support of family and friends were paramount to my success. I was highly motivated to keep up the momentum. I aspired to do more, develop myself further, and was focussed on making the RAF a full career. I had not even dreamt of doing anything different since I had joined. I also realised that I was a late starter in this swim lane, many of my peers were much younger than me. My age would be a factor a little further down track, but for now I was ready to move on to the next career challenge.

I had already voiced my desire to return to Cranwell as an instructor, as I had a real penchant for teaching. Occasionally, I had wondered over the years what I would have done with my life if I hadn't had the desire to join the RAF. At this juncture, I could have been tempted to consider becoming a schoolteacher. However, I recognised that my experience up until now had driven me towards that kind of profession. Had I not joined the RAF and took the opportunity in retail management with Asda, who knows what career track I would have been on.

Having received a glowing final report from my job on 74 Squadron, my wish was granted, and I would become the Engineering Management Common Module Instructor and EOT 2 Course Mentor within the Department of Specialist Ground Training, RAF Cranwell. I would be the professional administrator of the five-week course I had just completed prior to being posted to RAF Valley.

Although we were adept at packing up the house, we now had three children and the cat in tow, so it would take a little longer this time. We also realised that we would soon need a much bigger car.

Chapter 10
Balancing Act

We loved Cranwell, it was such a fun and family focussed place to live. The kids loved it too, and there was plenty of things for everyone to get involved with. Our married quarter was on the main site where we had been living during previous postings. You could let the kids roam around freely knowing that it was a safe and secure environment. There were plenty of secure walks, wooded areas for the kids to cycle and play. It was just a great place to raise children and the social side for the parents was equally as much fun. There was about a core of six to eight families and we would each take it in turns to open our homes during the week, normally on a Thursday, where we would eat, drink and just socialise. We loved it and so did all the children. Of all the places we had lived, we felt that Lincolnshire would be our home for good. It just felt right.

There is no doubt that having kids keeps you young at heart. You can have fun and do all sorts of childish things with kids and nobody bats an eyelid. Such events also give you some of the most unforgettable memories ever. Do those same things as a solo adult and everyone thinks you are bat shit crazy. It is also important to encourage kids to do a range of different activities for three reasons. Firstly, it helps kids decide for themselves what they would like to do whilst promoting their self-development. Secondly, it gets you as a parent, involved and engaged with them as they grow, and thirdly, it keeps the little buggers out of trouble. I have always had the firm belief that if a child can play at least one musical instrument and play a team or individual sport, those two skills together will promote the child's social development and make them a more rounded person, able to be successful in any environment. Teaching a child to swim and ride a bicycle (not at the same time of course) should be core parental responsibility - the younger they learn these skills the better.

Witnessing Josh ride a bike that was far too big for him whilst pulling his older brother around the streets when he was sat on a skateboard at the end of a piece of rope, is a memory I will remember forever. The communication between the two brothers about speed and direction was hilarious. Also, having kids makes you extremely comfortable around other people's children and in social circles. The ability to mix, relax and enjoy other people's company with children running around is awesome. Also, kids allow you to develop a patience you never thought you could have. Kids put 100% trust in their parents, they know no different. One great example of this trust was the game I used to play with them called simply *'throwing you on the bed'*. The kids in turn would run across the bedroom landing as fast as they could, into our bedroom where I would sit on the floor with my back against the base of the bed. The kids would literally launch themselves at me (arms in the air, feet leaving the ground) into my outstretched arms where I would catch them, follow through with their momentum throwing them higher in the air so they would fly over my head before belly flopping onto the bed and into a pile of pillows. They would then roll off the bed and the next one would start their run up; repeat until everyone is tired out or someone gets hurt. Pulling the kids around the living room with some string wrapped around a cardboard box pretending it's a car or a bus or anything you like is also good fun. You don't need expensive toys; all you need is an old box and some imagination. I used to tease my kids with the fact that all I had as a young boy was my mother's clothes pegs and her peg basket to play with. It was my equivalent to having Lego bricks. I could make anything with a little bit of imagination and a bunch of mum's pegs.

We did not know this at the time of moving, but this tour would be our longest tour to date. I would be at Cranwell over two years finishing on 13th December 1996 with some good career news; a promotion to Squadron Leader. This promotion would extend my career, but we had to make some changes to our family plans. I passed the year-long Individual Staff Studies Correspondence Course in September 1994, which was significant for me as writing has never been a strength of mine. I can give credit to Diane for coaching me through some of the more challenging aspects of this English writing course. Although, I still struggle with stringing a properly constructed sentence together either verbally or in writing, so you can imagine how much I struggled writing this book. I put that down to my upbringing and education in the Welsh Valleys. This Welsh-ism is a real advantage when listening to other dialects of English speakers, be they Irish, Scottish or from some other part of the British Isles. I can understand them all. Success on this writing course meant that I could now officially write my own letters and had met the standard of service writing required for promotion.

Much of my new job was face to face instructing students in the classroom and the RAF had a great course for people who were going into these *'teaching'* positions. I attended Number 665 Ground Instructional Techniques Course at RAF Newton, colloquially called the *'GIT'* Course, an intense two-week course about different ways to get students to learn stuff in the classroom. The course would not make military teachers, but instructors. Instructors specialize in areas of expertise; they are not teachers.

The RAF did employ academically trained educators who were specialist, i.e. teachers. The lines between an instructor and a teacher was always a little blurred to me, I often felt that depending on the background and knowledge of my students, I could be both a teacher and an instructor. I had specialist knowledge of the subjects, and I had been given a toolbox of common techniques to get a message across to the students. I did observe that some of the less motivated instructors adopted a single *'lecture'* type approach to everything. This approach required little effort on behalf of the instructor. I really enjoyed the GIT course and was keen to build on my experience as an instructor. I graduated the course on 29th July 1994 with a 'B1+' Classification. The highest classification you can obtain as a rookie coming off the course was a 'B1+'. I was eligible to apply for a recategorization to 'A2' Classification after a minimum of six months' instructor experience. There was never any pressure on anyone who successfully graduated the GIT course to be re-categorised if they didn't want to. To me, that was a wasted opportunity, why wouldn't you want to be your best and get some recognition for your training and experience.

I was already fired up to be the best instructor I could be, but my ability to get the message across in the classroom was only half the story. The other half was credibility. I wanted to be a credible and respected instructor as this was also important to me. I would research my subject matter thoroughly and often call upon my own experience either as an airman or as an officer and add that experience to the mix in the classroom. I also had an inquisitive side to learn more about my specialist topics from others who perhaps had more or a better experience of the subject matter, so I was keen to learn from the very people I was instructing. Many of my students did have more knowledge than I, and some also had vastly different experiences to myself on many of the topics being taught.

The RAF was just getting into 'Quality Assurance' when I arrived as an instructor, and I was going to be the Subject

Matter Expert (SME) for the whole department. I got myself upskilled quickly before completely revamping the syllabus. I had been given almost a free rein to develop the training in accordance with the training objectives (which I also helped develop). The result was two separate courses: one of 20 hours classroom tuition and one of 14 hours. Both concluding with a two day role-playing consolidation exercise. My master stroke as a training developer was modularizing the subject, a sort of smorgasbord of quality depending on the experience of the audience. I went on to adapt this training for non-technical students, senior leadership and even did a few road shows. I had become known as 'Captain Quality' - the magnifying glass in the cover caricature being the symbol of quality.

The ability to listen to a student's experience and then use that to guide my subject matter was genius. No one else was doing that at the time. Although I was the teacher, it seemed that I was doing most of the learning. I was growing my professional knowledge from the very people I was instructing whilst at the same time building up my credibility as an instructor. I also felt that this approach gave me the edge on many of my instructor colleagues in terms of positive student feedback. There was a bit of a competitive aspect to this job. In fact, competitiveness was rife throughout the RAF and the other services, and in many ways, the service thrives and benefits from generating a competitive environment. People will often go further than just wanting to do their best and can feel obliged to be the best in their field. Promotion competitiveness is a great example, there seemed to be constant pressure to get to the next rank, it was almost an obsession for some people and they would do all sorts of things to make themselves look good (often at the expense of others) just to be one step ahead of their contemporaries. Although I never did anything underhand to further my own career, I certainly felt the competitiveness and was always conscious of where I sat on the promotion ladder. It may have been healthy for the service, but I was never convinced it benefited the individual or was conducive to a good work/life balance. But, when you are part of it, it is hard to imagine an alternative way to manage your career.

Over the two and a bit years I spent as an instructor, I had taught over half the junior engineer officers in the RAF. In total, I had instructed over 500 students for the courses I directly administered, about 100 of these students would have been international guests from Asia and the Middle East. One of my international students from Thailand wrote me a nice note in broken English. In the note, he thanked me for making the course enjoyable for him, making him laugh and getting him through. This guy would fall asleep in seconds on sitting down in the classroom and I had to spend a lot of 'one on one' time with him. I would always let him sleep when he did fall asleep in class and when he woke up, I would pretend I never noticed. I had briefed all the other instructors on this student, so he was never singled out. He missed so much of the shit we were teaching, I had to be with him when he sat the tests. These are the kind of things you did for the *'paying'* international students. He clearly appreciated my help and I still have that open invitation to Thailand to visit him.

I successfully passed my instructor re-categorization assessment from 'B1+' to 'A2' on 15th December 1995 and then went through and passed a tough series of assessments in October/November 1996 that allowed me to achieve my goal of becoming an 'A1' instructor. Very few people in the ground instructional world become 'A1' instructors, it was normally the purview of aircrew on flying appointments, so I was particularly proud of this achievement. I was ready to take the assessment earlier, but the RAF educational system had difficulty finding someone who could assess me.

Although I was pleased with my RAF achievement, I also wanted to get formal civilian academic recognition for my experience as an instructor, so from January to July 1996, I undertook a City and Guilds Adult Education Teachers Certificate which could only be completed if you were employed in a teaching environment. Having both service and civilian assessors critically evaluating your teaching performance keeps you on your toes. I successfully passed the course which had its own tough assignments and personal assessments and was formally recognised with my Adult Education Teachers Certificate in August 1996.

In May 1995, I had been notified that I had not been accepted for *'Assimilation'*, that is, to serve up to age 55. Therefore, I was due to leave the RAF on my 38th birthday, in just three years' time. The service would evaluate my performance and consider me one more time, just 18 months before my discharge date. The odd thing here was that as a sergeant I was enlisted to serve until age 55 which is considered a full career. Once commissioned as an officer, you were only required to serve to age 38. Thereafter, further service was on merit and service demand. It was a bizarre set of circumstances for bettering myself in my career, I was rewarded with less time to serve.

The children were growing up fast and were ready for external stimulus outside the family unit and it would be during this tour at Cranwell, that my sons Dan and Josh would pull me into other *'secondary'* areas of life. Namely Boy Scouts, swimming, football, music and the RAF Cranwell Woodwork Club. To be fair, the Woodwork Club was my secondary duty, nothing to do with the kids, and offered a contrast to my primary duties. As an officer, both your primary and secondary duties make up your annual appraisal which is used for promotion considerations and further service. It was always better to do a secondary duty you liked rather than one you didn't or one that may have been chosen for you by your boss.

Both Dan and Josh were keen to be involved in the Scout movement, or rather the younger pack called, Beaver Scouts. I had never been involved in the Scout movement as a child. Although I did join the Boys Brigade for a short while as a teenager. The Boys Brigade was a Christian movement for young adolescents, and they had uniforms, hats and everything a young lad would crave in being part of a group. But I got into a bit of a fight with a couple of the more established boys in the group and it was suggested to me that I may want to consider something else. So that was the end of that.

I took both Dan and Josh along to the 1st Cranwell, Beaver Scouts, and very quickly got roped into helping the group. I didn't mind, the boys were there anyway, and it was another opportunity for me to use my professional educational skills and techniques. Although colouring, making stuff with glue, paper and sticks, telling stories and playing games isn't quite what these qualifications were designed for. As a helper, I was clearly in the wrong place at the wrong time and quickly became the Officer in Charge of Scouts (yes, all the 1st Cranwell Scout Troop – Venture Scouts, Scouts, Cubs and Beavers). Then in no time at all, I also became the Chairman, then the Secretary and finally Acting Scout Troop Leader whilst still holding down the Beaver Scout helper position. I seemed to be doing everything. Talk about whipping a willing horse. To be fair, the District Commissioner for Scouts recognised my hard work which included my hosting the St Georges Day parade at RAF Cranwell for all of the Sleaford District in 1996. It was a pretty full on couple of years in the Scouts and I learnt a lot about other families who were perhaps not as well off as my own. We (Dan, Josh and I) had a huge amount of fun and it gave us some very fond father and son memories. I tip my hat to the volunteers who do this year, after year, after year. It was hard work. The kids get so much out of these activities and I was proud to be part of the movement for two years. Though, I had had enough in the end. It was time for someone else or rather several others to take the baton/s from me. I would finally hand it over just a couple of weeks before we left Cranwell.

Scouts was just one day a week - normally. RAF Cranwell also had a highly active swimming club called *'Dolphins'* and on a Friday the kids had swimming lessons. The swimming fees would be waived if you volunteered to become a Dolphins Swimming Club helper. The club paid for training. Well, what a great deal, where do I sign? The club professionally trained all its swimming teachers and I undertook the Amateur Swimming Association (ASA) Assistant Teacher Certificate in September 1996, which meant that I could now run my own small swimming class under overall supervision of a fully qualified swimming teacher.

I was never a great swimmer myself but could teach the basics of survival in the water. After all, I had a few other teaching qualifications, one more would be another string to my bow. Indeed, I found myself putting more effort into one of my 30 minutes swimming lessons than I had to put into a couple of hours instructing at work. I never mixed the two but thought on many occasions that I should introduce a contrasting activity like jumping and playing horses with foam sticks at the end of my professional lessons like I did with the kids in the pool. Teaching swimming was a huge learning curve. Controlling six, six-year olds in a very noisy and busy swimming pool with several other classes going on at the same time is not easy. Once again, hugely rewarding but very tiring particularly if a few instructors didn't turn up on the night. At times, I ended up running several back to back classes on a

Friday night for a couple of hours when all I wanted to do was rest and have a few beers. I never went for the full teaching certificate as that involved grown up kids and strong swimmers who required coaching on their technique and more fitness training. This was not what I wanted to do. I just wanted to have a bit of fun teaching the basics to kids learning to swim. The swimming qualification would come in useful during my next tour.

Apart from Scouts and Swimming, the other activity, which also begins with the letter 'S', that the boys got involved with was Soccer or rather Football. I had little capacity left for helping out with the soccer club during this tour, but would get involved big time when we returned to Cranwell for a fourth time in the late 90s. Both the boys loved football/soccer and it would be the singular activity that they would both do consistently throughout their informative years and into adulthood.

Cranwell primary school and the teachers were excellent, and it was through the school and private tuition from one of the members of the RAF Cranwell, College Air Force Band, that the boys (and eventually Sian) got into music. Both Dan and Josh learnt to play the recorder, read music and move onto the clarinet. Dan went on in life to learn the saxophone and guitar and Josh headed off to play bass guitar and drums. Both would play in the school band and indeed their own rock bands later down track. Sian would just stick with the clarinet. All three enjoyed their music and I can still picture Dan playing what I think was that classic recorder song *'Frère Jacques'* on both his and Josh's recorder at the same time, one stuck up each nostril. As parents, we suspected from that moment onwards Dan might just go onto bigger and better things with his music.

Sticking with the music theme. As a family, we were visiting the historic and beautiful local Lincoln Cathedral one day. The cathedral itself is an amazing piece of architecture and was claimed to be the tallest building in the world for 238 years; an awfully long time ago from AD 1311 to 1549 to be precise. It trumped the Great Pyramid of Giza on the day. One of the more modern modifications to the cathedral was the introduction of a public-address system.

On this occasion, there were several organ recitals throughout the day by a guest organist. We had been in the cathedral a little while and had explained to the children how people would come here to worship and pray to God. A being no-one could see, but God was everywhere, and this was Gods house. That was all well and good until a few moments later when a deep voice came over the public-address system, reverberating off the massive walls and high ceiling, filling the cathedral with sound when all we could hear previously was our own voices. The announcement was telling people to make their way to the main hall for the organ recital which would start in five minutes. Josh immediately froze on hearing this very loud deep voice and the look on his face was one of pure fear. He was the classic startled rabbit in the headlights. *'What's up Josh?* We asked. *'Its God, he's talking to us'.* We can only imagine how scary that moment must have been to Josh as a youngster. Another priceless and memorable moment courtesy of the children, and another example of children believing in everything their parents tell them - literally. How that would change a few years down the line.

My office mate for my second year at Cranwell was a fellow motorcyclist named Matt. Matt only had one testicle. I knew immediately because one of his desk tidies when he unpacked his office belongings was a ping pong ball painted like a testicle with red veins. He had lost his testicle through cancer just a few years earlier. The painted ping pong ball was a reminder of a life-threatening event is pretty typical of the type of leaving gift you get from your RAF friends. With such an open sense of humour and being a fellow Celt (albeit Scottish), I knew this work relationship was going to be a good one. Matt and I would become great work colleagues and very good friends. We had developed a ritual that we would go through each morning, just before the first coffee of the day and after Matt had finished ironing his uniform shirt and had changed out of his bike gear. One of us would salute the raising of the office venetian blinds (just like the raising of the camp ensign every day) as the other one slowly pulled the draw strings of the blinds. Childish yes, but we did it anyway and we did it with our uniform hats on. It was our way of starting the day and reminding ourselves that we were in the military. Not surprisingly, when we were not talking about work, we were talking about motorcycles.

One day the subject of a Land's End to John O'Groats (or End to End) run came up. I had done this trip before with Diane in a brand-new Ford Sierra hire car back in April 1987 but had always hankered doing it again on a motorcycle. The journey in the car had taken us 13 hours and one minute over a distance of 876 miles. I had the tie, badge and certificate and was a fully paid up Member of the Lands' End to John O'Groats Association; membership number 118. The return journey home from John O'Groats to South Wales seemed to go on forever and was a killer to drive. It was only 876 miles one way, but we had to get to Land's End to start and then get home afterwards. We ended up completing over 2000 miles in under two days. It was absolutely exhausting and by the time we had reached the midlands on the way back (less than 150 miles away from home), I had started to hallucinate through lack of sleep. I had to stop for a little while whilst I power napped. It was dangerous and stupid to be driving for so long and being so tired, but Diane could not drive at that time and we were keen to get back home. We did it and it was fun. Diane would keep herself and me awake by feeding me something to eat every 15 to 20 minutes for the whole journey - there and back. The hire car company didn't believe the mileage when I handed back the car. Luckily, it was an unlimited mileage special deal.

Matt was very keen to do the trip on a motorbike too but wanted to raise money for charity at the same time. So that was it then, an End to End run for charity done in less than a minute of meaningless conversation. Normally these things are discussed and decided over a beer or two when you are tipsy or full on drunk and then you both conveniently forget the discussion in the morning. This was different with a decision being made over the innocent morning coffee – and it wasn't even an Irish coffee. There was no backing out now. I was not keen to do exactly the same route on a motorbike, the motorways were boring in a car, they would be even more so on a bike. A computer route planner (there was no Google Maps in 1995) suggested 24 hrs would be needed non-stop avoiding motorways. With extra time added for the five RAF stations we planned to visit, time for refuelling and a three-hour rest break for safety, we reckoned that 30 hours would present a reasonable challenge.

Me, Matt, Talking Pages Rep, and Ian, DSGT Cranwell, England, 1995

We decided to help the charity that had benefited the least from RAF Cranwell's many fund-raising events. This ended up being the Sleaford & District Talking Newspaper for the Blind.

This charity transferred newspaper and magazine articles onto audio tape for those who the written word couldn't reach. A visit to their premises in Sleaford left us impressed by the dedication and devotion of the volunteers who selected and recorded the written material. We were also impressed by their enthusiasm for our bikes and motorcycling in general. Many local and national organisations were approached for help and we had a relatively successful hit rate which, when coupled with the RAF Cranwell staff contributions, allowed us to make 440GBP for the Charity (worth about 750GBP in 2018).

We had decided to do it over a long weekend and set off on Thursday 8th September from work and got back on the Sunday. Combining a passion with a purpose is extremely rewarding and the experience is almost addictive. It was so much fun. There was much discussion afterwards about what we could do next. Unfortunately, life got in the way. We really wanted to do more, but it just seemed too hard for us to arrange. That inability to get it together a second time was a learning experience all of its own. You really need to be committed to planning such adventures. I would remember this some years down the line in planning other motorcycle activities.

A few fun facts of the trip were:
Money raised - £440.00 (all money raised given to charity - none subsidised the trip in any way)
Bikes - Kawasaki GTR1000 (Matt), Yamaha XJ600 (Nigel) and Honda VFR750 (Ian).
Total round-trip mileage from Cranwell and back - 1847 miles.
End to End mileage - 919.5 miles.
Total End to End travelling time - 27 hrs 15 mins.
End to End travelling time spent on road - 20 hrs.
Total round-trip fuel used - 38.9 gallons = £97.25.
Total End to End fuel used - 19.37 gallons = £48.42.

Total End to End average speed - 33.74 mph.

Total End to End average speed while on the road - 45.97 mph.

On the morning of 13th February 1996, the pilot of a Hawk took off from RAF Valley to perform the weather check sortie for the day. Immediately after take-off, the aircraft rolled to the right at an ever-increasing rate. The pilot realising that he no longer had control of the aircraft ejected, hit the ground and was killed. The aircraft continued rolling until it impacted the ground and was destroyed. A board of Inquiry was convened immediately, and I was selected as the engineer member to work alongside the aircrew member and the President of the Board.

Unlike the Chipmunk crash, this time I had relevant and recent aircraft experience, knowledge of local engineering and maintenance practices and was still part of training command. An advantage for me at the time was that I could transit back and forth to RAF Valley from Cranwell with the President of the Board who also lived at RAF Cranwell and was himself a Hawk pilot. Flying back and forth saved us a laborious four hour drive each way. It was during the flight to the crash site that the President introduced me to the term Gifted Amateur for the first time.

During his career, he had the privilege of being the very last Lighting aircraft display pilot and had some great stories to tell about his time flying that amazing aeroplane. He had also been involved in investigating a number of incidents and accidents with the aircraft and had done a number of other duties in his flying career, all of which he had received no training, yet he was expected to do a great job. He classified himself as a Gifted Amateur. I remember that really resonating with me at the time. I could do all sorts of things then, many to a competent level, but I never considered myself an expert at any of them.

But what the military had taught us both, is that we are never afraid to have a go at something new. We both had enough skill, experience, and common sense to be able to adapt to any new professional or personal challenge. I could add instructing, scouts, swimming, and a whole raft of other activities to the Gifted Amateur list. The ability and confidence to just have a go at stuff is a great skill in itself and a perfect description of any military officer - commissioned or non-commissioned. Give it a go and give it your all.

It was less than three years since I had been involved in the investigation of the Chipmunk crash at St Athan, so the investigative process was still fresh in my mind. The Chipmunk investigation was heavily laden with Human Factors (aircrew). It was suspected that the Hawk crash may be Human Factors (maintenance), and it was, big time. My involvement in both these investigations influenced my career choices going forward and I would become a core member of the Defence Aviation Safety Centre, Aviation Safety Review Team in 2002. The Hawk accident had a profound effect on me personally which resulted in my developing and implementing a Human Factors in Aircraft Maintenance program later in my career. Academically, I choose the topic of Human Factors as my sole focus for my dissertation during my Engineering Management degree in 2011.

The experience from these two fatal accidents coupled with my career experience as an instructor and technician allowed me to put together a series of presentations on airworthiness, human factors and valuable lessons learnt. I was also able to relate these experiences to other civilian industries and work environments, a skill set I would use extensively as a safety consultant later in my career. My experience supported the research in that tragic (and avoidable) accidents are always the result of an unbroken chain of events. Identification and subsequent breaking of any one of these events (links in the chain) would have prevented the accident – full stop. The Hawk accident investigation was not very demanding from a technical perspective. We had plenty of professional witnesses who had seen the crash unfold so we were pretty sure what had happened to the aircraft just from eye witness statements. We found the physical evidence in the wreckage within an hour of arrival at the crash site. Getting to understand the reason behind what we had found was the difficult bit. I was in disbelief at times when we started to uncover the chain of events and the various contributory aspects of the accident. I learnt so much about people, their influence on others, personality types and decision making. In particular, the reasons why people do or don't do things when they know better, and of course, the consequences of these poor decisions. I was grateful for the professional experience but was deeply saddened (again) by the tragic loss of life. I never knew the pilot personally but meeting the people who did was very sad and upsetting. He was just doing his job – a job he loved to do.

With impending forced retirement at age 38, I had written to the RAF in March 1996 notifying them of our desire to remain in the Lincolnshire area (Cranwell specifically) and requesting a last tour of duty there. Diane had been accepted for nursing training commencing September 1996, the kids were enjoying their schooling and we were now seriously considering buying a house locally. Somehow magic then seemed to happen and I was notified on 12 July 1996 that the RAF had considered and subsequently offered me assimilation to age 55 (Service until 2015) with an optional retirement date of 7th June 2004. However, to take the optional retirement date of 7th June 2004 I would need to notify the RAF by 8th June 2003. Not a problem in 1996, but we would think a little differently in June 2003, and that date would cause us some stress.

There was no doubt that the hard but enjoyable work at Cranwell had paid off. After some serious family consideration, on 6th September 1996 we decided that I should accept the offer of further service. My final report from Cranwell in October 1996 was a *'Spec Rec'* a Special Recommendation for promotion. These reports were very rare in a person's career and getting one now was perfect timing for me. I was to be promoted to Squadron Leader and posted on promotion to RAF Linton-On-Ouse, Yorkshire as the Senior Engineer Officer and Contract Monitor on 16th December 1996. Everything had now changed for us in the last four months of 1996, my last tour of duty was no longer required as I had a career for the next eight years at least. Something that in June 1979 had been a bit of a pipe dream after my bike accident.

On reflection, the Cranwell instructional tour had been the busiest, most diverse and enjoyable job I had done to date. It added real strength to the adage; *'you only get out of something what you put into it'*. The rewards really do come when you put in the hard graft. That was certainly true this time around at Cranwell. The family commitments (children's activities) quite rightly, had been the number one priority. As parents, we got to meet and spend time with other likeminded parents, and it made for a fulfilling lifestyle. I loved my work as an instructor and the whole package at Cranwell cemented our desire to return and settle in the area. Lincolnshire was a great area to live and offered the right balance between urban and rural living. Cranwell was also close enough to both families in South Wales to go and visit for a weekend. Had I not been offered further service, promoted and posted; we probably would have been living there today.

We were rapidly approaching the end of 1996 and we had already decided that we were not going to move immediately before Christmas, this meant that I would commute for a short while. I also had to undertake some pre-employment training courses for the job so I would live in the Officers Mess until the family moved across to join me. RAF Linton-On-Ouse was the home of Number 1 Flying Training School (FTS) providing basic fast jet training on the turbo-prop tandem-seat Tucano aircraft for student pilots that have been selected to fly fast jet aircraft. On completion of the course, successful students are awarded their brevet wings and move on to Number 4 FTS, RAF Valley for their advanced fast jet training. I began to think that the RAF Flying Training System was dominating my career.

Linton-on-Ouse also operated relief landing grounds at Dishforth and Topcliffe which would also come under my purview. I was excited at the prospect of a new job and a complete change in environment in my new rank. But it wasn't quite the dynamic job I thought it would be. When I pitched up at Linton, the whole base had been operating under a civilian contract for almost 10 years and my position there was more about Contract Monitoring than maintenance engineering. The Station Armoury and a few other aspects like Secure Communications, Photographic Section and the Firing Range were still operated by the RAF, so an engineer officer was the best person to head up the small team. Also, most of the contract was about the maintenance of the aircraft and producing aircraft to meet the flying programme, so once again it was appropriate to have an engineer officer to monitor those core contractual activities. Finally, I was the only uniformed engineer on the base and was required to provide specialist advice to my boss, who was an administrator, for those uniformed units under my command. All other contractual matters required me to go directly to the Station Commander who was a pilot.

In all honesty, if I was to rank all the jobs I have done throughout my careers for job satisfaction, professional challenges and fun, this one would probably be sat at the bottom. However, it did present a major training opportunity for me which I would grasp with both hands and which would help me develop my skills and knowledge just in case I decided to leave the RAF. Three significant events happened during our short time at Linton, all were bad; proving mums' philosophy of life that bad things happen in threes. The first event happened during the first two days on the job, the second event involved Josh being hospitalized and the third event involved my mother.

Picture this. My boss was a very polite, tall, well-spoken and big boned lady in her early fifties. She always had a reputation for being a stickler for standards of behaviour. An archetypal RAF administrator you would be foolish to cross. She was the consummate professional. For example, you wouldn't dare drink straight out of a beer bottle in the Officers Mess bar. Such behaviour was not fitting of an officer. If she saw you, you would be crucified there and then. She wouldn't care who was around, it was her job, she was the enforcer of standards. If you rode your bicycle around the base in uniform without wearing a hat, once again you were dead. If she didn't catch you but had seen and recognised you, you would be summoned to her office immediately and she would tear a strip off you. You really didn't cross this lady. On the other hand, she had a real soft spot for the Senior Engineer Officer - my position, as she had no idea about the technical stuff that went on over the base. I had arrived on the Monday and met my team, my boss and the other Station executives I would work with, including the sitting contract manager, a civilian. This guy had a bit of a reputation as being a company man and would pose a real relationship challenge for me. The following day (Tuesday) I had been invited to the Northern Region Police Club by the Senior RAF Police Officer. The Police Club was a club for RAF Police from all over the northern part of England, not just Linton-on-Ouse, and of course any special guests who had been invited. On this Tuesday night, I would be the special guest. The club was just a five-minute walk from my office and the Officers Mess another five minutes from the Police Club, but in a different direction.

I arrived at the Police Club about 5:30pm, in uniform, expecting to have a few beers then I would walk back to the Mess for dinner before bed. Next thing I remember I woke up in bed at around 9am the following morning with a massive hangover, still in my uniform. Oh my God! We still had batting staff (room service) in the Mess and when the batting lady knocked my door and asked if I wanted a hot drink, I realised I couldn't speak properly. I must have got absolutely hammered the previous night and was still drunk. What the hell! How on earth did I get back to my room in this state. To say that a sense of panic came over me would be an understatement. I managed to sort myself as best I could and then dragged my sorry arse as quickly as I could into work, trying to avoid the prying eyes from my boss's office, which was on the way. I looked like a complete down and out, was shaking with dehydration and wishing it was the weekend. If there was a *'back to the future'* card you could play in life, I would have played it that morning. My new team were as shocked and surprised as I was, they couldn't believe that their new boss pitched up at work completely drunk and hungover and it was only day three.

I tried my best to explain what had happened in my dribbling broken voice, but we all knew that their actions over the next few hours would be critical in forming the fundamentals of our working relationship for the rest of my tour. There were only three people in the office that day, the admin lady, the female logistic sergeant, and my deputy, who was a flight sergeant. The sergeant and the flight sergeant took control immediately and started covering my arse throwing my new boss off the scent saying I was out and about when she rang to speak to me. They also successfully diverted all my other phone calls and set about re-arranging all my meetings planned for the day. The logistics sergeant took off in her car and got me two of the biggest bacon and egg sandwiches I had seen in a long while, they were washed down with a large Coco-Cola and strong coffee. She got me two instead of one because she thought one was never going to be enough. She was spot on, I ate them both in no time at all, in fact, I could have eaten a third. I was starving, I had not eaten since lunchtime the day before. That was why I was feeling like this. Note to self – eat before you drink. A life lesson that seems to fade with time and one that you must re-learn time and time again. After my belly had something to work with, they locked me in my own office with the lights off and blinds closed so no-one could see me in there and they just left me to sleep it all off. For some reason Diane had rung me later that morning and they felt obliged to put that call through. Diane would never ring me at work unless it was urgent, but this day she just wanted to see how the new job was working out for me. I could not talk properly even then, Diane seemed concerned at first because it must have sounded as if I had suffered a stroke. But that all changed when I tried to explain myself; she was not happy. The day was a complete nightmare and I wondered how this would play out over the next few days.

    I found out that I had been drinking whisky. What an idiot! I don't do whisky drinking well. I also found out I had been singing with the small folk group who were performing in the Club, so that explained the rough voice. Luckily, the folk group were also made up of Policemen, so my secret was safe. In my enthusiasm, I had accidently smashed a few glasses too, but was clearly enjoying myself and having a great time - according to the people who were there. I eventually left the club around 3am (9hrs later) and was one of the last to leave. The police seemingly enjoyed my company and I had left some kind of impression on them. I still have no idea how I got back to my room or indeed when I got back. The five-minute walk could have taken me hours. The following are the notes and lessons I took from this experience:

Note 1. The RAF Police run RAF Police clubs for the RAF Police and have no set opening and closing times. It really is an exclusive club.

Lesson 1: Keep a tab on the time and don't overstay your welcome, even if you are encouraged to stay.

Note 2. As a guest and first timer, drinking glasses are continually being topped up free of charge. I had no fricking idea how much I had drunk that night.

Lesson 2: Always finish your drink before starting the next one - and keep count.

Note 3. They don't serve food other than bar (packet) snacks. So, getting something to eat before you go drinking in the police club is a very good idea.

Lesson 3: Salted peanuts on their own does not constitute a main evening dinner meal.

Note 4. The band liked me and asked if I would perform with them in the club again.

Lesson 4: I think I can sing even when I am drunk - maybe I can.

The major lesson and take away here were beware of policemen who are nice to you - just kidding. My boss never did get to find out about that night, and I knew that I owed my team a huge debt of gratitude for the way they handled me and the situation the following day. In a way, the episode worked in everyone's favour. Inadvertently, I had built a great team literally overnight and although the tour for me was not that demanding and rewarding, they really were a great bunch of guys – even the senior policeman who thought very little of the episode, he had clearly witnessed such behaviour many times before. Finally, although I had been promoted, my promotion was in an acting rank, i.e. it was provisional. It would not be made substantive until 1st July 1997. I really needed to keep my nose clean from now on. It was time to grow up - again.

I have never drunk whisky to excess since this event. Indeed, I only drink whisky these days if I have a cold or flu like symptoms or maybe have a small glass with ice and water after a formal dinner in the mess or a quiet meal with friends. I learnt a lot about myself from this episode and quite frankly, it frightened me because I really had no recollection of what had happened. In reading it now it's quite funny, and if it had happened to someone else it would be even funnier, but it happened to me. I swore then, that this would never, ever happen to me again, and to this day I have been true to myself.

A similar (never again) moment happened when I was around 12 years old. We would call into the local fish n' chip shop and ask Alwin (the fish n' chip man) if we could have a bag of *'scrumps'*. Scrumps were what we kid's called bits of fried batter that had fallen off the fish whilst it was being fried. Depending on what part of the country you were from, the kids had given these batter bits different names but to us, they were scrumps. Scrumps had absolutely no nutritional value whatsoever but they were free and Alwin didn't mind given them away to the kids. One night I ate around four portions of these scrumps and was violently sick pretty soon afterwards. When I say sick, I mean throwing up not just what I had eaten but everything in my stomach. I remained unwell a few days later. I think I literally poisoned myself with used cooking fat. To this day, I struggle with eating fried fish and would prefer to have it crumbed or just baked with nothing on it. As soon as I smell fish batter, my stomach sends an amber warning signal to my brain which in turn selects my appetite switch to off. It is similar to my experience from smelling and drinking warm milk in primary school. I am sure there is research on this but in my mind *'over dosing'* on something is a sure way to prevent and maybe even stop an addiction. Although, having said that, I have over dosed on chocolate many times, but it has not had the same effect. Then again, I always stop eating chocolate just before I am physically sick.

My secondary duties at Linton were twofold; officer in charge of *'Linton Ladybirds'* a pre-school playgroup/kindergarten and the officer in charge of the November Fayre. Both were a pain in the arse for me. The playgroup duty was plagued with staff problems, external (regulatory) inspections, national changes to a subsidised voucher certificate system and my trying to get the playgroup recognised charitable status. The November Fayre was in effect a Station Open Day with stalls and entertainment all set out around part of the base which was then opened up to the paying public. The entrance fees along with the trader stall charges, would go to various local, national and RAF charities. All for a good cause but it really was nothing more than a project management nightmare. It was also my first exposure to planning big events with lots of moving parts including the handling of non-public money, safety, emergency procedures, security, publicity and everything else that these events generate. The centrepiece of the Fayre was a massive bonfire that my Armourers would build and light and then set off several hundred fireworks over a 20-minute period in front of over two thousand people. Not much to go wrong there then.

It was the biggest event in town. Organising this event took more effort than my day job and my master plan was to only arrange the Fayre in 1997. I really wanted to be out of the job before the 1998 Fayre. Sometimes you make your own luck and my cunning plan to escape worked out just fine. I had accepted a job at RAF Wyton on 20th April 1998 having just completed 16 months of a not-so-great two-year appointment. I considered it my greatest achievement of the job.

As the base Senior Engineer, I was also the Deputy Health and Safety (H&S) Officer. The base had its own dedicated H&S Officer, who was a civilian. My position was purely a back-up. Well, I thought to myself, If I am responsible for something, even if it is just a secondary appointment, I am going to make sure I know what I am doing. Therefore, I really should upskill myself if I am going to be called upon to carryout H&S duties or be the Service expert on such matters. I completed the Basic H&S Course run by the local Selby college which whetted my appetite for more. I could see the benefits of this training for me in the RAF, but perhaps more importantly, recognised it as a potential career opportunity outside the military. I had already started to think of training opportunities in these terms. For the first time in my career, I had become a little disillusioned with the RAF and it was all down to this job.

The RAF had its own training school at RAF Halton for H&S and I had completed the Introduction to Environmental Protection Course in March 1997, followed closely by the Managing Safely course in April 1997. This latter course was a recognised IOSH (Institute of Occupational Safety and Health) so it carried some weight outside the RAF, but I had decided that with a little more effort and sponsorship money from my secondary appointment as the Deputy H&S Officer, I could undertake the National General Certificate in Occupational Safety and Health (NEBOSH). This national qualification would be the minimum requirement to operate as an independent contractor or as an associate to a H&S consultancy company. I got financial approval from my very nice boss and managed to just complete the year long course and assessments before my posting. It was perfect timing. I was awarded the NEBOSH qualification in May 1998. I had something in the bag for a second career as a safety consultant – if I needed it.

Domestically, it was not a great time at Linton which is perhaps why this tour was not that pleasurable overall. The local area was beautiful and two of the most popular TV programmes at the time were filmed in and around that area. *'Heartbeat'*, a police drama set in 1960s and *'Emmerdale Farm'* a long-running soap opera set in a fictional village in the Yorkshire Dales. Emmerdale started on TV in 1972 and was still going in 2019. We were lucky to experience and visit both sets in our time at Linton. Our married quarter did get brand new double-glazed windows and the house overall was nice and in a lovely area of North Yorkshire. I had swapped my treasured Yamaha XJ600 for a bright Yellow, 900cc Triumph Speed Triple some months earlier on 9th July 1996. This bike was bloody awesome. It sounded beautifully and was very quick - wide grin on the face, quick. The roads around Linton and York were perfect for this naked street bike – I loved it. The bike was bright yellow, my favourite colour, but in summer, living in a rural area it would be a magnet for flies, bugs, bees and just about any insect around. Clearly the bike looked like a flower, albeit a fast and noisy one.

Socially, the kids were very active, but we did get a big wakeup call one day, it was Wednesday 13th May 1998, Dan came down stairs and reported that Josh had gone floppy and was lying on the floor of the bedroom twitching. The next few hours were a complete blur for everyone. I would spend the next two days in hospital with Josh who had suffered a seizure of some kind, but he was ok and recovering well.

Actually, Josh had contracted a right lower lobe pneumonia. I think the feeling of seeing your own flesh and blood suffering, in any capacity, is the worst feeling in the world. I can feel myself filling up with tears just writing this passage, so vivid is the memory even after all these years. You would sacrifice a limb or more just to see your own children fit and well and not suffering in any way. The strength of the love you have for your own children is incredible which is pretty visible and surfaces when shit like this happens. It was bloody awful for all of us. Yet, it would not be the last time I would hang out in hospital with Josh, or Dan come to think of it. Sian seemed to be less prone to hospital visits.

Josh, Sian and Dan, Linton-On-Ouse, England, 1996

If what had happened to Josh was not bad enough, we did suffer a worse event whilst at Linton and it was before Josh fell ill with pneumonia.

I don't remember the exact time or even where we were when we got the call, and I think the call was from my brother, telling us that my mum had passed away. Mum had been found by her sister and had died at home on 19th September 1997. The death certificate said ischaemic heart disease and atherosclerosis which was not a surprise considering what had happened to dad and the lifestyle they had lived with smoking and eating fatty foods. Much like at dad's passing, I don't actually remember much about Mums funeral, but I do remember going to see her on my own at the funeral home and I wish I hadn't. It wasn't the vision of mum I wanted to remember her by.

Mum had suffered from agoraphobia in her final years and had hardly left the house before she died. Although she didn't mind going outside to argue with her neighbour Mrs Barrett. Nobody knew what was going on in mum's mind. Anyway, that was mum. It was comforting for me to know that I had done my bit for mum over the years. After all, she had certainly done her bit raising me.

Sometime after dad had died, mum did not do so well with managing her money and with Jayne still living at home, she struggled. Over a period of time she had run up quite a bit of credit card debt and had no real means to pay it off, and it was worrying her a lot. I don't remember how I found out about it, but once I did, and realized how much it was worrying mum, I had to do something. I took mums credit card away from her and slowly started to pay off her debt until it was completely paid off about a year later. I knew she hated the fact that we (Diane and I) were paying off her debt, but she really did not have any other option. She could have re-mortgaged the house I guess, but we never would have suggested she did that. Thinking that would just compound her worries. In any case, it was not a common thing for people to do back then. I like to think that our actions added days to her life, relieving her of the stress that debt can cause. It was the right thing to do and I was so glad we could do that for her. It made me feel good too. Dad would have been proud. A bit of Karma there perhaps for my stressing them out after my shoplifting exploits as a teenager.

Mum was a mere 64 years old when she died. The house was sold, and her estate settled almost exactly a year later, on 2nd September 1998.

The posting away from Linton-on-Ouse was welcome but a move to RAF Wyton, caused us a bit of a dilemma as a family. Where would we live? Wyton was in Huntingdon. It was closer to South Wales than Yorkshire, but we had not lived in that area before and quite honestly, we were getting a little tired of moving the family around, plus the boys would need some stability for their education in the coming years as Dan was rapidly approaching 10. Also, we had sold our house in Llantwit Major, so we were in a good financial position to buy our own home once again. We had no idea what my next posting would be after my two years were up at RAF Wyton, so we decided that we would return to Cranwell, occupy married quarters for a short while whilst we looked for a new family home. It didn't really matter what would happen in two years' time, we needed to put some roots down in the place we loved most. I would commute daily to RAF Wyton for two years from Cranwell then hopefully get a posting back to the Cranwell area afterwards. Brilliant plan we thought, and it did require a lot of effort from us, but it was all worthwhile. Our endeavours worked out very well in the end. Sometimes in life, you make your own luck. This was one of those times.

The RAF allowed us to move into a surplus married quarter at Cranwell for six months whilst we looked around for somewhere to live in the local area. This would be our fourth time living at Cranwell. My Course officer from EOT 1, and a few other RAF Cranwell officers had recently bought houses on a new estate in the nearby village of Caythorpe called *'Kings Hill'*, which was just five miles away from the base. We loved the area and the local school and were lucky to be able to pick one of the best plots on the development. We would have a brand new four-bedroom house that would be built in re-used brick and completed to our specification and within our budget. We would occupy the house some time in 1999. It was during the time of the house build that Diane's father was diagnosed with cancer of the oesophagus. The disease took a hold of him very quickly and sadly he would never get to see our completed home. He died on 25th March 1999.

37 Kings Hill, Caythorpe, Lincolnshire, England, 1999

It was absolutely tragic, and it all happened so, so quickly. I have never known a man, husband, father and grandfather who was loved as much as he was. He was just a great man – period. Another one taken from us well before his time. He passed away peacefully at the family home where he had raised four children. It was exactly the end he wanted. At the actual time of his passing, he had all his family around him, including myself. Many, if not all of us in the room experienced something very special in the moment he passed away. We felt what I can only describe as his spirit leaving his body. A presence of some sort seemed to go around the stillness and silence that was in the room. It lasted just a few seconds, but it happened. You could not see, hear or touch it, but you felt it as a sort of draft, but a draft that seemed to pass right through your whole body. It was not a breeze that is felt on the surface of the skin caused by the wind, it felt much deeper than that. I had never experienced anything like that before or since and was convinced it was his spirit. As this presence left the room, the curtains seem to gently sway in what seemed to be a final wave goodbye and then it was no more – just stillness and silence.

Seconds afterwards we all just looked at each other and without saying a word everyone's reaction was as if they were saying; *'did you just feel that?'* It was one of life's unforgettable spiritual moments. It was very comforting and reassuring, not at all morbid or frightening. I felt immensely proud to have shared that experience with the family. The passing of a loved one affects everyone, and people grieve in different ways. I had underestimated how much Diane had been affected by her father's passing. Everyone feels and deals with death differently. I knew how I felt when my own father had died and how quickly I seemed to move on. I was wrong to think others would feel the same way. It would be a tough lesson for me to learn. I was an 18-year-old boy when my father passed away and felt that I was only just getting to know him. This relationship was very different; a 34-year-old woman with her own family had just lost her dad, with whom she was very close. She had known her dad almost twice as long as I had known my own father. I should have done much more to support her emotionally in the coming weeks. Her relationship ran much deeper than the relationship I had with my own father. I don't have many regrets, but this was one that haunted me for a long time afterwards and to this day, still frames my thinking towards others who are suffering grief from the passing of a loved one.

Since commissioning, I realised that my life had become a constant balancing act, and I struggled to squeeze everything in. I didn't always get it right and even when I did, it never stayed in equilibrium for long. Conflicting priorities of home, career, money, children's activities and a bundle of other things all jostled for my time and attention. These conflicts would often occur when I had the least amount of mental capacity to be able to deal with them properly. The one thing that makes you hit the pause button of life is the serious illness or death of loved ones. For a while nothing else matters and you reflect on your own life. Then, just as quick as it stopped, you release the pause button, and your life spins up again at the crazy speed it used to be. This is not a great way to go on, but if you use the brief period of reflection and act on it, you will think differently about risks and life. This in turn, can lead to some life changing outcomes. I know this to be true, because that's exactly what happened to me just a few years down the line.

Chapter 11
Samsonite Warriors

The commute to RAF Wyton was a mere 61 miles (98 Kms) each way from Caythorpe. The trip was a straightforward trek due south, 80% of which was on the A1. The A1 is the main artery running north/south of the country from London to Edinburgh. The traffic was always busy but some days it was just appalling. On a good day, I could get to work in about 80 minutes. On a bad day coming home, the same journey could take between two and three hours. Over a week, the commute was at best tiring, over a month exhausting, so to do it over two years was brutal, and I was feeling it. Not just on me but also my little Citroen ZX car. I bought the car from my then brother-in-law's parents. They were proud that the car had so little mileage when they offered it for sale. I certainly corrected that anomaly; I don't think the engine had chance to cool down for the next two years once I had started commuting in it.

I was posted to SM23c with a start date of 20th April 1998 for a two-year tour that would be reviewed on 20th April 2000. The term SM23c stood for Support Management (SM) and the 23 was a numerical indicator specific for the Tornado aircraft engine. The 'C' was a subset of the engine which, in my case was engine accessories, control systems and specialist tooling. The term *'support'* encompassed both engineering and supply (logistics) responsibilities. Logistics for an engineer was a significant new skill if you hadn't done it before; and I hadn't. The whole support offices changed their names shortly after I moved there, and we would be part of the Tornado Integrated Project Team (Tornado IPT). We were now part of the team that supported the platform and the new title reflected that. What a great idea. A job title that reflected the work you did - Brilliant! Now everyone in the organisation knew exactly who we were and what we did, they never would have figured that out from SM23c.

My small team consisted of two technical and five supply personnel. It is fair to say that this job was the hardest professional engineering job I have ever done in my life - period. It was also the job that would give me the greatest professional satisfaction, once I eventually understood the scope of responsibility. The experience I gained in the 28 months I was there, gave me the professional confidence I needed for the rest of my career. No other job I have done since, has phased me as much as this one did. It was the only job I have ever done that required me to hold a professional licence. Technical judgement and engineering decisions had legal ramifications and was an integral part of the military airworthiness framework.

In my view, most jobs are either tactical or strategic in nature. Some jobs (like this one) have both a tactical and strategic element to them. The tactical tasks or elements are the right here, right now; things that need to be dealt with immediately or are on a pretty short time fuse. These tasks are measured in hours up to a few days for action and number around a dozen max. The tactical tasks change often and can rise to the top of the pile quickly, but they also fall away quickly as many of them tend to be time sensitive. These tasks normally go away completely once they have been dealt with. Few bounce back to bite you.

In this job, I needed to deal with the tactical tasks first thing in the morning or as soon as possible when they cropped up during the day. Up until now all the jobs I had done were basically tactical in nature (I am generalising a bit here so bear with me). The strategic jobs tend to be project or program management type jobs which can have a tactical element to them, but the tactical tasks are normally in support of an end game as the project or program is coming to completion. The strategic components of the Tornado job did not have an end game, it was continuous improvement of the product and the processes through the total life of the aircraft until its retirement. So, in my 28 months, some tasks I would start but not finish, some existing tasks would be managed to completion, but most tasks would be progressed through the process throughout my time there. The strategic tasks were more in number (around 30 to 40 in total), far more complicated and much bigger than tactical tasks but they didn't need to be resolved immediately. Nevertheless, they did need to be progressed in the coming weeks/months for things to move forward or for others to do their part in the process.

There were clear links between some of the tactical and strategic tasks, so my efforts often served both, but there was another dimension to the basic staff work that was required in the job. I had a complicated and dispersed user (customer) community that was spread over seven main operating bases, three forward operating bases (overseas) and three detachment locations (also overseas). The main operating bases alone were in two different countries; the UK and Germany (four countries if you consider Scotland and Wales as independent countries). On top of this, I was accountable for a large 11 million GBP operational and development budget and had numerous external contracts to manage, was the Chairman of several technical committees and was required to work within a legal framework. Budgets, contracts and customers are all part of project and program management jobs, but these requirements were often applied separately to each of the equipment's and I was responsible for a shit-load of equipment's.

The only real benefit I had going into the job was an appetite to learn and a lot of *'in-service'* experience of much of the equipment I was going to be responsible for. My time at St Athan had made me a subject matter expert on many components and my hands-on experience would give me credibility with my external contractors almost immediately on taking up the position. Indeed, I knew more about the technical details of the equipment than most of the contractor representatives; that was a first for many of them. The first three months in work were a bloody nightmare for me. The job often brought me to tears as I struggled with managing the enormity and physical number of tasks I had to complete (or thought I had to) on a daily basis. I had never done this type of work before and I was burning myself out pretty damn quickly. I was spending more of my own time doing work and I was literally worrying myself to death about shit, all this on top of a very long commute.

I requested a sit-down with my boss at around the 6-8 weeks stage and told him exactly how I was feeling. He smiled and chuckled (politely) at me before explaining that every engineer who picks up responsibility for logistics (engineering and supply aspects) of these Support Management jobs goes through feelings of helplessness. He gave me some tips, techniques and personal coping strategies to deal with my work load and the number of meetings I had to prepare for, which helped me enormously. Although, don't underestimate the power and effect of his acknowledgment of my issues had on my wellbeing. His acknowledgement was probably the single most thing that helped me turn the corner on the way I was feeling. I no longer felt hopeless. I was normal, everyone goes through this. A couple of major lessons I learnt here. Firstly, if you can't cope, go get help or at least tell your supervisor once you have exhausted all your best ideas on dealing with the job. Secondly, as a supervisor myself, I also became attuned to look out for people who worked for me and their ability to cope with their workload. My belief from this experience was that one of the main functions of a boss is the ability to know your people and having the experience and emotional intelligence to notice changes in their mood and behaviour. My boss should have noticed me working so late, so often, and looking depressed. He should have called me in rather than wait for me to reach my breaking point.

I had the privilege to travel extensively in this job all over the UK and at least three times a year to the beautiful city of Munich, Germany, where I would meet with my counterparts from Italy and Germany involved in the Tornado (tri-nation) project. I had received professional training on budgets, contracts, legal aspects, risk, airworthiness and managing a support management team. It was during my time in the Tornado IPT that I also completed Basic Staff Course, a month long military Staff Course from 1st to 26th March 1999; this course was a pre-requisite for promotion and covered a whole range of topics that were management focussed including finance, change, personnel, communication (oral and written), defence studies, project management and public relations. Due to the content of this course, it led to the award of a Diploma in Management from the Institute of Management on 29th July 1999. The RAF really does train you well to do the job they post you into, which in turn, allows you to progress your career in a lifelong learning type of way.

At about the six months marker, my confidence grew exponentially as I got to understand the intricacies of the work and the myriad of professional relationships I had to manage. To be honest, I could have done this job for five/six years easy, it was so diverse, challenging and rewarding all at once. I was loving it. However, I did feel it was starting to put a strain on my personal/married life. The commuting and being away often was hard on the marriage and even when I was at home the children's football, scouts and swimming activities and Diane's work kept us both busy. We seemed to have less and less time to spend with each other. I felt like I knew the people I worked with almost as much as I knew my own family. I thought this was just something every family went through, believing it was simply the phase of life we were in. After all, I had nothing to compare it with. We just needed to suck it up and get on with it, as it would eventually pass.

On reflection, letting it go on and doing nothing to address the changes was not the best philosophy. I should have realised things were different and I should have talked to Diane about the cumulative strain of the daily commute and the pressure that my work/career was having on me. My going away had been normalised and I should have focussed more on maintaining my marriage when I was at home. When you start to share aspects of your personal life with the people you work with, and your work colleagues do the same with you, then that should set off a few alarm bells. Having said that, sometimes it is easier to confide in a work colleague than discuss issues with your own family. It's a form of mutual counselling if the person you are confiding in is also going through something similar. In an insidious way, you start to become sort of kindred spirits, but such trust in sharing personal troubles is dangerous and has the secondary effect of muting any alarm bells that may be going off in your mind. I know this to be true. However, those alarm bells did go off for me and luckily, I recognised what was happening and brought things back on track. I needed to focus on what I had and what I had achieved not look for distractions to take my mind off what was going on at home. It scared me that things could have gotten out of hand so easily and an alternative life path pursued.

Life with the children growing up was as busy as it had ever been, and it was so much fun but there was a price to pay by being so busy at home. It is not a good omen when you take things and people for granted and fail to manage all the other little things that are important in life. Life itself is a metaphor for the game of snakes and ladders. You throw the dice and work hard to get where you are by progressing forward and climbing the ladders, but one poor throw of the dice and you find yourself rapidly slipping backwards down the snake. I had looked the snake in the face but luckily had thrown a six and just trucked on through.

I had done a really good job in the Tornado IPT and had earned my spurs in this very busy staff work environment with a positive *'Highly Recommended'* for promotion. These spurs would be my golden ticket to do the job every young Squadron Leader engineer wants to do; to be the Senior Engineering Officer on a front-line aircraft operating squadron; the SEngO (Sen-go). Lincolnshire was peppered with operating bases, so I was confident I would land a front-line job and be much closer to home. What I failed to realise at the time, which was clouded in my excitement of getting such a position, was that a front-line aircraft squadron job would require me to be away from home when the squadron was deployed. So closer to home but away from the family just the same.

On 2nd July 1999 I had reached a milestone in my career without even noticing. I had automatically crossed over to a full officer career. The 2nd July was my 38/16 optional retirement date. As an officer, you automatically get a natural retirement point at age 38 years or 16 years commissioned service. Although I had only been commissioned since 1988, I had seniority in my graduating rank of Flying Officer from airman service, so was eligible to leave if I wanted to. The onus is on the individual to exercise the option as it will lapse automatically if not notified to your career manager. These option points were important milestones in your career because if you decided to leave the RAF outside these designated dates, you would be requesting 'Premature Volunteer Release' (PVR) and PVR had a negative and permanent effect on your pension. This option point did not have any effect on my next optional retirement point of 44/22 (44 years old or 22 years' service) due on 7th Jun 2004.

The SEngO job I would have loved to have done was the one that was responsible for the maintenance of the Red Arrows Aerobatic Team operating the Hawk aircraft at RAF Cranwell. I had experience of the Hawk during my time at RAF Valley on 74 Squadron and had flown over 30 sorties in the aircraft. In fact, the timing of changeover was perfect for me and I was subsequently called forward for interview on 2nd March 2000. Not all jobs are subject to interview, but this one was, like my Queens Flight job back in the 70s. I had recent success in January for my professional interview with the Royal Aeronautical Society to get my Incorporated Engineer status and become an Associate Member of the Society (IEng, AMRaeS) so my confidence was riding high.

The interview went well for me but the person who landed the job had already worked with the team from a previous tour and was a known quantity to several of the aircrew team members. I came away satisfied that I had done my best but was a little concerned that I had been challenged during the interview on whether I would compromise my technical judgement for the pressure of putting on a public display. I felt that some of the interview questions was suggesting that the *'show must go on'* at all costs, the display was sacrosanct and only the operators have control. I think my response was a little more inflexible than what they were expecting. I may have even been slightly aggressive when I believed they were suggesting that my technical standards should come second to the display.

It was my experience with the Hawk accident investigation that was ringing alarm bells here and I knew that bad technical judgment costs lives. I would never put myself or allow others to put themselves in such a position. Or maybe, I just came across as over cautious because of my experience, who knows. I was disappointed that I was not selected, of course, but it was not the end of the world for me. I was also grateful for the interview experience and was chuffed with myself for giving it a go. Sometimes things don't go your way, when things like this happen it's a good idea to look closely at the positive and negatives, i.e. look at the disadvantages as if I had secured the position and then be thankful that they will never come to fruition. Working weekends and being away from home for extended periods of time would have been the norm in this job.

With the Red Arrows job now off the table, I would be posted to RAF Waddington as Officer Commanding, Sentry Maintenance Squadron (OC SMS) with effect from 8th August 2000. The E-3D Sentry aircraft is an airborne surveillance and command-and-control aircraft although the RAF operated it extensively in the Airborne Warning and Control System (AWACS) role. At the time of my posting there were seven aircraft in the whole fleet. Although belonging to the RAF, the aircraft were assigned to NATO (North Atlantic Treaty Organisation). This meant that the aircraft were considered a NATO asset and could be tasked by NATO. The aircraft was uniquely operated by two separate organisations, Number 8 and Number 23 Squadrons, but the maintenance and flight line operations were centralised in SMS. The aircraft was the last of the Boeing 707-320B airframes to be manufactured. Although the aircraft was an old design, it had been extensively modified and updated to accommodate modern mission systems,

systems that require a crew of 18 to operate. My team of around 200 maintenance engineers included a team of Ground Engineers or GE's. These were tradesmen/women who had been crossed trained in all other trade tasks for the aircraft type. When the aircraft went anywhere, even to local venues, a GE or maybe two went with them, it was a far more effective and efficient way of supporting the deployed aircraft than sending dedicated trade people away. The aircraft were hardly at home, most of their work was at deployed locations. For longer detachments and more intense flying programme detachments, other trades would support the GE's. Interesting fact about the Sentry; mission endurance is around 11 hours although this can be extended significantly using air-to-air refuelling. I was to learn quite quickly that although air-to-air refuelling can extend the mission time, the single toilet on board would be one of the limiting factors for those flying in the aircraft.

RAF Waddington was just 12 miles down the road from our home in Caythorpe. What a result. It was the next closest operational RAF Base to Cranwell, and I could cycle to work on good days. Days of long commutes in the car were behind me. The Sentry being a large and complicated aircraft was not like the cut and thrust of a fast jet Tornado, Harrier or even Hawk squadron. Life was a little more sedate with the Sentry. You could launch a Tornado or Harrier in minutes, but it would take a few hours to launch a Sentry. After all, organising a crew of 18 independent aircrew members can be like hoarding cats, then you had to switch on and warm up the aircraft and mission systems, load up the food (which was a critical task), download and then upload all the mission data, complete the flight plan and just take a bit of time; after all, you could be flying in the aircraft for most of the day, so you needed to make sure everything was done correctly and everything was in place. After all, coming straight back after take-off with a full fuel load because you forgot something just isn't going to happen. In contrast, fast jets tend to fly for an hour or two and there is a maximum of two to get organised, so the readiness time is somewhat shorter. My point is, the urgency of time is not such a major factor with big aeroplanes and so squadron life should not be as stressful. Right. Even in peace time, the Sentry was a NATO asset and could be called upon and operated 24/7, and during my time it was. I lost count how many times I had been called out at ridiculous times at night/early morning to resolve technical problems or sign paperwork to release the aircraft to fly. At the time of my arrival we had one long standing commitment to Aviano, a US Air Force Base in Italy in support of the Balkans war/crisis of the 1990s, but that was drawing to a close, so I needed to get my skates on if I was to experience this long-standing deployment and understand how we operated the aircraft away from its home base.

The first time I arrived in Aviano was on 8th November 2000 and I ended up staying a week to experience deployed operations. This was a well-oiled machine. After all, the Sentry had been operating there for 10 years, almost immediately since the aircraft entered service in 1990 and the infrastructure was very well established for the aircraft and crews. It had become a home from home and with the Americans allowing us to visit and shop at the Base Exchange, life was good in Aviano. People would fight to be selected to go on this deployment just before Christmas as it was common to go there to get cheap Christmas presents. Aviano is a beautiful little town located at the base of the Italian Alps, about 90 minutes from Venice. It is in a popular wine region called Friuli-Venezia Giulia which produced a red wine named *'Franconia'*. It was bottled in decent size one litre bottles, never exported to the UK (to my knowledge) and was the best red wine I have ever tasted. Clearly, quite a lot of other people thought the same because when the Sentry aircraft was due to return to the UK, it was loaded up with pallets of this stuff. It was much better to have the wine at home than your deployment uniform, that could be sent back in the C130 Hercules next week.

What I also experienced on the deployment was the fact that we seemed to have to many people on the ground supporting the operation. The deployed manpower had not been reviewed for several years and we were wanting people back home where the lion's share of the work was being carried out. You can imagine how that went down with the team. The mere suggestion of trimming back the Aviano deployment sent shivers down many spines and resulted in some pretty lame excuses why I shouldn't even look at it. *'Great experience for the new guys'* or *'we need to maintain our deployed skills'* all absolute bollocks. It was often the experienced people who would deploy, and the place was like being back at home because we had been there so long. The topic did touch a nerve for other deployments though. I had already observed that there had been a constant battle between my trade chiefs and the operators/aircrew that had gone on for years. When the aircrew were planning their deployments and operations away from RAF Waddington, if their proposals came under financial scrutiny, forcing them to cut costs, the groundcrew element of the detachment would always be the first to be cut to save money. This would lead to deployments being under resourced which would put pressure on the groundcrew that did deploy to perform and keep the aircraft serviceable for the detachment period.

This got me thinking, perhaps I could combine the two issues and get a result that would satisfy everyone. Not impossible, and it was worth giving it a try. So, I did. During my time in the Tornado IPT, we had a risk log that documented all the things that could possibly go wrong with the engine and against each entry were the things we could do to mitigate each risk. Each risk, depending on its probability of occurrence and the severity of failure, was colour-coded either red, amber or green. Risks spelt danger and, quite rightly, were the major focus of our management effort. With a little bit of imagination and assistance from the GE's we could come up with a Risk Matrix for detachment manning which would give the aircrew some choices to make when considering the ground support for any detachment. Then, depending on the aims and objectives and amount of flying required whilst on the deployment, they would determine the amount of risk they could afford to take on the ground support element. The red option would give them the least amount of manpower to safely conduct aircraft operations (without overworking the ground crew and no tricky faults to rectify). The green option all but ensures success for the whole deployment including additional tasks if required and aircraft serious fault rectification. It was a bit more involved than what I have just described, but the risks to the detachment as a whole were clearly defined and the success or otherwise of the deployment (from a ground support perspective) was clearly understood by everyone.

I presented the final version of the Risk Matrix to the Station Commander and the Squadron Executives who accepted the principle of what I was trying to achieve, and I subsequently put myself forward to try it out for real. We took the minimum (red option) amount of people to Anchorage, Alaska with one aeroplane for a week on a US Exercise called Cope Thunder (renamed Red Flag Alaska). I was the pseudo engine tradesman and boy; did I work bloody hard that week. I went back to my roots for a week, wore overalls and got covered in oil and shit and had a complete ball. I even had a bollocking from the Detachment Commander after about day three (who just happened to be the Station Commander) for taking my role too seriously. The Detachment Commander thought I had begun to look like a tired-out ramp worker rather than an Operational Maintenance Commander. Good times. The matrix worked and was used for all detachments during my time on SMS including the one in Aviano. Not everyone liked it, but it sure took the sting out of the debate on detachment manning.

Alaska in July is interesting. It is warm and does not get dark. It goes dusky around 1am then stays much like that until around 4am when it turns into a dawn and then gets light once more. It plays hell with your body clock and makes the decision to leave the night club particularly challenging. Sleeping was difficult, so when we got the aircraft airborne for the day, I would just grab some sleep in the team truck, on the grassy area near the ground equipment or, if in a social setting at the restaurant between menu courses or beers. This was my first time to Alaska, and it is truly one of the most amazing places I have ever visited. It is like witnessing nature in its naked state.

Me at Lunchtime in Anchorage, Alaska, USA, 2001

We took a glass top train ride from Anchorage to Seward and witnessed black bears, moose and wild birds in their natural environment. We took a boat trip and was fortunate to see a pod of Orca's stalking seals on some remote rocks. Although, the seals looked like they were in control, tormenting the orcas by swimming up onto the rocks if they got to close. It was an amazing experience to see natures game of 'cat and mouse' play out in the water. Detachments were not all like this one. I was to experience the other end of the spectrum in just three months' time.

What I learnt from this reflective experience with the manning matrix was that with a bit of rework and innovative thinking, experience gained from other jobs had relevance to my current position. It would be a life lesson and it motivated me to write an article for Air Clues, the RAF Flight Safety Magazine. My three-page article was published in Issue Number 4 of 2001. I had become an overnight sensation in the magazine world. Well, not quite, but it is very nice to see your ideas published in the RAF magazine. I also wrote about three other ideas in the same article which also helped me improve SMS. The first was a boarding/interview process for the GE's to ensure that they were making good airworthiness decisions away from home. The second was a simple tracking system to ensure people remain authorised at all times to do their job whilst employed on SMS, and the third was a short training course for engineering officers to enable them to carry out independent inspections on flight critical systems rather than relying on their rank as a means of competence. All these small changes were still being used successfully when I left SMS.

Over this period, the RAF were keen to promote self-supervision for aircraft trades, so we developed a series of tasks that could be undertaken by a self-supervised tradesman/woman. Self-supervision was simply the act of doing a job and then self-certifying the work yourself, a practice that had been done in the civil aviation world for some time. This was a relatively easy thing to do overall as we operated with GE's who worked in the main as self-certifiers away from base. I got the team to design a badge that people could wear on their coveralls once they had become self-certifiers. A small but very visible symbol of professional self-worth. That was another small point of difference for people who worked on SMS.

As the aircraft were assigned to NATO, it was important for me to understand what that meant when we deployed as a NATO asset. In my first year at Waddington I got myself onto a NATO tour where I was lucky to visit the other NATO basis in Greece, Turkey, Germany, and Norway where our deployed aircraft would operate from. It was also a great opportunity to experience some local culture and cuisine. In Greece it was the food. In Turkey it was the 'Whirling Dervish', a religious swirling ceremony of spirituality, love and faith. A dance that gradually increases in speed and intensity making it very difficult to watch for more than a few minutes. How these guys don't get giddy and fall over I never know. Germany was the beer of course, and Norway was the scenery and local all-night clubs. The base at Trondheim, Norway, was probably my favourite of the four. The cost of alcohol in Norway is prohibitively expensive. I took a bottle of whiskey on my second trip as a negotiation asset and hid it in the loft of the officer's mess in preparation for our deployment there in the first quarter of 2001. Unfortunately, in between these two dates the UK suffered a massive outbreak of Foot and Mouth disease in February 2001 which almost wiped out the agricultural industry in the UK and would last almost a year. Several cases were reported in Ireland and mainland Europe, following unknown transportation of infected animals from the UK. Everyone was twitching about a continent-wide pandemic, including the Norwegians, but these proved to be unfounded in the end. This extremely infectious disease required us to carry disinfectant and decontamination trays in the aircraft when we operated away from base. Norway got very concerned about having us there over this period and eventually refused us entry just days before we were about to deploy. I never made it back to the officers' mess and often wonder if my bottle of whiskey is still there, maturing in the roof space.

Most people remember where they were on Tuesday, September 11th, 2001. I was in work and having lunch watching the lunchtime news on the Bridge (Flight Line Control) at RAF Waddington. Breaking news that two aircraft had crashed into the New York, World Trade Centre, the Twin Towers. I remember it being like a spoof Hollywood movie scene, but it was real. Al Qaeda terrorists aboard three hijacked passenger planes carried out coordinated suicide attacks on the World Trade Centre and the Pentagon in Washington, D.C. Killing everyone on board the aircraft and nearly 3,000 people on the ground. A fourth plane crashed into a Pennsylvania field, killing all on board. Within the hour, it was confirmed as a terrorist attack on the mainland of the United States. I was thinking that shit is about to get real, and it's going to happen quickly.

As the political wheels spun up, it was about a day or so later that we were put onto 72 hours warning to move. We had no idea where we would be going or who would be going, we just had to get ready to go quickly. British security forces across the world were placed on maximum alert and the Prime Minister, Tony Blair, pledged that Britain would stand *"full square alongside the U.S."* in the battle against terrorism. That was it then. We would be involved in whatever the Americans would decide would be an appropriate response. I lost count how many local meetings we had on what the UK support to the US would mean to us at Waddington, but what did become clear was an initial deployment would take place sometime soon. I would be the Deputy Detachment Commander responsible for getting an aircraft and supporting ground troops and equipment ready to deploy and then lead them into theatre.

Our work up training was focussed on Nuclear, Biological, and Chemical (NBC) warfare, rifle drills, shooting practice and using the bayonet. I was not the only one who had concerns about RAF personnel deploying with bayonets fitted to their rifles. What the fuck! Where the hell were we going that required aircraft technicians to defend themselves with bayonets. What kind of danger are we expecting to be operating in. Holy shit! As we worked up our deployment skills it became clear that most of the military activity would be focussed on Afghanistan. We would work alongside the US, E3A (AWACS) aircraft, we just needed a place to deploy to.

As luck would have it (if you can call this luck), the UK were involved in Exercise Saif Sareea II, Arabic for *"Swift Sword II"*, which was a major military exercise involving the military of the UK and Oman. It was the largest single deployment of UK forces since the Gulf War and was in progress on 9/11. We already had a Sentry aircraft deployed on the exercise operating out of Thumrait, Oman. It was decided that we would initially deploy to the same place under *'Operation Veritas'*. We would effectively take over from the exercise which was coming to an end in October anyway. Operation Veritas was the code name used for all British military operations against the Taliban in Afghanistan during 2001, this morphed into *'Operation Oracle'*. On 3rd October 2001 it was decided that two aircraft would deploy to Oman and personnel were put on immediate standby. At 7pm the same day the message came through for deploying personnel to be at Number 3 Hangar, RAF Waddington by 23:59 hours Sunday 7th October 2001.

That Sunday was a memorable and emotional day. It sounds dramatic even writing it now, but I was leaving my home, wife and three children to go to war. Our neighbours and friends came out to send me off and I cried as I kissed my family goodbye. I knew we were going to Oman but had no idea if we were going to be staying there or getting closer to Afghanistan. I also had no idea how long we were going for, it was open ended. I was more than a little apprehensive about this deployment. I was a little scared. Still, this is what you train for. There were 150 of us in the hangar at Waddington that evening with all our combat kit, including weapons, respirators (gas masks), medication for chemical attacks and a complete range of other shit, including the fricking bayonets for our rifles. We were allowed very little personal stuff. I was the senior person and Detachment Commander for this part of the deployment as the Operational Commander would be flying with the aircraft the following day. I remember briefing everyone on the latest threat assessment in the hangar just before midnight and after a few questions directed that everyone load their stuff onto the trucks. With our kit loaded up, we boarded three buses and headed out to RAF Brize Norton where we would fly to Oman. Equipment that we could not take with us was loaded onto an Antonov and left for Thumrait via Turkey. Morale was sky high, it was incredible to experience the motivation of so many people who were effectively going to war. Every person wanted to be there, we were all volunteers (in that most had volunteered to be the first to deploy) and were keen to get on the ground in the operational theatre and get fighting this war on terror. But morale and attitudes would quickly change once in theatre.

We arrived at RAF Brize Norton and ended up spending several hours there. Everyone had time for breakfast prior to leaving on the Tristar aircraft at 9am. Flight time was 8 hours and 30 minutes to Royal Air force of Oman (RAFO) Thumrait, Oman. Thumrait was an extremely busy air base, and it took a considerable amount of time to get the detachment processed and located at the tented accommodation. The dramatic change in climate, poor accommodation (tents with no ground sheets), and the fact that we were all very tired made the situation difficult. We met up immediately with the guys on Saif Sareea II and got ourselves settled in. Our plush accommodation was a camp bed in a six to eight-man tent with no air conditioning pitched close to the runway.

Although Saif Sareea II was ending, local activity had already begun to switch into Operation Veritas/Oracle. The Americans had also started to arrive in theatre and they would also operate their E-3s from the same airfield. We knew they were staying because they brought a full complement of air-conditioned tents, a full suite of recreational items, cable television and fast food stalls. They sure put the UK to shame when it comes to giving support to their troops. The US is well rehearsed in setting up their deployment infrastructure and had quickly fenced it all off to everyone except US personnel. This looked like we would be staying in Oman and would be fighting the war in Afghanistan from here. Operating from Oman was a sensitive political issue at the time but offered a much safer environment for us to support such a high value asset in an extremely risky operational theatre. It also looked highly likely that we would not be needing our bayonets after all. That was the only good news.

High Street Thumrait, Oman, 2001

We were operational the day we had arrived although the aircraft was launched by Saif Sareea II detachment personnel. We took over the following day. The battle rhythm would be US-E3/UK -Sentry/US-E3. Each flight would provide an eight hour *'on station'* sortie therefore providing 24/7 coverage in theatre. We were in Oman and the action was in Afghanistan. That was at least a two-hour flight away, so overall sortie times were around 12 to 14 hours. Therefore, each sortie would require at least one air-to-air refuelling segment. We had committed two aircraft to the operation but would only fly one sortie a day. With a two-hour prep and at least an hour to refuel and prepare for the next sortie, assuming no faults, then each day would be a long one. It didn't take long for us to start feeling a little burnt out.

The realisation of living in field conditions and the effects of working in a hot and humid climate hit home immediately. We did not have time to acclimatize. We started with 12 hours on 12 hours off shift pattern, but the night shift just couldn't sleep once the aircraft had been launched so we swapped onto 24 hours on 24 hours off with a change-over daily at 8 pm from Day 5. That worked much better and people were getting better quality sleep too. The accommodation was awful for sleeping and most of us were tired before we even started work.

My Luxury Omani (shared) Home, Thumrait, Oman, 2001

We had successfully negotiated with the base commander permission to occupy a Hardened Aircraft Shelter (HAS) which was close to where our aircraft were operating from. The HAS had air conditioning, sleeping quarters, washing facilities and office accommodation – it was perfect. The only downside was that the HAS was three miles from the main operations, so communications and transport were a bit of an issue for us. Nevertheless, The HAS allowed us to keep all our equipment after the exercise and the additional shit we needed for Operation Veritas/Oracle. It was 100% improvement on the tents. The hangar quickly became our first home (rather than the tent) and a great place to sleep and just hang out. It was also dark and cool in places which attracted camel spiders, aka wind scorpions, so you had to be careful. Although not fatal to humans their bites are very painful. RAF people just don't do rough accommodation. I know we were at war and had to suck shit up, but the only stars we like to sleep under is the four and five stars of the Hilton and Marriot Hotels. RAF people are affectionately known as *'Samsonite Warriors'* and I can relate to that. If I had wanted to do my work in sand, dirt and muck I would have joined the Army.

Although the shift patterns took a time to settle, we got into the battle rhythm of getting the aircraft ready for the mission pretty quickly. Once the aircraft was successfully launched, we could relax a little, eat, do our washing (because that's what you do daily when its stinking hot and humid) and generally relax a bit. If the aircraft had a problem on start up or had to turn back early because of an in-flight problem, hell would break loose and it would be all hands to the pump to get the aircraft fixed and launched again. Remembering that we were taking over from the Americans and they could not come off task until we relieved them, so every minute we were late getting on task would be an additional minute the Americans would have to stay on task. It worked the other way as well of course, and in my time in theatre we never missed a task, we may have been a little late once or twice, but we never missed a task. Yet, several of our missions were extended because the Americans had a few issues of their own. We even picked up a few additional missions when we had the capacity to do so with our spare aircraft if it wasn't being robbed of parts. You train for this kind of stuff all the time during peace and, I have to say, with few exceptions, the work is pretty much the same during war. The real difference is the priority that is put on the mission.

It is worth mentioning that the Sentry and E-3s were critical to the overall mission in Afghanistan. This single platform controlled all the air assets in theatre. There were literally thousands of sorties being launched every day into Afghanistan. Close Air Support missions for the troops on the ground, bombers, tankers and everything else in between. The inventory of hardware was like reading a Jayne's *'All the World Aircraft'* every one of which were controlled by the Sentry or E3. The ATO (Air Tasking Order) that was taken on board the aircraft before launch was reams and reams of fanfold paper, it looked like a couple of encyclopaedias some days. There was so much ordnance being used in Afghanistan in those early days I am surprised that the country still exists. The campaign almost certainly would have changed the topography of parts of the country.

As the aircraft was flying for so long the aircraft flew with an augmented crew, this allowed for a fresh pilot to bring the aircraft home safely after such a long mission. Crew duty hours were being stretched but safety was paramount. This is also where I really got to learn about the limiting factor of the aircraft and only having one toilet. When servicing the toilet, we would only partly fill it with chemicals afterwards allowing more room for waste, even then after such a long sortie we would need to take caution when emptying. Not the most pleasant job in aircraft servicing but an important one nonetheless.

It was about the two-week point once we got sorted and were into a work routine that people started to ask how long we were going to be there, and how long the campaign was likely to run. There was little for people to do in their down time and the camp was dry (no alcohol - initially) with few facilities. I played a round of golf once on an all sand golf course. You had to carry a square mat of AstroTurf around with you to play. It was quite an experience but not something you wanted to do all the time in the intense heat of the day. We had phone cards, so we could ring home and we also had internet access for 30 Minutes at a time that had to be booked like the phone in advance. The calls home was such a morale booster. To be able to talk about everyday things at home and to just hear Diane and the kid's voices put everything into perspective. It kept me connected and allowed me to recharge my sanity batteries. I was always a little teary eyed at the end of the call, but it was all that was needed to make life in the operational field much more tolerable.

RAF Sentry E3D on the Flight Line, Thumrait, Oman, 2001

Oddly, this deployment seemed to bring the family much closer together. Email and phones were a God send. I guess the distance and the risky work we were doing made us all think hard about what was important in life. It was in complete contrast to my being away and travelling to RAF Wyton during my last job. Later in the detachment we had the opportunity every few weeks to go downtown to Salalah, Oman, to shop and chill in one of the hotel pools or go swimming in the rip tides of the Arabian Sea. It was here that I had the idea to buy the perfect Christmas gift for Diane, having named our boys from the bible, I bought her the gifts of the three wise men; Gold (bracelet), Frankincense and Myrrh. How cool was that. Even with excursions away from Thumrait, there is no doubt that morale had started to wain quickly once we had established the routine. People were starting to report sick and you could just feel the change in attitude and social behaviour. This was no Aviano. I couldn't help feeling that some of the younger guys had been spoilt by the Aviano detachment experience and comparisons were being made. This was very different.

It became clear, through the daily operational briefs, that the campaign was going to run for some time and the management at Waddington were already thinking about a rotation of people. I wrote to my boss back at RAF Waddington requesting that they send some R&R (Rest and Recuperation) items out to us that would be helpful in keeping up morale and occupying people's minds during their down time. Tv's, videos, games anything. Cleaning sand out of your personal weapon is not a great pastime for aircraft technicians. Also, I asked for some bicycles as the aircraft were parked a little distance away from where we were located, and we had limited ground transportation. It worked. Local businesses in Lincolnshire did us proud and donated all sorts of stuff and that came out on the next rotation of aircraft. It was a huge boost to morale to get this stuff. Also, it motivated everyone to build a proper rest area, so we could set all this recreational stuff out.

As the maintenance commander, I acquired my own personal bicycle which allowed me to get around the base and meet with various entities we needed to deal with without tying up the ground transportation for the groundcrew. It was perfect if not comical. I had gotten an infection in my left foot and had to wear training shoes. Not very war like to see an Engineer Officer in combat clothing and bright white Nike training shoes riding a bicycle.

On the shoe issue, we had been sent desert coloured combat boots, 300 pairs of them, but the soles could not stand the surface temperature of the concrete, by day three they were completely useless. No such issue with my Nike trainers. Along with the R&R stuff arriving, we had also gotten local permission to build a social bar out of a 20-foot ISO container. That was also a great project to absorb spare time. We called it the 'Talybar'. The use of the bar was under strict operation instructions particularly as we were looking to open it during Ramadan.

Me & Sentry CFM 56 Engine, Thumrait, Oman, 2001

Technically, we had a couple of thorny issues to deal with which I needed to get endorsement from the UK Sentry IPT to approve. I was operating outside the bounds of my airworthiness authority in certifying the aircraft fit to fly. Whether it was poor communications or something else, I was to learn that such authority was either not forth coming or would come far too late for us to meet the mission. Grounding the aircraft and not doing the mission was not really an option in this environment unless there was a real danger to the aircraft or crew. My thinking quickly turned to that of stating an *'intent'* rather than asking for permission/authority to do something. I would discuss with my engineers and the aircrew, a safe and workable short-term solution to the technical problem and then document that as a novel limitation to operating the aircraft. I would then send the details in a fax to the UK stating that *'unless I hear differently from you, then this is what we are going to do'*. Not the best way forward but I found myself between a rock and a hard place.

As an engineer I always think of the worst possible outcome and mitigate the risk by working backwards from that. My thought process in this case was if I acted in a reasonable manner with the information I had, if anything did go wrong and there was litigation, a reasonable person would say, *'Yes, under the set of circumstances he found himself in, he did the right thing'*. I never got any feedback from my approach and luckily nothing went wrong. Nevertheless, it was not a great situation to be in. I felt professionally isolated but learnt a lot about myself working and making decisions under pressure, whilst recognising and accepting the weight of responsibility of my actions.

E3D Flight Line (Aircraft Shelter & Office in Background), Thumrait, Oman, 2001

On 3rd November 2001 we moved into our new tents; well different tents, they were the same as the old ones we were leaving but in a different area of *'Tent City'*. Tent City was the name given to the site where all 1,600 British Forces were located. The Army were transiting through at that time and although the camp was dry (no alcohol), they seemed to find an alternative source which resulted in a drunk Army soldier borrowing a Land Rover and rolling it over several times, writing it off and fracturing his skull in the process. It was determined that the alcohol was a factor. Army, Alcohol, Vehicle, Soldier with nothing to do = Accident. Indeed, there had been a number of deaths due to bad driving in Oman since Saif Sareea II had started. Not great statistics. The weather was a constant, belting out 40+ degrees C during the day, dipping to around 17 degrees C at night. The burning sun and blowing sand allowed me to renew my body skin several times over during the detachment. My arms seemed to be shredding skin every other day, even though I was applying sun factor 45. Around 500 to 600 people were transiting through Thumrait on their way back to the UK every day, but were being held up for up to 48 hours waiting for their transport home. That meant the cue for food at meal times was horrendous, one big kitchen tent with some 2000 people to feed. My mate was the catering officer, and he was telling me that his team were working in kitchen temperatures exceeding 70 degrees C (158 degrees F). After the second week, every day for me was roughly the same. I was living a real *'Groundhog Day'*. The following is how I described my day to my family at home. I was the detachment boss so did not operate on any one shift, rather I was present and available for both shifts. After all, what else did I have to do.

6am *Get up, put on shorts and trainers (after checking for spiders), grab towel, razor, mirror, shower gel, toothbrush and toothpaste and bottle of water and walk about 50 metres to toilet (wash hands before* *and after). Go to communal wash area and pick up a plastic bowl. Dip the bowl in disinfectant and fill from the standby tap. Return to wash area and wash. Clean teeth with bottled water (and toothbrush and toothpaste of course). Empty bowl into communal drainage dustbin and dip it into the disinfectant before placing back onto bowl pallet. Walk back to the tent, put my stuff away, fold up sleeping bag and hang above bed (less likely to attract spiders). Get dressed trying not to get dirty feet on the dusty and dry plastic flooring. Go to breakfast about 6.30am. Food is great, but I just have a bowl of sugar puffs (lardy or full breakfasts are a bit too much everyday, so I have one now and again). From the mess tent I either get picked up by the duty shift or, if they came early to breakfast they would have left the land rover in the car park with the other 60 odd vehicles (most of which are land rovers). That's a laugh and a challenge trying to find ours – they really do all look the same. When I say car park what I actually mean is a piece of desert that has been allocated as a car park and not even cordoned off. Anyway, I travel the 3 to 4 miles into work by land rover arriving at about 7am. There is a shuttle bus service that is operated by the camp and the buses are driven by the Omanis (nicknamed 'Jinglies' which was a term of endearment not a racist or nasty term). Unfortunately, the Jinglies don't follow the common-sense rule and the thought of following a timetable is not in their culture. So, there is usually 3 buses, the first one is full and the other two empty and they all set off together. Really bizarre, as they are all going to the same place - it's a shuttle bus. Then if they think that it is time for them to rest, they just stop the bus - anywhere. And there is nothing you can do. Hence most people sort themselves out with alternative transport in the morning.*

7am *Arrive at work and get the rundown on the previous night's work and see how the aircraft are holding up. Then I either cycle or drive to operations and have a brief with all the other Operation Veritas and Saif Sareea II Engineers at 7:30. I then check on the daily* *flying programme before getting back to work about 8:30. Depending on the flying, I do my washing, writing or whatever needs to be done. I keep a detachment diary on domestic and operational issues. Lunch is 11:30 to 1:30, which is usually a very nice meal and dinner is 6pm to 8pm which is even nicer. There is a shift handover everyday starting at 7:00pm where I brief both shifts on the ever-changing scenario (Shift work 24hours on 24hours off).*

8pm *After dinner I go for a shower – what a laugh. You fill up a large black plastic bag with smelly water the day before and leave it in the sun all day to heat the water up. You then hang it above your head (shoulders actually), open the little on/off tap and dance around underneath it to get wet. There are 6 hangers in the shower tent and with the movement of the frame coupled with the swilling plastic bag and its dangling tube with spray nozzle, it is quite a sight to behold seeing up to 6 naked men prancing around crouched under their shower bags trying to wash their hair with a pathetic spray of water that changes direction every second. It looks more like a pub game than a way to maintain personal hygiene. A good full bag would last around three minutes (if you were lucky) and the strongest spray was always at the start. Gravity was the only thing that emptied the bag and you almost had to squeeze the last pint of water out if you still had soap in your hair. I had 3 bottles of shower gel – I have one left. The thieving gypsies nick everything. I always forget to take the gel back to the tent, sometimes I'm lucky but twice I have not been. In fact, it was less than the time it took me to walk from the shower block to the tent when the first bottle got nicked (5 minutes max). Anyway, I'm learning fast but need to learn faster. By the time I have walked back to the tent I'm almost as dirty as when I set off. Kids would love this routine, me not so much.*

8:45pm *Sometimes I will go to the BFOT (Big F*ck Off Tent) Yes that's it's name. Or to the FU Bar (You can guess that one), The FU*

Bar is about a ¼ mile away from the main site and is the only place you can drink at the moment (Talybar under construction). And people do drink, but you only need a third of what you drink at home to become a bit tipsy. As the ¼ mile walk is across desert and in complete darkness, I don't think I have ever walked back the same way twice. I eventually arrive back at about 11 pm. I then crawl into my sleeping bag and try to sleep. Waking up in the middle of the night for a pee is one experience you just don't want to know. And then the cycle starts all over again at 6am.

We had worked hard to make the domestic environment better than the one we inherited from the exercise. Hard cabin accommodation was on its way to replace the tents, but I would not experience such luxury. This was no Aviano, but it was not a bad place to be when you consider the shit that was going on in Afghanistan. We got the nod that the initial deployment of personnel would be rotated on 20th November 2001. That was without doubt the biggest boost to morale we could have had. I must admit I was tired and jaded at the end and missed my family so, so much. Hearing their voices on the phone was at times heart breaking for me but along with the email messages and letters from home, it got me through.

I couldn't wait to get back home to see my family. They had been through the mill as well. Life went on for them, but they missed me too and I was so proud of them all. I was also proud of what we all had achieved both operationally and locally in making the detachment environment a much better place to be. We had also accomplished all the missions that we were asked to do every single day, seven days a week. We also moved the location of our house tents several times away from the noise of base operations, so the next crew would be better served. We would be home for Christmas having been in theatre just 63 days. That 63 days seemed like six months. In the end, it was the monotony of routine that was the hardest to deal with.

It turned out that although I was much closer to home working at Waddington, in the two years and a bit I was there, I was away from home just as much as I was in the Tornado IPT. There is no doubt that when you are away from home so often there is an insidious change in the family dynamics that happens in your absence. The family get to cope very well without you. This is a good and a bad thing depending on which way you look at it. From my perspective, it was great that the family survived without me, but the bad news was that the family survived without me. Being away from home can put a strain on relationships that is not immediately apparent when you get home as everyone is so pleased to see you, and you them. Being the person who was away, you feel as though you have missed out a little on the progress of everyday life and indeed you have, even a few weeks can make a difference but in a couple of months the gap can be huge. Unfortunately, being in the military, life is like that and you just come to accept it. This acceptance is really a failing, there are things that you could and should do to keep the family relationship on track once you get back. But there are usually 101 reasons why this doesn't happen, and before you know it life has moved on, and you are back into a different routine - plodding along.

My overall success at Waddington led to a highly recommended for promotion and for advanced staff course but it was clear that my age and my desire to remain in the local area would work against me in the competitive environment of promotion and academic progression. I was now within a month of being in my last two years of service and I would be required to let the RAF know my career intentions. I didn't know if I was going to exercise my final leave point option which would be on 7th June 2004. It was a huge decision and it required some serious consideration. I was formally *'Dined Out'* at Waddington on 19th April 2002, my dad's birthday, he would have been 72. I didn't know it at the time, but this would be the last time I would attend a formal Officers Mess dinner in the UK.

As a secondary duty at Waddington, I was the Officer in Charge of the Warrant Officers and Sergeant's Mess. This was an awesome secondary duty and was well sought after by the officer cadre. The mess had around 500 members and was a great community to be a part of, offering me a fond reminder of my time at RAF St Athan. The social functions were always well attended and a huge amount of fun. It was through my connections in the Sergeants Mess that I got involved with the Lincolnshire Air Gunners Association. These were a diminishing group of gentlemen who had been Air Gunners during World War II. They were some of the humblest gentlemen I have ever had the pleasure to meet and they had some great stories to tell.

The Air Gunners and their wives would have monthly lunches in the Sergeants Mess. During my last social occasion with them I suggested to the Chairman that I could try and get a visit arranged to RAF Coningsby where the Battle of Britain Memorial Flight was located. Coningsby had the only operational Lancaster bomber at that time. They were so excited about the opportunity to reminisce their war time memories. I continued to work with my contacts after I had left Waddington in the May of 2002. I eventually got a plan together, so the Air Gunners could visit RAF Coningsby on 25th September 2002. On the day itself, myself, the Air Gunners and their wives were picked up early in the morning by an RAF coach at Waddington and transported to RAF Coningsby which was about an hour down the road. Our first visit of the day was to the Tornado F3, Operational Conversion Unit;

Number 56 (Reserve) Squadron. Here they experienced a modern-day air defence squadron and had the opportunity to sit in the cockpit and imagine what flying would be like in a very tight and cluttered environment. Afterwards, we climbed back on the bus for a quick ride to the Battle of Britain Memorial Flight. Here the Air Gunners could look around and climb into the Lancaster bomber.

I will never forget the reaction of these guys when they climbed into the aircraft hull and the gun turrets. Many of them just sat there in a reflective pose, silent. Some of them openly crying. It was one of these incredibly special poignant moments, and they had earned it. Who knows what they were thinking or reflecting on. I felt so humble to have given them this opportunity to re-live their memories. From the Memorial Flight we headed off to the Officers Mess for lunch to relax and talk about what we had seen. At the lunch, everyone was so grateful for the opportunity they had to visit RAF Coningsby. Many of them recognised that it was probably the last time they would climb into a Lancaster bomber. I don't think anyone had done anything like this for this small group of gentlemen and their wives, which made it even more humbling for me. I heard them talking amongst themselves about some of the more enjoyable adventures they had experienced in the aircraft before moving to the ante room in the mess for coffee and a small afternoon nap before the trip back to Waddington. The ride back in the bus was a quiet but happy affair. I got so much pleasure in seeing these war heroes and their wives reminisce. It would be the last time I would be part of the Air Gunners Association.

The children were growing up fast and our house in Caythorpe was certainly starting to look like a permanent family home. I loved the house and it was so refreshing to have some family stability and a place where we could do things to the house to make it our home. We had a vastly different mindset to living in married quarters. I had a small workshop in the garage where I could make stuff for the garden and we had a small garden front and back for the cat and myriad of rabbits and guinea pigs Sian would have whilst we lived there. The children were socially active almost every day of the week and Diane and I had made some great friends in the local area. Our best friends had moved next door and it was difficult to even imagine things changing anytime soon.

We made so many memories in this house over the years, but it's funny how you tend to recall the not so great but funny ones. It is perhaps the learning that takes place from the memory that pushes it to the front of your mind when reminiscing. Once such memory involved my cooking. I don't remember the year, but it was Christmas time. We had turkey for Christmas day and with the left overs, I had made some turkey soup. It was New Year's Eve and we were having a party with our friends next door. At lunch time, I warmed up the soup and we all ate it with some bread. Within the hour Sian had tummy issues and had started to vomit and had the runs, I don't remember the order, but Dan, Josh and Diane went down with the same thing one after the other in quick succession. I was in denial about the soup because I was feeling OK. We had three toilets in the house and now we needed four. It got very untidy. Then whatever the bug was, took its hold on me too. All five of us vomiting and shitting like it was a family Olympic sport. Then it seemed to pass almost as quickly as it came, but by then we were all physically exhausted. We all needed to lie down and rest for a few hours, which we duly did. By evening time, we were over it and ready to party after consuming several slices of dry toast washed down with plain old water. To this day, the kids are incredibly careful about eating turkey soup – and who can blame them. Me, well, it was not one of my greatest cooking achievements for sure. Of all the great meals I can and did cook over the years including Chinese and Indian dishes, the turkey soup will forever be my master disaster dish.

We also had a few good parties in this house. One of our friends who lived a few doors away was just leaving after a social evening when she collapsed at our back door because she was so drunk. The real funny part was not seeing her collapse in a heap on the floor as she was smiling and waving goodbye; although that was pretty funny, the funny part was helping her husband load her into a wheelbarrow, so he could take her home. Friday evening wine and music nights that ran into Saturday were also popular in the Sainsbury's house. It was just a great family home. One of the more bizarre things that happened within our little community was one of our neighbours become a national celebrity over night when he found a new born baby wrapped in a blanket in the hedgerow of a lay-bye on his way to work one morning. He had stopped in his car to take a phone call and had seen something moving in the hedgerow. He got out to look and found a baby. Well that's what he told the police and his wife. His wife believed him, but the police were not so sure, so they took him and the baby into custody. It was quite a story and it made the National nightly news. The baby was a new born, just hours old and had been abandoned by its mother. Stopping the car to take that phone call saved the baby's life.

I didn't know it at the time, but my posting to the newly formed Defence Aviation Safety Centre (DASC) on 7th May 2002 would be my last posting in the RAF. The DASC was a tri-service organisation formed at RAF Bentley Priory on 1st April 2002. It was to provide defence aviation safety policy and advice focussing on aviation safety matters, education, and publicity. I had asked specifically to be posted into this job for two reasons; firstly, it was new, and I thought it had great potential for me to make it my own. Secondly, it would potentially be my last tour of duty in the RAF and it would be good to finish in a job that consolidated all my training and experience whilst being a major stepping stone into a civilian job. I had already been looking for alternative employment opportunities in the aviation safety sector and had gotten one step closer to leaving by securing an interview at RAF Boscombe Down with a company called QinetiQ. They were prepared to put me through a master's degree in Safety Engineering as part of my transition to their employment. However, that meant a family move or my living away from home. Neither were attractive to us, so we passed that opportunity up, but we had still not discounted doing something different with the family and it was looking highly likely that I would be exercising my option point to leave.

My job in the DASC was a newly established position within a small team that carried out aviation safety reviews on military aircraft. The first complete review I would get involved with was on the Sentry Aircraft. I had just left RAF Waddington, and the review would be specifically focussed on the deployment at Thumrait, Oman. The operation I had set up and had recently left. I was about to hit the ground running. The first day on the job I did all my arrival paperwork at RAF Wyton. Day two I was on an aircraft flying to Cyprus to assist other team members finish off the review of the Hawk aircraft. This particular aspect was reviewing the deployed operations of the Red Arrows Aerobatic Team (RAFAT). I would be in Cyprus a week before flying onto Thumrait, Oman to conduct the review on the Sentry detachment.

The week in Cyprus was a baptism of fire. I was in at the deep end and found it both professionally and personally challenging. It was the first time I had to look critically at an aircraft operation I was very familiar with, my approach and attitude here would prepare my thinking for the Sentry review. The RAFAT deploy to Cyprus during winter assuring themselves of the best weather and preparedness for the display season to follow. I found myself thrust into a known environment and aircraft type but did not find it difficult to be critical of the operation. I did think that some of my critical observations were a reflection of my disappointment of not landing the Red Arrows job previously rather than my professionalism. All the risks and observations of any review had to be quantified, which I could, so it turned out to be more professionalism than envy, but I wrestled internally with the conflict initially. I certainly felt from this first and brief encounter with the RAFAT that I had a penchant for this kind of work.

The Sentry aircraft fleet had already been subjected to a safety review some 18 months previously. Our review of the Thumrait detachment would be an addendum to that review as there seemed to be some concerns about the operation in Oman (I wonder who raised those concerns – Nigel). This was a strange situation for me to be in, but it was not lost on me that I had a great professional opportunity to highlight the shortcomings I knew existed. Additionally, I had not completed any training for my role. Knowing the shortcomings of the operation was one thing, but critically examining the processes I set up in my time there was something else. I felt like a poacher turned gamekeeper.

I knew all the people on the deployment, and it was a little uncomfortable at first particularly as I didn't know exactly what my job was all about at that time. I did of course understand deployed operations. I also found myself becoming a little defensive to criticism from other members of the review team. Who were they to pick holes in my old work environment? I was clearly a little touchy. Overall, our visit and final report added real value to the Sentry review and made recommendations that not only made the deployment safer but addressed many of the communication problems I experienced when I was there as the Deputy Deployment Commander. It was during this time that I really got to know who my new boss was. I had heard that he was not the easiest person to work for, or with, and I had already seen some of his confrontational management style. His controlling behaviour was unacceptable, and it made our relationship more than a little strained. I had begun to question what I had gotten myself into for my last tour of duty. I was hoping it would be a happy posting, but my first contact with my new boss was not giving me the warm fuzzy feeling that I was craving.

I worked hard in this appointment despite working for a controlling boss, and I made the most out of the professional training I received. I completed a Flight Safety Officers Course in June 2002, Management of System Safety in Acquisition in September 2002 and a Civil Aviation Authority Audit Techniques Course in October 2002. These courses coupled with my Health and Safety Courses, my experience in aircraft accident investigations, and teaching at RAF College Cranwell all bundled together nicely for me to do this job. During my time in the DASC, I would present to various technical and non-technical courses at RAF Cranwell on general aviation safety and airworthiness matters, relating it to real life taken from my own experiences. These opportunities also meant that I had a great excuse not to travel to work that day being one less day to be with my boss. Perhaps the greatest learning for me, was that I realised I could transfer these skills and knowledge into other areas in the civilian sector. Indeed, I did work with the rail industry, logistic warehousing, motor vehicle repair shops and food packing industries as an associate of my old work colleague's safety consultant business.

My part time work as a safety consultant was a dipping my toe in the water for stepping into civilian life. The idea of eventually becoming an independent Safety Consultant was quite attractive and I was led to believe through my work colleague that it would lead to bigger and better things, so I worked really hard in my final year consolidating my training and experience to give myself the best chance of success. Working as an associate in my colleague's company would mean that we could remain in our home in Lincolnshire. I would just commute daily to clients as required around the North of England – that was very doable and of course an attractive proposition.

Sometimes things just don't turn out the way you want them to. This business venture into safety consultancy was one of those moments. Perhaps I was a little naïve, or just misunderstood our conversations. What I thought I was getting into was more of a partnership with my colleague once I had gained more experience earning my consultancy spurs. I had underestimated how precious he had become about his business and it was HIS business after all. I would learn this fact a few months down the line. As time went on, I picked up more clients, but it looked like I was just going to be one of his associate workers, and not be his business partner which is what I thought we had discussed. I didn't have the financial backing or experience to start up on my own so was dependent on him to get work for me.

Many of my clients required me to travel significant distances to meet with them and work through whatever was required. After about four months, I realised three things. Firstly, it had become clear that my mate had no real intention of sharing his business, I was only ever going to be a worker and he fed me a few clients just to keep me engaged so I could earn some money. That was how this relationship was going to work for him. Secondly, I realised that I was nothing more than an insurance policy. Many of my clients just wanted me as the safety face of their company to front up to insurance representatives and to spout the good work and safety record that was required to obtain good insurance coverage.

I also had to prove that the company I was representing was compliant with all the relevant Health and Safety regulations by producing company documentation. This included the management commitment in the company policy. As a consultant, I would draft most of these documents and of course many clients had no interest in spending money or committing to things that either slowed them down or added little value to their outputs and bottom line.

Thirdly, this job was affecting my health. I had started to lose sleep over several of these business clients and decided that this kind of work, in the long term, was not for me. I am an honest person. I learnt that giving people the benefit of the doubt is one thing but when they bluntly disregard their own documented practices and procedures that they knew existed, I could no longer turn a blind eye. I decided that I would no longer be telling little white lies or giving the benefit of the doubt to insurance companies. I had to stop. I enjoyed the training aspect, but the consultancy aspect of generating pointless policy documents for companies who played lip service to them and would glibly hand them over to insurance underwriters just to get reduced premiums, was over. If I were to leave the RAF, I needed an employment Plan B. By this time, even if I had been offered partnership in this business, I would have refused it. My conscience couldn't take it.

During my time in the DASC, in concert with safety related topics, I had developed further my interest in Unmanned Aerial

Vehicles (UAVs) and worked with the Army, Phoenix UAV team in reviewing their Safety Management System. Such experience piqued my interest further in understanding the role of the human in the aviation operating environment. I attended a conference in London with the Aeronautical Society in October 2003 which just reinforced my interest to explore this science further, and after my experience with the Hawk accident investigation, I felt that I was developing a bit of an expertise in the field of Human Factors.

In my two years as part of the DASC team I also reviewed the Phoenix, Unmanned Aerial Vehicle operated by the Army, and the Royal Navy Jetstream. I did the Jetstream aviation review all on my own (five-man team down to one) and was commended on the quality of the report and its findings. The Jetstream review allowed me to engage with other operators of the aircraft including the RAF and a civilian charter company. This was a huge boost to my confidence and would serve me well for my next career. I just didn't know it at the time.

As mentioned previously, my boss was the worst supervisor I have ever worked for and it would be fair to say that the only thing I liked about him was his chair and teapot. The work was new and interesting, but he seemed afraid to let us get on with it and develop further the process of conducting aviation safety reviews. He made even the simple things in life a challenge for everyone. I would start a piece of work and his input and criticism would be almost immediate. He could not help himself to give such specific instructions that it left no room for initiative or any external input. It was an awful environment and he was dragging me down. I had got to the stage where I was becoming depressed and anxious about going to work. On top of this, I had restarted the balls aching 61-mile commute to RAF Wyton so had plenty of time to think about how things would eventually turn out.

When we were out in the field auditing and reviewing, we would not be together, so it made life a little easier; but office life was not good. I would hope and wish that he had an accident or was ill and could not come to work. Sometimes my wishes were answered, we would laugh about his controlling behaviour when he was not there, but in reality, it was no laughing matter. My heart would sink when I heard his car pull up outside. I just could not work with this man and I was not the only one who was having difficulty with him.

One day I had been pushed to my limit which resulted in my telling him to go somewhere and abuse himself. I just walked out of the office and went home. I don't even remember what he had done, it really didn't matter, he had pissed me off. I could take it no longer and all this played out in front of the others in the office. I felt so guilty and horrible afterwards and couldn't wait for the following day to say sorry. My outburst was unprofessional and unacceptable. But the strange thing was that the following day, nothing happened. It was as if the event of the day before had never occurred. It was bizarre. I never felt there was an opportunity to apologise and clearly, neither did he. I did notice a slight shift in his attitude towards me, so there was something positive to come out of this event.

It was at a rare social function at his home that he admitted to me that throughout his RAF career he would get to know the aircraft on his squadron better than he knew members of his own family. I thought that was a very sad admission indeed and left me feeling sorry for him. How is wife and family had put up with his antic's goodness knows, perhaps he kept those just for work. It was a time for me to do some self-reflection. I would never want to become such a controlling person. I did wonder how he had survived so long without someone punching him in the face. I was to learn from my office mate at another social function that he had indeed come close to hitting him after a heated confrontation several weeks before I had arrived. He had taken out his anger on the office door instead. What surprised me about this whole episode, was how one person can have such a detrimental effect on your self-worth and how it affects both your work and home life. A major career decision was about to be made and he was pushing me away from a career I had loved for so many years. It would be a real shame if it was to end like this. Things needed to change for me, and they did.

At home, we were still deliberating on whether I would leave the RAF, and if I did leave, what would be next? I wrote to my career manager in March 2003 asking for a deferment of my decision to leave from 6th June 2003 to 6th December 2003 citing that the review team I was working with had changed three of its four members (I was the only one left) and I just had one of the most difficult and damaging reporting periods in my career with my old boss. Thankfully, the career manager accepted my deferment.

My new boss in the DASC was a Navy man, and against all odds, successfully rescinded the previous report from my old boss and submitted his own appraisal of me which was considerably better. His assessment not only reflected the work I had done in the team, but the development work I had done to improve the business. Part of me was hoping that I would be selected for academic advancement and/or promotion in my last year, but I knew the chances of that were now pretty slim. As mentioned previously, it was a bit of a rat race for promotion and being in my early 40s, my age was working against me. I was also trying to string out deciding whether to leave or not. My indecisiveness could be construed as a lack of commitment and also work against me. The odds of my continuing with an RAF career were now 50/50.

I found myself working hard on my RAF career when I was in work and working hard on a second career when I was at home. It was not an easy decision to make one way or the other. This rapidly approaching career option point would allow me to leave with a lump sum of money and a small, but immediate military pension. The financial situation would be a game changer in removing any risks involved in shifting careers. I was 43 years old, had a young family and a hefty mortgage. I felt I wanted to do something different, but I had served over 26 years in the RAF and had become institutionalised to some extent. I loved my career, but I recognised that it had to end at some point and because of my age, I was wavering towards leaving, believing I was still young enough to start a new career. My consultancy business could be the buffer between the RAF and my second career.

Reflecting on my 26 years' service in the RAF, I realised that I had crammed quite a bit in. I had married, raised three children, deployed to war, completed 49 professional and personal training courses (ranging from adult education, to airworthiness management). I had been an auditor, accident investigator, contract manager, safety consultant and maintenance commander. Personally, I had qualified as a Football Association (FA) referee and junior team coach, been a scout troop leader, swimming instructor and was privileged to play keyboards for a few years in a very cool rock band. I started out as a teenage junior airman, was a corporal at 20, sergeant at 24 and a commissioned officer at 28. I had moved home 23 times, 12 of which with a family. All against the backdrop of a bad motorcycle accident that almost killed me and my career even before it had started. If I had a dream at the start of what my career would look like, my wildest imagination would not have produced the story thus far, and there was more to come. I was proud of everything I had done and achieved. I was not an expert at anything, but I give my all to everything I did. I was the consummate gifted amateur. Even my failures were a success because they too helped form my character. So, what was going to be next?

We had been living in our own house for four years and my wife Diane and I had seriously been considering a lifestyle change. Life was rather good in Lincolnshire, but it was full on and we felt we needed more family time together. I had been commuting over 120 miles a day on and off for nearly six years and was physically exhausted. Diane was working hard for a local company too, and we only seemed to be together briefly at mealtimes. If I stayed in the RAF for the next 11 years to full retirement at age 55, it looked as if my commuting would continue. That was not an attractive proposition. There were lots of other things to consider as well, but whatever the decision, it would be a family one and not based purely on my career choices. We felt that we were well prepared to do just about anything. Although, none of us would have guessed what was about to play out, and the changes that would happen in our family and to our life…….

About the Author
Nigel M Sainsbury

Fairfax, Virginia, USA, 2020

Nigel's passion for non-fiction writing started in 2016 when he wrote a chronological diary of his life for his children. Realising that many of the turning points in his life were centred around motorcycles, he had an epiphany to write his first self-published memoir, One Down Four Up; My Bikes My Life. That success spurred him on to write about other aspects of his life in an honest *'no holds barred'* kind of approach. His critical reflections on his experiences influence his judgement, and he is the first to admit that he is the sum of his own decisions. In his writing he encourages readers to reflect on their own life and experiences, not as a comparison, more of an endorsement that we are all a sum of our own thoughts and actions.

Born a Welshman but is a naturalised Kiwi, Nigel now lives in Fairfax, Virginia, USA and is on route to his hattrick of passports.

Websites:
www.mybikerauthor.com
www.nigelsainsburyconsulting.com

www.ingramcontent.com/pod-product-compliance
Lightning Source LLC
Chambersburg PA
CBHW021054080526
44587CB00010B/252